T0137056

Big Data in Emergency Management: Exploitation
Techniques for Social and Mobile Data

Rajendra Akerkar

Editor

Big Data in Emergency Management: Exploitation Techniques for Social and Mobile Data

 Springer

Editor
Rajendra Akerkar
Big Data Research Group
Western Norway Research Institute
Sogndal, Norway

ISBN 978-3-030-48101-8   ISBN 978-3-030-48099-8   (eBook)
https://doi.org/10.1007/978-3-030-48099-8

This Springer imprint is published by the registered company Springer Nature Switzerland AG.
The registered company address is: Gewerbestrasse 11, 6330 Cham, Switzerland

The book is dedicated to first responders—who are all out there every single day for anyone who needs them.

Preface

The term *emergency management* can be defined as the organization and management of resources and responsibilities for dealing with all humanitarian aspects of emergencies or disasters, in particular preparedness, response, and recovery in order to lessen the impact of disasters. Earthquakes, floods, terrorist acts, and catastrophic infrastructure failures are events that cause huge physical destruction, loss of life and property around the world. The frequency, intensity, and impact of catastrophic events have significantly increased in recent decades. Faced with such events, public authorities have recognized emergency response and disaster management as major concerns in need of concerted efforts, in collaboration with business and academia. The emergence of extremely large and complex datasets (i.e., big data) made it possible to utilize advanced techniques to reveal patterns, trends, and associations. Data-driven emergency rescue and response have been efficiently applied in several recent hazardous events.

Big Data provides valuable insights into all main phases of emergency management: prevention, preparedness, response, and recovery. There are two major sources of big data, sensor networks (e.g., earthquake detection using seismometers) and multipurpose sensor networks (e.g., social media such as Twitter using smartphones), both have proved their effectiveness in emergencies such as the hurricane Sandy, coronavirus outbreak, and so on. However, significant big data research challenges arise because of emergency management requirements for quality of service (e.g., highly available real-time response) and quality of information (e.g., reliable communications on resource availability for the victim).

The Transnational Partnership for Excellent Research and Education in Big Data and Emergency Management (BDEM) is a research and education network coordinated by Western Norway Research Institute. The BDEM aims through a cooperation between Western Norway Research Institute, University of Bergen, and six world-class universities from Hong Kong, Japan, and the USA, to establish a long-term partnership where excellent education is to be embedded in high-quality research in big data for emergency management. The field of data-driven emergency management involves cross-domain terminology and methodologies and should be carried forward by multidisciplinary and international efforts. This edited book is based on a specially designed topic on big data in emergency management by the BDEM project team. The master level course also launched at the University of Bergen, Norway from autumn 2017.

This edited textbook has been designed to meet the needs of individuals wishing to pursue a research and development career in emergency management and big data, specifically techniques for social and mobile data.

Overview of the Book

Particularly, every chapter is based on graduate lectures or research seminars delivered by authors over the last several years for a wide variety of courses in various universities and research venues. The feedback from participants and colleagues at these venues has helped them to improve the text significantly.

A brief description of the contents found within each chapter of the book is as follows:

- In the chapter "Introduction to Emergency Management," we examine basic concepts of emergency management and provide its brief history. In addition, the concept of data-driven emergencies is described by considering the unique characteristics of big data.
- The chapter "Big Data" reviews the sources of big data and their characteristics. Further, it discusses the potential benefits of big data for emergency management along with the technological and societal challenges it poses. Also, central technologies for big-data storage and processing in general are reviewed, before presenting the Spark big-data engine in more detail. Finally, the chapter explains the ethical and societal threats that big data pose.
- Next, the chapter "Learning Algorithms for Emergency Management" deals with the fundamental machine learning techniques to support the decision-making processes for emergency management. Then the practices and exercises of the learning techniques with real tweet datasets in real emergencies are discussed.
- Emergency-relevant data comes in many varieties. It can be high volume and high velocity, and reaction times are critical, calling for efficient and powerful techniques for data analysis and management. Knowledge graphs represent data in a rich, flexible, and uniform way that is well-matched with the needs of emergency management. The chapter "Knowledge Graphs and Natural-Language Processing" explains the most important semantic technologies and how they support knowledge graphs. The chapter discusses their benefits and challenges and gives examples of relevant semantic data sources and vocabularies. The chapter concludes with an overview of techniques for processing natural-language texts.
- Next, the chapter "Social Media Mining for Disaster Management and Community Resilience" describes the role of social media during disasters as how platforms like Twitter and Facebook facilitate communication for both the public and response agencies during the time-critical events. Specifically, it

introduces the concepts of social media mining for disaster events, provides the use-cases to mine social media for helping public and emergency services, and describes different methods of user, content, network, context, and visual analytics to process and analyze social media data for emergency management and community resilience.

- Human mobility modeling for emergency management plays a critical role in guaranteeing people safety and saving people's life. However, many traditional techniques for regular human mobility modeling fail on emergency management, because human mobility differs significantly from routines. The chapter "Big Data-Driven Citywide Human Mobility Modeling for Emergency Management" elaborates the challenges and reviews the state-of-the-art technologies to cope with the three fundamental tasks of human mobility modeling for emergency management.
- Emergency communication networks (ECNs) are designed to provide reliable communications under emergent scenarios. Recently, smartphone-based networks have attracted remarkable attention on the management of ECNs. The chapter "Smartphone based Emergency Communication" presents the state-of-the-art research efforts devoted to the establishment and management of smartphone-based ECNs. The related key techniques and their significant roles for disaster relief in ECNs are discussed. Further, the chapter also presents several real-world applications and case studies. Finally, it summarizes the open issues and future research directions.
- Finally, the chapter "Emergency Information Visualisation" is the final puzzle piece to complete a big picture of big data in emergency management. A good visualization can transfer big emergency data into a way that is easier and more comprehensive to discover underlying patterns and valuable insights, which are useful for either other analyzing tasks or end users.

Throughout the book, cases and exercises are given to highlight certain aspects of the covered material and to stimulate thought. The BDEM website (https://www.bigdata.vestforsk.no/resources) also has a dedicated webpage containing various pointers about emergency datasets, tools, and software.

Intended Audience

The book can be used at the graduate or advanced undergraduate level as a textbook or major reference for courses on Big Data and Disaster Management.

- Advanced undergraduate and PhD students and other early-career researchers who seek to conduct research on data-driven emergency management.
- Researchers, engineers, data analysts, and data managers who need to deal with large and complex sets of data.
- Besides, the goal is to help policymakers and other individuals navigate the new data-driven emergency response landscape.

Prerequisites

To appreciate fully the material in this book, we recommend the following prerequisites:

- A basic course in R programming and related database systems.
- A sophomore-level course in data structures, algorithms, and discrete mathematics.

The organization and the contents of this edited book have benefited from our outstanding contributors, members of the BDEM network. I am very proud and happy that outstanding researchers agreed to join this project and prepared a chapter for this book. I am also very pleased to see it materialize in a way as we originally envisioned. I hope that this book will be a source of inspiration to the readers. I especially wish to express my sincere gratitude to all the authors for their contribution to this book.

I am grateful to the Research Council of Norway (RCN) and the Norwegian Agency for International Cooperation and Quality Enhancement in Higher Education (Diku) for supporting the BDEM initiative through INTPART programme.

Springer Verlag, especially Susan Lagerstrom-Fife, production editor, production staff, and reviewers of this book in bringing out in an orderly manner.

I wish all readers a fruitful time reading this book and wish they experience the same excitement as I did—and still do—when dealing with *Big Data*.

Sogndal, Norway   Rajendra Akerkar
March 2020

Contents

Contributors

Rajendra Akerkar Big Data Research Group, Western Norway Research Institute, Sogndal, Norway

Zipei Fan SUSTech-UTokyo Joint Research Center on Super Smart City, Southern University of Science and Technology, University of Tokyo, Tokyo, Japan

Song Guo Department of Computing, The Hong Kong Polytechnic University, Hung Hom, Hong Kong

Minsung Hong Big Data Research Group, Western Norway Research Institute, Sogndal, Norway

Huawei Huang School of Data and Computer Science, Sun Yat-Sen University, Guangzhou, China

Hoang Long Nguyen Big Data Research Group, Western Norway Research Institute, Sogndal, Norway

Vimala Nunavath Department of Information Science and Media Studies, University of Bergen, Bergen, Norway

University of Agder, Kristiansand, Norway

Andreas L. Opdahl Department of Information Science and Media Studies, University of Bergen, Bergen, Norway

Steve Peterson National Institutes of Health, Bethesda, MD, USA

Hemant Purohit Department of Information Sciences and Technology, George Mason University, Fairfax, VA, USA

Ryosuke Shibasaki SUSTech-UTokyo Joint Research Center on Super Smart City, Southern University of Science and Technology, University of Tokyo, Tokyo, Japan

Xuan Song SUSTech-UTokyo Joint Research Center on Super Smart City, Southern University of Science and Technology, University of Tokyo, Tokyo, Japan

Glossary

Analytic hierarchy processing   The analytic hierarchy process is a structured technique for organizing and analyzing complex decisions, based on mathematics.

Anomaly detection   Anomaly detection is the identification of rare items, events, or observations which raise suspicions by differing significantly from the majority of the data.

Cloud-based service   A cloud service is any service made available to users on demand via the Internet from cloud service provider's servers.

Collective intelligence   Collective intelligence is shared or group intelligence that emerges from the collaboration, collective efforts, and competition of many individuals and appears in consensus decision-making.

Community   A group with a commonality of association and generally defined by location, shared experience, or function.

Competitive intelligence   Competitive intelligence is the systematic collection and analysis of information from multiple sources and a coordinated program.

Content analytics   Content analytics defines a family of technologies that processes digital content and user behavior in consuming and engaging with content, such as documents, news sites, customer conversations (both audio and text), and social network discussions, to solve specific problems.

Critical infrastructure   The physical structures, facilities, networks, and other assets which provide services that are essential to the social and economic functioning of a community or society.

Crowdmapping   Crowdmapping is a subtype of crowdsourcing by which aggregation of crowd-generated inputs such as captured communications and social media feeds is combined with geographic data to create a digital map that is as up-to-date as possible on events such as wars, humanitarian crises, or natural disasters.

Cyber-physical system   A cyber-physical system is a system in which a mechanism is controlled or monitored by computer-based algorithms.

Data aggregation Data aggregation is any process in which information is gathered and expressed in a summary form, for purposes such as statistical analysis.

Data-driven approach A data-driven approach means it makes strategic decisions based on data analysis and interpretation.

Decision-making system Decision-making system is a system for computer applications that help individuals and organizations make choices and take decisions, typically by ranking, prioritizing, or choosing from a number of options.

Emergency An event, either man-made or natural, sudden or progressive, the impact of which is such that the affected community must respond through exceptional measures.

Emergency management system Emergency management system refers to the legislation, regulations, plans, standards, policies, technology systems, guidelines, and associated reports in place to facilitate effective emergency management across the four phases of prevention, preparedness, response, and recovery.

Emergency risk management A development approach to emergency management focuses on underlying conditions of the risks which lead to crisis occurrence. The objective is to increase capacities to effectively manage and reduce risks, thereby reducing the occurrence and magnitude of emergencies.

Event An event may be natural or caused by human acts or omissions, for example: a cyclone, hurricane, earthquake, flood, storm, storm tide, tornado, tsunami, volcanic eruption, or other natural happenings, and an infestation, coronavirus outbreak, or epidemic. An explosion or fire, a chemical, fuel, or oil spill, or a gas leak. A failure or disruption to an essential service or infrastructure. A terrorist attack against the state or community and another event similar to an event mentioned here.

Event detection The goal of event detection is to detect the occurrences of events and categorize them.

Geospatial Relating to or denoting data that is associated with a specific location or that has a geographic component to it. It can be in the form of coordinates, addresses, or postcodes.

Hazard A potential or existing condition that may cause harm to people or damage to property or the environment. The magnitude of the phenomenon, the probability of its occurrence, and the extent and severity of its impact can vary.

Impact assessment The analysis of the consequences of an event, including psychosocial, economic, natural, and built environment.

Information system Information system is a formal, sociotechnical, organizational system designed to collect, process, store, and distribute information.

Level of risk Magnitude of a risk, or a combination of risks, expressed in terms of the combination of vulnerability, consequence, and their likelihood.

Machine learning Machine learning is a method of data analysis that automates analytical model building. It is a branch of artificial intelligence based on the idea that systems can learn from data, identify patterns, and make decisions with minimal human intervention.

Mobile communication   Mobile communication is the use of technology that allows us to communicate with others in different locations without the use of any physical connection. Mobile communication makes our life easier, and it saves time and effort.

Mobile computing   Mobile computing is a technology that allows transmission of data, voice, and video via a computer or any other wireless-enabled device without having to be connected to a fixed physical link.

Preparedness   Arrangements to ensure that, should an emergency occur, all those resources and services which are needed to cope with the effects can be efficiently deployed.

Prevention   Regulatory or physical measures to ensure that emergencies are prevented or their effects mitigated.

Radio-frequency identification   Radio-frequency identification is a method of automatic identification that relies on storing and remotely retrieving data using RFID tags.

Real-time sensor data   Real-time sensor data is information that is delivered immediately after collecting from sensors. Real-time sensor data is often used for navigation or tracking.

Real-time system   A real-time system can serve real-time applications that process data as it comes in, typically without buffer delays.

Recovery   The coordinated process of supporting emergency-affected communities in reconstruction of the physical infrastructure and restoration of emotional, social, economic, and physical well-being.

Relief   The provision of immediate shelter, life support, and human needs for persons affected by an emergency incident.

Resilience   A system or community's ability to swiftly accommodate and recover from the impacts of hazards, restore essential structures and desired functionality, and adapt to new circumstances.

Response   Actions taken in anticipation of, during, and immediately after a crisis event to ensure that its effects are minimized and that individuals affected are given immediate relief and support.

Risk   The expected losses (lives lost, persons injured, damage to property, and disruption of economic activity) due to a specific hazard. Risk is the product of hazard and vulnerability.

Sensing data stream   A sensing data stream is a sequence of digitally encoded coherent signals used to transmit or receive information from sensors.

Sensor data   Sensor data is the output of a device that detects and responds to some type of input from the physical environment. The output may be used to provide information or input to another system or to guide a process.

Sensor web   Sensor web is a type of sensor network that is especially well suited for environmental monitoring.

Situational awareness   Situational awareness is the perception of environmental elements and events with respect to time or space, the comprehension of their meaning, and the projection of their status after some variable has changed, such as time, or some other variable, such as a predetermined event. It is also a field of study concerned with the understanding of the environment critical to decision-makers.

Smart grid   The "smart grid" is basically an intelligent communications network that overlays the electric grid making optimal decisions on allocation, routing, utilization, and spend of electricity.

Social networking service   A social networking service is an online platform which people use to build social networks or social relationship with other people who share similar personal or career interests, activities, backgrounds or real-life connections.

Spatial analytics   Spatial analytics includes any of the formal techniques which studies entities using their topological, geometric, or geographic properties.

System modeling   System modeling is the process of developing abstract models of a system, with each model presenting a different view or perspective of that system.

System reliability   Systems reliability describes the ability of a system to function under stated conditions for a specified period of time. Reliability is closely related to availability, which is typically described as the ability of a system to function at a specified moment or interval of time.

Ubiquitous computing   Ubiquitous computing is a concept in software engineering and computer science where computing is made to appear anytime and everywhere.

Volunteers   People who are formally affiliated with an emergency service organization or nongovernment organization and act under the respective organizations direction and authority.

Vulnerability   Degree of loss resulting from a possible damaging phenomenon.

Wireless sensor network   Wireless sensor network refers to a group of spatially dispersed and dedicated sensors for monitoring and recording the physical conditions of the environment and organizing the collected data at a central location.

Introduction to Emergency Management

Rajendra Akerkar and Minsung Hong

1 What Is Emergency?

In the contemporary society, various emergencies occur more and more frequently and have threatened to human life, environmental protection, social stability, and even political relationship of different countries around the world [14]. Indeed many emergencies killing thousands and destroying enormous amount of properties and infrastructure [7, 19]. For example, the 2010 and 2011 Queensland floods has caused the economic losses about A\$ 6.8 billion [36], and the economic impact of 2016 Japan's Kyushu Island earthquake were estimated to about US\$ 25 billion and US\$ 30 billion. This 9.0 magnitude earthquake resulted in 15,889 deaths, 6152 injuries, and 2601 people missing and caused 127,290 building collapses, 272,788 buildings half collapsing.[1] Insurance firm Swiss Re which makes this calculation every 6 months estimated the economic loss in 2017 to be US\$ 306 billion, which is almost double 2016s loss of \$188 billion [50].

The World Health Organisation (WHO) defined the emergency as "an occurrence disrupting the normal conditions of existence and causing a level of suffering that exceeds the capacity of adjustment of the affected community."

There is one broad consensus that emergencies are social phenomena characterised by a disruption of routine and of social structure, norms, and/or values [41]. This definition implies that the severity of a disaster is more related to the extent of the disruption of social life, than to the measurable physical magnitude of the hazard that may have triggered the emergency.

---

[1]Wikipedia. 2011. Tohoku Earthquake. Retrieved July, 2018 from https://en.wikipedia.org/.

R. Akerkar (✉) · M. Hong
Big Data Research Group, Western Norway Research Institute, Sogndal, Norway
e-mail: rak@vestforsk.no; msh@vestforsk.no

© Springer Nature Switzerland AG 2020
R. Akerkar (ed.), *Big Data in Emergency Management: Exploitation Techniques for Social and Mobile Data*, https://doi.org/10.1007/978-3-030-48099-8_1

Table 1 Emergency categories and sub-categories, adapted from [38]

Category	Subcategory	Examples
Natural	• Meteorological	• Tornado, Hurricane
	• Hydrological	• Flood, Landslide
	• Geophysical	• Earthquake, Volcano
	• Climatological	• Wildfire, Heat/cold wave
	• Biological	• Epidemic, Infestation
Anthropogenic	• Sociological (intentional)	• Shooting, Bombing
	• Technological (accidental)	• Derailment, Building collapse

Emergency is a sudden, calamitous event that seriously disrupts the functioning of a community or society and causes human, material, and economic or environmental losses that exceed the community's or society's ability to cope using its own resources. Though often caused by nature, disasters can have human origins. The above Table 1 shows, two taxonomies used in Europe and the United States, as well as the traditional hazard categories listed in [18].

Furthermore, an emergency could be a major disaster or crisis that goes beyond a small geographic space and requires help from the outside. Thus, there are four levels of emergency:

- **First (lowest) level**: this is about routine events, e.g. a vehicle accident or a heart attack in a public place
- **Second level**: emergencies that can be dealt with within the municipality or local level without requiring significant resources from outside areas. This includes severe flooding or a power outage.
- **Third level**: a major incident or crisis requiring regional resources and higher levels of coordination. Examples include a airline accident.
- **The fourth level**: refers to a national or international disaster, an event of such magnitude and seriousness that it can be managed only with the complete engagement of the national government, and perhaps also international aid. Examples include an earthquake or an act of terrorism.

Peculiar characteristics of most emergencies are its complexity and unpredictability. During emergencies, unexpected problems, dynamic changes of situations or environmental and knowledge limitations often lead to the need for improvisation. Based on an analysis of the response to the 2001 World Trade Centre attack, the following characteristics of emergency management can be considered as reasons for improvisation:

- Time pressures force a convergence of planning and execution
- Uncertainty is present because developments within emergencies are rarely predictable
- The rarity of incidents limits opportunities for training and learning
- Multiple decision makers and responding organizations may negotiate while responding to the event

– Extreme events have very broad consequences leading to complexity, which necessitates a need to manage interdependencies among a wide range of physical and social systems

In spite of these complexities and unpredictability, emergency services have built systematic approaches to deal with these uncertainties and to carry out planned and coordinated activities in emergencies. Yet, many situations require spontaneous, ad-hoc decisions and short-term (re-)planning and the need for skills in improvisation. The ability to improvise is therefore a valuable asset for individuals and organizations, and is usually cultivated in emergency training and grows with experience. Computer-based systems can support these processes, if the design is informed by an understanding of the cognitive processes involved in responding to unanticipated contingencies.

In this chapter, we focus on the natural emergencies, without medical emergencies. Natural emergencies refer to a natural processes that occur in the ecosystem, which can lead to the losses of stability of the social-economic system, and serious imbalance between supply and demand of social resources [59]. A brief technical description of the upper major natural disasters is as follows [22]:

– **Tornado:** is a rapidly rotating vortex or funnel of air extending ground-ward from a cumulonimbus cloud, exhibiting wind speeds of up to 300 miles per hour. Approximately 1200 tornadoes are spawned by thunderstorms each year in the United States. Most tornadoes remain aloft, but a few that do touch the ground are devastating to everything in their path. The forces of a tornado's winds are capable of lifting and moving huge objects, destroying or moving whole buildings, and siphoning large volumes from bodies of water and ultimately depositing them elsewhere. Because tornadoes typically follow the path of least resistance, people living in valleys have the greatest exposure to damage.
– **Hurricane:** are cyclonic storms that begin as tropical waves and grow in intensity and size. Tropical waves continue to progress in size and intensity to tropical depressions and tropical storms as determined by their maximum sustained wind speed. The warm-core tropical depression becomes a tropical storm when the maximum sustained surface wind speeds range from 39 miles per hour to 73 miles per hour (mph).
– **Flood:** is an overabundance of water that engulfs dry land and property that is normally dry. Floods may be caused by a number of factors, including heavy rainfall, melting snow, an obstruction of a natural waterway, and other generative factors. Floods usually occur from large-scale weather systems generating prolonged rainfall or onshore winds, but they may also result from locally intense thunderstorms, snow-melt, ice jams, and dam failures.
– **Landslide:** occurs when masses of relatively dry rock, soil, or debris move in an uncontrolled manner down a slope. Landslides may be very highly localised or massive in size, and they can move at a creeping pace or at very high speeds. Many areas have experienced landslides repeatedly since prehistoric times. Landslides are activated when the mechanisms by which the material was

anchored become compromised (through a loss of vegetation or seismic activity, for example).

- **Earthquake:** is a sudden, rapid shaking of the earth's crust that is caused by the breaking and shifting of rock beneath the earth's surface. This shaking can cause the collapse of buildings and bridges; cause disruptions in gas, electric, and phone service; and trigger landslides, avalanches, flash floods, fires, and huge, destructive ocean waves (tsunamis).
- **Volcano:** is a rupture in the crust of a planetary-mass object, such as Earth, that allows hot lava, volcanic ash, and gases to escape from a magma chamber below the surface. Earth's volcanoes occur because its crust is broken into 17 major, rigid tectonic plates that float on a hotter, softer layer in its mantle.[2]
- **Wildfire:** can be occurred by human, here we consider the naturally occur wildfires. It can be characterised in terms of the cause of ignition, their physical properties, the combustible material present, and the effect of weather on the fire. Wildfires can cause damage to property and human life.[3]

2 Emergency Management

Emergency Management is a strategic planning and process that is administered and employed to protect critical infrastructures from severe damages when natural or human made calamities and catastrophic even occur. Emergency management plans are multi-layered and are aimed to address such issues as earthquakes, floods, hurricanes, fires, terrorist attacks, and even mass failures of utilities or the rapid outbreak of disease. Some interpretations of the term emergency management are as follows:

- IEM is "a discipline that deals with risk and risk avoidance." It illustrates broad definition of the EM, since risks represent a wide range of issues, and the range of its situations are also vast. This supports the premise that EM is essential to the security of everyone's daily lives and should be integrated into daily decisions and not just called on during times of emergencies [22].
- More modern EM includes processes to exploit the modern technologies which contribute to effectively and efficiently monitoring, response to, handle, and process the emergencies, with integrating various resources and analysing scientifically the cause and process of emergency and its negative impacts [13].
- According to the definition of the Federal Emergency Management Agency (FEMA), the EM consists of preparing for, mitigating, responding to, and recovering from an emergency when it happens [2].

---

[2]Wikipedia. Volcano. Retrieved July, 2018 from https://en.wikipedia.org/wiki/Volcano.
[3]Wikipedia. Wildfire. Retrieved July, 2018 from https://en.wikipedia.org/wiki/Wildfire.

– EM deals with the emergency events by the serious activities such as detection, preparation, planning, mitigation, response, and recovery [22].

The traditional approach to EM is referred to as bureaucratic or command and control [3]. In other words, in traditional methodologies, EM has been addressed from a single authority's perspective. For instance, the traditional emergency response is recognised as an approach which focuses on a strict set of norms, and it consists of bureaucratic policies and processes where emergent norms are not accepted [48]. Therefore, adaptation to unexpected tasks and involvement of other groups is not recognised as the necessary factors. Also, classic approaches are characterised by adopting a hierarchical structure. With an increase of complexity and a decrease in the predictability of operational scenarios, the traditional EM activities, which follow a hierarchical approach, have difficulty in following factors: (1) needs of rapidly developing scenarios, (2) increased numbers of participants, (3) suitable adoption of new technologies and (4) huge amounts of data collection and analyse [35].

Whereas, **a professional approach** of the FEMA [4] recognises that EM is a decentralised network of organisations that collaborate to mitigate the impacts of emergencies. For example, local police and fire stations, public enterprises, volunteers and government entities carry out tasks across the board of emergency life-cycle. Also it accommodates the civilians support for recovery strategies. In contrast to the traditional approaches, it acknowledges that public information and resources may support emergency activities. For instance, the public is able to be recognised as the first emergency responder because they directly experience the event. In addition, the flexibility of professional approach allows the implementation of its strategies to multiple types of emergencies. That means the strategies are not constrained to one specific emergency any more [35].

The recent approaches use Internet technologies to gather and disseminate information in emergency situations, as well as to communicate among stakeholders [27]. There were number of websites being set up in response to emergencies in beginning 2000s [39]. For example, a user-generated content website was used in response to a crisis in 2004. In addition, significant activities of emergency response have took place on MySpace, which is social networking service, during the occurrence of Hurricane Katrina which struck the city of New Orleans in the United States in 2005 [49]. One of the earliest famous cases of people using the micro-blogging service such as Twitter in an emergency is severe wildfires that took place near San Diego, California in 2007. Since then, it has become common practice for affected people and concerned others to use Twitter to communicate, ask questions, collect and spread information, and organise response efforts (among overall tasks) [16, 26, 47, 53, 54, 56]. On the other hand, with the Gartners' hype-cycle 2014, the Internet of Things (IoT) has just reached the top of public awareness and focus. Although it is entering the phase of disillusion, there is a clear longstanding technological trend that will affect the amount and type of information that is available in EM. In fact various research projects in the EM domain rely upon such open geo-spatial services and IoT paradigms and varied possibilities it provides in visualising, analysing, and predicting emergencies [55]. For example, TRIDEC[4] focuses on new technologies for enable intelligent information management in real time in order to efficiently find, merge, evaluate, and manage huge amounts of information and data for EM.

Moreover, in a response and recovery situation, numerous actors will be on site. The emergency management services have "specific responsibilities and objectives in serving and protecting people and property in emergency situations". Emergency management services "include agencies such as civil protection authorities, police, fire, ambulance, paramedic and emergency medicine services, Red Cross and Red Crescent societies, and specialized emergency units of electricity, transportation, communications and other related services organizations." The following broad types of emergency management services can be identified:

- First responders
- Governmental agencies or bodies
- Non-government organisations
- Businesses
- Media.

3   Emergency Management in Social Media Age: Information Flows

Social media platforms, including Twitter, Youtube, Foursquare, and Flickr have been contributing significantly to emergency management. Geotagged social media data can be collected by streaming harvest from the APIs provided by the social media firms. Social media services have contributed significantly to emergency management as a tool to communicate information during emergencies. There are many ways of using social media in emergency management, including data collection, analytic workflow, narrative construction, crisis related information extraction, geolocation pattern/text/image analytics, and the broadcasting of information through social media platforms.

By supporting both directions of information flow, it will be better positioned to study the full impact of the entire communication between public authorities and citizens via social media tools, apps and platforms.

Considering the citizen-to-authority (C2A) interaction, citizens can share information, for example, through social media channels as normal but with the knowledge that their contribution may help ES. All information sent by citizens on social networks selected by the emergency response system will be usually filtered

---

[4]TRIDEC: Collaborative, Complex and Critical Decision-Support in Evolving Crises, http://www. trideconline.eu.

and gathered. The processing and analysis system skims the list of messages in order to retrieve concise and accurate information to be communicated to ES.

Although emergency response systems are usually not equipped for social media, they use interoperability alerting protocols through which they can delegate the Authority to Citizen (A2C) communication to the system. In this way, emergency response systems can be both uncoupled from social media and yet able to use it for the broadcast of messages. The social media information to be shared by the system adapts CAP-format messages. The emergency response system extracts information from alerting messages and routes them toward social media using available APIs. Citizens therefore both read and feed social media information during an emergency.

4   Emergency Management using Big Data

Undoubtedly, Big Data has opened new options for natural EM, primarily because of the varied possibilities it provides in visualising, analysing, and predicting emergencies. In this regard, emerging technologies associated with levering this new ecosystem of Big Data to monitor and detect emergencies, mitigate their effects, assist in relief efforts, and contribute to the recovery and reconstruction processes are critical [57].

However, stakeholders who try to apply Big Data technologies to EM are facing the biggest challenges to manage large volumes of data exponentially generated at emergency. Due to huge amount of data, traditional data storage and processing techniques are very difficult to fulfil performance in aspects of real-time processing, scalability and availability [21]. As shown in Fig. 1, in addition to the techniques, analytics to extract useful data and information from the huge data are particularly challenged due to the combination of following unique characteristics (5 Vs such as *volume*, *variety*, *velocity*, *veracity* and *value*) of Big Data.

- **Vast data** generated by a huge number of the people who affected or related to emergency,
- **The high time sensitivity** due to data and events which must be detected and be responded in real time,
- **Integration techniques of static and dynamic data** (e.g., maps and crowd emotion) which are essential for effective and efficient EM [33, 46],
- **Heterogeneous data** ranging from raw data (e.g., sensors) to structured and unstructured data (e.g., metadata and multimedia) [42],
- **Disparate levels of trustworthiness** of the data sources (e.g., newspaper, government data and rumour in social media) [23] and
- **Valuable information** that may be extracted from data created by people who are affected by emergency event in real time, via crowdsourcing [32]

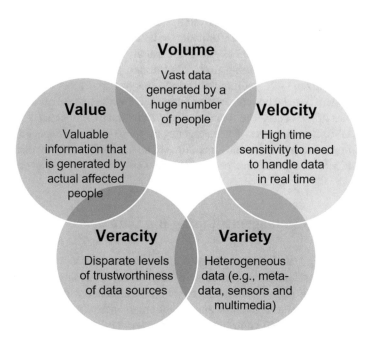

Fig. 1 Characteristics of emergency data according to the 5 Vs of big data

5   Tasks in Data-Driven Emergency Management

The concept of data-driven EM became common that uses a number of emerging technologies—e.g., big data analytics, participatory crisis mapping, crowdsourced translation, social media, and mobile technology. For successful data-driven EM, it is essential a variety of tasks based on an appropriate technologies (ML, DL and AI) within across the three phases (i.e. pre-/in-/post-emergency). Figure 2 shows the tasks for which the vary techniques of ML to be used, in each phase of emergency life-cycle. In the phase of "pre-emergency", the occurrence of potential emergency is predicted and early informed. For "in-emergency" stage, events caused are detected and tracked, and situational awareness are conducted using collected data to response the events or relief the affected people. The "post-emergency" phase is also important. In this stage, evaluating the loss caused by the events and the execution of response are carried out for the effective restoration and the preparation of next emergency. Moreover, as the usage of social media is growing, crowdsourcing-based approaches are attracting more attention to recover from an emergency and simultaneously adjusting distribution of volunteer efforts.

– **Event prediction** can achieve forecasting potential emergencies using technologies and interpretation methods which extract inherent feature or pattern of an emergency [37]. Although there is still no prediction method with perfect

Fig. 2 Tasks of emergency management in emergency life-cycle [Source: BDEM[5]]

accuracy, it is one of the most important tasks since early detection of the emergencies makes us prevent or avoid many dangerous situations [15, 28, 45].

– **Warning systems** to detect impending emergencies can give that information to make decision and early take actions such as prepare and evacuate people at the before or early part of emergency [52]. These systems have significantly improved using advanced techniques such as AI, DM and ML in recent years than the past but they are not perfect yet [17, 40].

– **Event Detection and Tracking** is one of the tasks in which researchers and practitioners have tried to apply the techniques of ML. Some events are often associated with specific location and time, however the events may or may not be necessarily related to the physical locations due to the online nature of collected data [12, 43, 51].

– **Situational Awareness** uses social media data related to specific information (e.g., caution, advice, donation, causalities and damage) and smart-phone which typically mount various sensors such as camera, GPS and accelerometer to take the appropriate decisions and actions in managing such emergency [46, 58].

– **Emergency Evaluation** is one of the most critical and complex tasks in EM [14], in post-emergency, current activity outcomes (e.g., loss of resources, recoverability, performance and social influence) should be measured to suppress the deterioration of next emergency. There were several tries to make measurements for the evaluation of EM [10, 20, 34, 44].

– **Crowdsourcing** has being utilised by both researchers and practitioners in EM for collecting, processing and sharing information across organisations and affected populations. Crowdsourcing might be considered with citizen participation and digital neighbourhood as complementary mechanisms to give an appropriate and sustainable response [8, 25, 30].

Valuable insight obtained from data during emergencies is highly dependent on data and its quality [37]. Numerous amount of data will be collected in emergencies, however, it's a mixture of informative and non-informative data. Furthermore, data related to emergency are gathered from multiple channels such as existing records, sensors, satellite networks or social media. Hence, the core of Fig. 2 is data processing (i.e., data collection, data filtering, data integration and information extraction) which is required in all the tasks in EM cycle.

– **Data Collection:** The Internet Technology (IT) has being arisen the innovative collection methodologies from the traditional data collection such as the use of processors, spreadsheets and forms to enter data directly into the databases [24]. It ranges from the automatic collecting sensors' data (e.g., temperature, humidity and wind strength) to gathering micro texts from blogs, SMS, email and social media as a new way of communication in the course of emergencies [11]. In other words, a major difference between data which is able to be collected with recent technologies and traditional sources is the possibility of receiving feedback from the affected people in real-time [37]. In addition to the real-time, data collection in EM should consider the processing of gathering data which is coming from multiple heterogeneous sources. Moreover, due to characteristic of emergency data which is rapidly increasing, scalability and availability are also important issues in data collection.
– **Data Filtering:** The objective of data filtering is removing redundant or unwanted data from an data stream using (semi) automated or computerised methods prior to provide it, to manage the data overload and increment of the meaningful data. If all the emergency data were presented to the users, it would cause an overwhelming workload. Therefore, the data should be filtered based on the specific purposes of the users [32]. Furthermore, data quality is the key for developing pre-emptive EM in .png environment [29]. Poor quality data makes it difficult to assess and use for emergency services [9]. The potential of emergency related data can be capitalised by addressing the risks of inaccurate and redundant data [6].
– **Data Integration:** Emergency services sometimes should handle a massive amount of data arriving from multiple channels such as existing records, sensors, satellite networks or social media [1]. Hence, one of the biggest challenges in EM is to integrate data from heterogeneous sources into one protocol for provide the user with an unified view of data [31]. Data integration includes the following steps: (1) converting contents of different formats into a standard format, (2) verifying the reliability of a variety of data sources and attempt to leverage it to produce meaningful information for emergency decision-making, (3) mapping

---

[5]https://www.bigdata.vestforsk.no/.

images or texts with the corresponding geo-locations to better capture the current situation and (4) processing and analysing the unified data for the proper purposes [32].

Big Data is a great global opportunity for emergency management. Big data has already demonstrated its usefulness for both dedicated sensor networks (e.g., earthquake detection during the earthquake) and multi-purpose sensor networks (e.g., social media such as Twitter). However, significant research challenges remain, particularly in the areas of Variety of data sources and Veracity of data content, which will be discussed in this book. Big Data and emergency management's latest growing relationship opens up new career opportunities also for those who want to find innovative ways to help others.

Acknowledgments The work is funded from the Research Council of Norway (RCN) and the Norwegian Agency for International Cooperation and Quality Enhancement in Higher Education (Diku) grant through INTPART programme.

References

1. Agarwal, R., Dhar, V.: Editorial—big data, data science, and analytics: the opportunity and challenge for IS research. Inf. Syst. Res. **25**(3), 443–448 (2014)
2. Agency, F.E.M.: Federal response plan (FRP). Technical report, Federal Emergency Management Agency, Washington (1999)
3. Agency, U.S.F.E.M.: A whole community approach to emergency management: principles, themes, and pathways for action. US Department of Homeland Security, Federal Emergency Management Agency, Washington (2011)
4. Agency, U.S.F.E.M.: Theory, Principles and Fundamentals of Hazards, Disasters, and U.S. Emergency Management, Approaches to Emergency Management. US Department of Homeland Security, Federal Emergency Management Agency, Washington (2012)
5. Akerkar, R.: Processing big data for emergency management. (Ed.) Liu, Zhi, and Kaoru Ota. Smart Technologies for Emergency Response and Disaster Management. 1–316 (2018), https://doi.org/10.4018/978-1-5225-2575-2
6. Akter, S., Wamba, S.F.: Big data and disaster management: a systematic review and agenda for future research. Ann. Oper. Res. **283**(1-2), 1–21 (2017)
7. Altay, N., III, W.G.G.: Or/ms research in disaster operations management. Eur. J. Oper. Res. **175**(1), 475–493 (2006)
8. Anbalagan, B., Valliyammai, C.: # chennaifloods: Leveraging human and machine learning for crisis mapping during disasters using social media. In: Proceedings of the IEEE 23rd International Conference on High Performance Computing Workshops (HiPCW), pp. 50–59. IEEE, Silver Spring (2016)
9. Beath, C., Becerra-Fernandez, I., Ross, J., Short, J.: Finding value in the information explosion. MIT Sloan Manag. Rev. **53**(4), 18 (2012)
10. Bernal, G.A., Salgado-Gálvez, M.A., Zuloaga, D., Tristancho, J., González, D., Omar-Darío: Integration of probabilistic and multi-hazard risk assessment within urban development planning and emergency preparedness and response: application to manizales, colombia. Int. J. Disaster Risk Sci. **8**(3), 270–283 (2017)
11. Boccardo, P., Tonolo, F.G.: Remote sensing role in emergency mapping for disaster response. In: Engineering Geology for Society and Territory, vol. 5, pp. 17–24. Springer, Berlin (2015)

12. Brants, T., Chen, F., Farahat, A.: A system for new event detection. In: Proceedings of the 26th Annual International ACM SIGIR Conference on Research and Development in Information Retrieval, pp. 330–337. ACM, New York (2003)
13. Chen, N., Liu, W., Bai, R., et al.: Application of computational intelligence technologies in emergency management: a literature review. Artif. Intell. Rev. **52**, 2131–2168 (2019)
14. Chen, N., Wenjing, L., Ruizhen, B., Chen, A.: Application of computational intelligence technologies in emergency management: a literature review. Artif. Intell. Rev. pp. 1–38 (2017)
15. Chen, W., Xie, X., Peng, J., Wang, J., Duan, Z., Hong, H.: Gis-based landslide susceptibility modelling: a comparative assessment of kernel logistic regression, naïve-bayes tree, and alternating decision tree models. Geomat. Nat. Haz. Risk **8**(2), 950–973 (2017)
16. Cobb, C., McCarthy, T., Perkins, A., Bharadwaj, A., Comis, J., Do, B., Starbird, K.: Designing for the deluge: understanding and supporting the distributed, collaborative work of crisis volunteers. In: Proceedings of the 17th ACM Conference on Computer Supported Cooperative Work and Social Computing, pp. 888–899. ACM, New York (2014)
17. Fersini, E., Messina, E., Pozzi, F.A.: Earthquake management: a decision support system based on natural language processing. J. Ambient. Intell. Humaniz. Comput. **8**(1), 37–45 (2017)
18. Fischer, H.W.: Response to Disaster: Fact versus Fiction and Its Perpetuation: The Sociology of Disaster. University Press of America, Lanham (1998)
19. Galindo, G., Batta, R.: Review of recent developments in or/ms research in disaster operations management. Eur. J. Oper. Res. **230**(2), 201–211 (2013)
20. Gao, J.: Analysis and assessment of the risk of snow and freezing disaster in China. Int. J. Disaster Risk Reduct. **19**, 334–340 (2016)
21. Grolinger, K., Mezghani, E., Capretz, M., Exposito, E.: Knowledge as a service framework for collaborative data management in cloud environments-disaster domain. In: Managing Big Data in Cloud Computing Environments, pp. 183–209 (2016)
22. Haddow, G.D., Bullock, J.A., Coppola, D.P.: Introduction to Emergency Management. Butterworth-Heinemann (2017)
23. Howard, C., Jones, D., Reece, S., Waldock, A.: Learning to trust the crowd: validating 'crowd'sources for improved situational awareness in disaster response. Procedia Eng. **159**, 141–147 (2016)
24. Hristidis, V., Chen, S.C., Li, T., Luis, S., Deng, Y.: Survey of data management and analysis in disaster situations. J. Syst. Softw. **83**(10), 1701–1714 (2010)
25. Huang, Q., Xiao, Y.: Geographic situational awareness: mining tweets for disaster preparedness, emergency response, impact, and recovery. ISPRS Int. J. Geo Inf. **4**(3), 1549–1568 (2015)
26. Imran, M., Castillo, C., Lucas, J., Meier, P., Vieweg, S.: Aidr: Artificial intelligence for disaster response. In: Proceedings of the 23rd International Conference on World Wide Web, pp. 159–162. ACM, New York (2014)
27. Imran, M., Castillo, C., Diaz, F., Vieweg, S.: Processing social media messages in mass emergency: a survey. ACM Comput. Surv. (CSUR) **47**(4), 67 (2015)
28. Kim, S.W., Melby, J.A., Nadal-Caraballo, N.C., Ratcliff, J.: A time-dependent surrogate model for storm surge prediction based on an artificial neural network using high-fidelity synthetic hurricane modeling. Nat. Hazards **76**(1), 565–585 (2015)
29. Kiron, D., Prentice, P.K., Ferguson, R.B.: The analytics mandate. MIT Sloan Manag. Rev. **55**(4), 1 (2014)
30. Kurkcu, A., Zuo, F., Gao, J., Morgul, E.F., Ozbay, K.: Crowdsourcing incident information for disaster response using twitter. In: Proceedings of the 65th Annual Meeting of Transportation Research Board (2017)
31. Lenzerini, M.: Data integration: a theoretical perspective. In: Popa, L., Abiteboul, S., Kolaitis, P.G. (eds.) Proceedings of the Twenty-first ACM SIGACT-SIGMOD-SIGART Symposium on Principles of Database Systems, pp. 233–246. ACM, New York (2002)
32. Li, T., Xie, N., Zeng, C., Zhou, W., Zheng, L., Jiang, Y., Yang, Y., Ha, H., Xue, W., Huang, Y., Chen, S., Navlakha, J.K., Iyengar, S.S.: Data-driven techniques in disaster information management. ACM Comput. Surv. **50**(1), 1:1–1:45 (2017)

33. Liang, J., Jacobs, P., Parthasarathy, S.: Human-guided flood mapping: from experts to the crowd. In: Companion Proceedings of the The Web Conference 2018 (2018)
34. Liu, M., Wei, J., Wang, G., Wang, F.: Water resources stress assessment and risk early warning– a case of Hebei Province China. Ecol. Indic. **73**, 358–368 (2017)
35. Luna, S., Pennock, M.J.: Social media applications and emergency management: a literature review and research agenda. Int. J. Disaster Risk Reduct. **28**, 565–577 (2018)
36. Menhart, M.: How much can Australia's economy withstand? Technical report, Munich Re (2015)
37. Nazer, T.H., Xue, G., Ji, Y., Liu, H.: Intelligent disaster response via social media analysis a survey. ACM SIGKDD Explorations Newsletter **19**(1), 46–59 (2017)
38. Olteanu, A., Vieweg, S., Castillo, C.: What to expect when the unexpected happens: social media communications across crises. In: Proceedings of the 18th ACM Conference on Computer Supported Cooperative Work and Social Computing, pp. 994–1009. ACM, New York (2015)
39. Palen, L., Liu, S.B.: Citizen communications in crisis: anticipating a future of ICT-supported public participation. In: Rosson, M.B., Gilmore, D.J. (eds.) Proceedings of the 2007 Conference on Human Factors in Computing Systems, CHI 2007, pp. 727–736. ACM, San Jose (2007)
40. Pengel, B., Krzhizhanovskaya, V., Melnikova, N., Shirshov, G., Koelewijn, A., Pyayt, A., Mokhov, I., et al.: Flood early warning system: sensors and internet. IAHS Red Book **357**, 445–453 (2013)
41. Perry, R.W.: What is a disaster? In: Handbook of disaster research, pp. 1–15. Springer, Berlin (2007)
42. Poblet, M., García-Cuesta, E., Casanovas, P.: Crowdsourcing roles, methods and tools for data-intensive disaster management. Inf. Syst. Front. **20**(6), 1–17 (2017)
43. Pohl, D., Bouchachia, A., Hellwagner, H.: Social media for crisis management: clustering approaches for sub-event detection. Multimed. Tools Appl. **74**(11), 3901–3932 (2015)
44. Rong, H., Xuedong, L., Guizhi, Z., Yulin, Y., Da, W.: An evaluation of coordination relationships during earthquake emergency rescue using entropy theory. Cad. Saude Publica **31**, 947–959 (2015)
45. Salehi, M., Rusu, L.I., Lynar, T., Phan, A.: Dynamic and robust wildfire risk prediction system: an unsupervised approach. In: Proceedings of the 22nd ACM SIGKDD International Conference on Knowledge Discovery and Data Mining, pp. 245–254. ACM, New York (2016)
46. Salfinger, A., Girtelschmid, S., Pröll, B., Retschitzegger, W., Schwinger, W.: Crowd-sensing meets situation awareness: a research roadmap for crisis management. In: Proceedings of the 48th Hawaii International Conference on System Sciences, HICSS, pp. 153–162. Kauai, Hawaii (2015)
47. Sarcevic, A., Palen, L., White, J., Starbird, K., Bagdouri, M., Anderson, K.: Beacons of hope in decentralized coordination: learning from on-the-ground medical twitterers during the 2010 haiti earthquake. In: Proceedings of the ACM 2012 conference on computer supported cooperative work, pp. 47–56. ACM, New York (2012)
48. Schneider, S.K.: Governmental response to disasters: the conflict between bureaucratic procedures and emergent norms. In: Procedures and Emergent Norms' Public Administration Review, pp. 135–145 (1992)
49. Shklovski, I., Burke, M., Kiesler, S., Kraut, R.: Technology adoption and use in the aftermath of hurricane katrina in new orleans. Am. Behav. Sci. **53**(8), 1228–1246 (2010)
50. Sigma, S.R.I.: Financial report—4 traders. Technical report, Swiss Re Institute Sigma (2017)
51. Singh, J.P., Dwivedi, Y.K., Rana, N.P., Kumar, A., Kapoor, K.K.: Event classification and location prediction from tweets during disasters. Ann. Oper. Res. **283**, 737–757 (2019)
52. Sorensen, J.H.: Hazard warning systems: review of 20 years of progress. Nat. Hazard. Rev. **1**(2), 119–125 (2000)
53. Starbird, K.: Delivering patients to sacré coeur: collective intelligence in digital volunteer communities. In: Proceedings of the SIGCHI Conference on Human Factors in Computing Systems, pp. 801–810. ACM, New York (2013)

54. Starbird, K., Palen, L., Hughes, A.L., Vieweg, S.: Chatter on the red: what hazards threat reveals about the social life of microblogged information. In: Proceedings of the 2010 ACM conference on Computer supported cooperative work, pp. 241–250. ACM, New York (2010)
55. Uslä, T., et al.: The trend towards the internet of things: what does it help in disaster and risk management? Planet@ Risk **3**(1), 140–145 (2015)
56. Vieweg, S., Hughes, A.L., Starbird, K., Palen, L.: Microblogging during two natural hazards events: what twitter may contribute to situational awareness. In: Mynatt, E.D., Schoner, D., Fitzpatrick, G., Hudson, S.E., Edwards, W.K., Rodden, T. (eds.) Proceedings of the 28th International Conference on Human Factors in Computing Systems, CHI, pp. 1079–1088. ACM, Atlanta (2010)
57. Yu, M., Yang, C., Li, Y.: Big data in natural disaster management: a review. Geosciences **8**(5), 165 (2018)
58. Zagorecki, A.T., David, E.J., Ristvej, J.: Data mining and machine learning in the context of disaster and crisis management. Int. J. Emerg. Manag. **9**(4), 351–365 (2013)
59. Zhou, L., Wu, X., Xu, Z., Fujita, H.: Emergency decision making for natural disasters: an overview. Int. J. Disaster Risk Reduct. **27**, 567–576 (2017)

Big Data

Andreas L. Opdahl and Vimala Nunavath

1 What Is Big Data?

There is already much more data available on the internet than humans can meaningfully process. Spread out among this data may lie central keys to prevent and better manage emergencies. To unlock the knowledge they contain, big data sets must become effectively processable by machines and the results easily interpretable for humans [2].

Big data is a broad term with many related meanings on the technical, computing, data, and usage levels. On the *technical-infrastructure level*, big data has often been used about data collections that are too large to be straightforwardly handled with traditional mainstream data-processing techniques and tools. Starting in the 2000s, big internet companies like Google, Amazon, and Facebook found they needed new ways and new software tools to store and process the enormous data collections they were amassing at the hearts of their businesses. The result was a new generation of distributed technologies we will review later in this chapter: file systems such as HDFS; grid and cloud technologies such as Amazon's Web Services (AWS); big-data stores such as Cassandra; and big-data processing engines such as Spark.

A. L. Opdahl (✉)
Department of Information Science and Media Studies, University of Bergen, Bergen, Norway
e-mail: Andreas.Opdahl@uib.no

V. Nunavath
Department of Information Science and Media Studies, University of Bergen, Bergen, Norway

University of Agder, Kristiansand, Norway
e-mail: Vimala.Nunavath@uia.no

© Springer Nature Switzerland AG 2020
R. Akerkar (ed.), *Big Data in Emergency Management: Exploitation Techniques for Social and Mobile Data*, https://doi.org/10.1007/978-3-030-48099-8_2

15

On the *computing level*, big-data computing methods also differ from past mainstream approaches. Most importantly, they need to be highly distributed because computing, networking, and storage demands can go way beyond the abilities of single computers. In consequence, computing must also be fault-tolerant because, when a distributed system consists of hundreds or thousands of computers, failing components become the norm rather than the exception. To achieve this, big-data computing must therefore be highly redundant, so that each computation is carried out and each piece of data stored in several places simultaneously, and so that computation can go on even when some of the computers, disks, or networks fail. While solutions to each of these problems have existed for a long time, big-data computing has brought them together in new techniques and tools and moved their use from the fringe into the mainstream [6, 7, 10, 14].

On the *data level*, big data refers to *"the three Vs"*: data that has large *volume*, arrives at high *velocity*, and has great *variety*—consisting of both structured data, natural language, images, audio, and video [9]. While earlier mainstream approaches could deal with two of these at the expense of the third, the ability to support all three "Vs" at the same time is a central requirement of big data. Two more "Vs" are that big data must be *valid* or true (*veracity*) and provide *value* to users. In addition, big data aims to be *exhaustive*, by representing each and every relevant phenomenon rather than just a sample. It tends to be *fine-grained*, by representing every available piece of information in the life-cycle of a phenomenon. It is *indexical*, in that it uses, as much as possible, standard identifiers for phenomena, attributes, and events. It is *relational*, in the sense that information about different phenomena are connected by use of standard identifiers. It is also easily *extendible* to new types of phenomena, attributes and events and *scalable* in size as more information is added. It is *historical*, by representing not just current but also all previous states of phenomena. And it can be *opportunistic*, in the sense that data is stored exhaustively, historically and in full detail because it can potentially generate value in the future, even if it is not yet needed today [9]. Despite including the word "big", *data size* is less used as a central characteristic of big data. Although the big global players today manage data collections in the peta- (10^{15}) and exabyte (10^{18}) range, many smaller- and medium-sized companies find big-data techniques essential for creating value from datasets with high variety and velocity, even when the volumes are much smaller.

Finally, on the *usage level*, big data refers to new data-driven ways of managing and organising private, public, and ideal enterprises. So-called *data-driven projects, businesses/organisations, and societies* continuously harvest exhaustive, fine-grained data about their inner workings and environment. They process the data in real time, using machine learning techniques on historical data to continuously describe and diagnose the past and present in order to optimally predict the future and prescribe optimal actions in advance [9].

2 Big Data Sources for Emergency Management

Several organisations provide online overviews of big and other data sources that can be useful in emergencies. The Humanitarian Data Exchange (HDX[1]) indexes more than 6000 crisis-relevant data sets, searchable by features, location, format, organisation, license, year, and general tags. CSV-tables is the most common data format by far. PreventionWeb[2] offers a portal to disaster-related datasets and sites across the globe, focussing on past disaster loss and damage, historical and synthetic hazard catalogues, socio-economic factors that can impact vulnerability and resilience on a local level, and exposure data about populations and buildings in particular locations.

General open data sources can also serve as useful references in emergencies. GeoNames[3] is a global database of geographical features that is searchable and browsable through a map interface. OpenStreetMap[4] is similar, but provides more detailed information about populated areas. The Humanitarian OpenStreetMap[5] is an international network dedicated to humanitarian action and community development through open mapping, for example of refugee situations, volcanic eruptions, and ebola outbreaks. Wikipedia is an important source of open reference data, along with its more recent sister project Wikidata[6] for factual and structured data. Google Crisis Map and Person Finder[7] are examples of proprietary data resources that can be leveraged in crisis situations through well-defined interfaces.

Public authorities on the international, national, and local levels are also important providers of reference data, for example census and map data. Many authorities also maintain emergency-relevant data about buildings (kindergartens, schools, hospitals, care facilities) and statistical data about their population. More sensitive governmental data include data about critical infrastructures: water supply and sewage, electricity, communication, roads and railways, and military installations and operations. Some local governments may also maintain information about vulnerable citizens that need particular assistance. In many countries, a wide variety of emergency-related data sets are already available through portals and data hotels such as http://data.europa.eu in the EU and http://data.gov in the US. Unfortunately, many datasets provide only static, aggregated, historical statistics. There are fewer live web APIs that offer minute-to-minute information.

There are also many closed (for-pay or restricted) data sources provided by businesses and governments. Some of them have higher quality than their open

---

[1] https://data.humdata.org.

[2] http://www.preventionweb.net.

[3] http://geonames.org.

[4] http://openstreetmap.org.

[5] http://www.hotosm.org/.

[6] http://www.wikidata.org/.

[7] http://www.google.org/crisismap, http://www.google.org/personfinder.

counterparts in terms of completeness, correctness, precision, timeliness, etc. Examples of private and semi-private companies that maintain potentially emergency-related information are: mapping agencies (maps, buildings, critical infrastructure); telecommunications companies (location and movement of subscribers, communication patterns, habits, pictures); transport companies (movement patterns, locations of people and vehicles); and app providers (many of the above and more). In some countries, previous government agencies have been privatised or semi-privatised in recent years, making emergency-relevant data sources less accessible.

The Internet of Things (IoT) is another source of big data, whose importance is rapidly growing [1]. There are already many times more things connected to the internet than there are people. These things can be sensors that measure and observe, such as a thermometer or surveillance camera, or they can be actuators that change the state of physical things, such as an alarm or a traffic light. Many things on the internet, such as mobile phones, can be both sensors and actuators, and they are quickly becoming smarter. Some of them have enough processing power and storage capacity to run heavy computing tasks locally, and others run apps that collaborate tightly with software agents running on more powerful computers in the cloud. As the Internet of Things continues to grow, it will offer enormous opportunities for preventing, detecting, limiting, managing, and recovering from emergency situations, which we discuss in the following section.

Of course, social media is another central source of big data. It is so important that we devote a separate chapter to it. For research purposes, CrisisLex[8] contains brief descriptions of downloadable emergency-related social-message collections from the past. In a later chapter we will also discuss emergency-related datasets that are available in semantic formats (such as RDF and OWL).

3   Big Data Benefits and Challenges

3.1   *Benefits*

Big-data analytics can be helpful in all phases of emergency management, from preparation, through detection and response, to recovery [3].

For *preparation* purposes, big data can be used to create baseline models that describe and diagnose (explain) normal conditions, such as the normal movement of people and goods in a city; normal consumption of transport services, power and water; normal geographical and meteorological conditions; and normal physical conditions inside a building. Diagnosing these and other conditions calls for big-data analytics because they may be highly dependent on contextual factors, not only on the most obvious ones, such as the location, time-of-day, day-of-week, and part-of-year, but also on weather, holidays and their types, public health situation,

---

[8]https://www.crisislex.org/data-collections.html.

state of the economy, accidents and emergencies, culture and sports events (both local and global, such as the football World Cup finals). Baseline models can be used to quickly identify deviating conditions and as input to simulating likely consequences of deviations, such as choke points or single points of infrastructural failure. Baselines can also be used for emergency preparation and training and for post-hoc analysis after the crisis or emergency. Baselines can be created from measurements and physical-observations from IoT devices and from social media sensors (see another chapter) that gauge people's moods and concerns, augmented with contextual information from private and public data sets, such as maps and information about buildings, infrastructure, population, vulnerable citizens, etc.

For *detection* purposes, potential emergency situations can be identified early by continuously monitoring people and their environments. In some cases, a quick response can even prevent an unstable or crisis situation from evolving into a full-blown emergency. Useful common sensor types include: surveillance cameras, mobile phones, wearable devices, and social media messages that signal people who are dangerously crammed together at a public event; all kinds of indoor heath, humidity, temperature, and light sensors that can inform about deviations such as break-ins, fires and leakages; positioning devices in vehicles, combined with mobile phone positioning data, social media messages, traffic sensors, road cameras, and live weather data that indicate traffic accidents—or increased risk of such; and, of course, all kinds of weather sensors combined with satellite images that give the earliest warning possible about looming deviations from normal geophysical and meteorological conditions.

For *response* purposes, similar types of information can be used during an unfolding emergency both to gain (strategic) situational overviews and (tactical) actionable insights [3], for example using map-based visualisations and interfaces. Information from physical and social sensors can be corroborated with open and reference data to improve data-quality attributes such as correctness and trustworthiness. Actuators can be repurposed to actively relieve and improve the situation. For example, a traffic light or gated crossing can be taken out of normal operation and instead be used to direct traffic around an affected area. Remote-controlled drones and other vehicles can be used to collect detailed information and to disseminate medical equipment and food. Social media and other communication technologies can be used in a similar manner (as *social actuators*) to disseminate results of big-data analysis and other information back to responders, victims, and their families and friends.

For *recovery* purposes, big-data technologies can be used to make full data traces of the emergency available for post-mortem analysis, both of the unfolding disaster itself, of its preconditions, of the detection and response effort, and of their impacts. Of course, emergency-data traces, when combined with physical and social baselines and reference data also have numerous uses in the aftermath of an emergency: for rebuilding and to prevent or prepare for similar situations in the future.

3.2 Challenges

Properly leveraging big-data technologies for emergency management also poses many challenges. Most of all, big-data harvesting, preparation, curation, analysis, and interpretation is a skill intensive process and demand for big-data competency is vastly greater than supply. Recruiting people with the right competencies, both as professional emergency workers and as volunteers, is therefore a challenging task. Global networks-of-networks are in place for recruiting, training, and coordinating volunteers in various types of emergency and environment related activities, for example in global-mapping activities or satellite-image analysis. Subnetworks of volunteers with competencies in big-data analytics are called for.

Availability of computing infrastructures is a also an issue, both at the emergency site and remotely. Cloud computing makes it feasible to create big-data infrastructures in advance. After they have been set up and tested, the cloud resources and services can be paused until an emergency occurs. Then they can be restarted quickly and easily scaled when computing demands increase. However, advance-preparing for an emergency is hard. Some of the data and processing needs that arise during an emergency will always be unexpected, and preparations must therefore focus on flexibility and responsiveness to change. Availability of computation and communication facilities near the emergency site can be a bigger issue. For example, local sensor networks may be damaged or disconnected due to network or power failure. Aerial-network drones and store-and-forward networking are possible ways to temporarily reinstate networking capacity in affected areas. Disseminating analysis results to the affected people is also a challenge, because most of the techniques and tools have been developed for highly-trained scientists, business people, and other skilled decision makes. Communicating the results of complex big-data analyses to emergency workers, victims, and their families and friends most likely requires different presentation techniques. In a crisis, criminals, terrorist groups, or hostile powers may try to exploit or destabilise the situation further. Social media, which can be used to spread disinformation (misinformation deliberately intended to deceive), has become a well-known attack vector. Cyberattacks are another possibility, for example to interfere with critical computer-controlled infrastructures, to hi-jack or cut off sensors and actuators, or to compromise the emergency-computing infrastructure itself.

Other challenges are less specific to emergency management. High-velocity data must be collected in real time from different data sources, of different types, in different modalities (audio, written text, images, structured data, etc.), using different formats and access methods (social media, the web, FTP, web APIs, etc.). Widely heterogeneous data sets must be recombined and corroborated to create richer situational overviews and facilitate more reliable actionable insights. The data, in particular from social media, must be filtered to clear large amounts of noise. Trustworthiness and other quality features (timeliness, completeness, etc.) must be assessed.

The many ethical issues of big data will be discussed in a later section.

4   Big Data Techniques and Tools

Although it builds on theories and techniques that are much older, the big-data wave gained momentum in the mid 2000s, when data-driven businesses and big internet companies like Amazon, Facebook, and Google needed new ways to store and process the rapidly growing data sets they had amassed. The result was a new generation of techniques and tools for big-data processing that includes: cloud and grid computing technologies, distributed file systems, new types of database management systems, and new distributed computing engines. Many of the ideas they build on are old, but the tools themselves are new, and big data has made their use much more widespread.

Big data is made possible by improvements in computing power, storage capacity, and network bandwidth [9]. In addition, new sources of large data sets have emerged, such as social media, the Cloud/Internet of Things (IoT/ClouT), and ubiquitous and pervasive computing. Important enablers on the computing side are cloud and grid techniques. *Grid computing* lets many loosely-coupled computers distributed across the net perform large computing tasks together. *Cloud computing* leverages grids to offer highly scalable services to end-users, such as massive data storage, powerful virtual and remote servers, big-data analysis services, and much more.

For example, Amazon Web Services (AWS[9]) uses large grids to offer a wide range of scalable storage, computation and analysis services in the cloud. AWS' Elastic Compute Cloud (Amazon EC2[10]) servers appear to their users as regular computers accessible over the net, but they are virtual: each of them may be running on only a small part of a physical machine, or it can run on a large grid of machines. Virtual servers can be quickly and easily created, started, stopped, restarted, resized, replicated, and even moved between data centres on different continents as computing demands change. A new cloud server can be instantiated in minutes, either as a clean Linux or Windows computer or by instantiating an existing Amazon Machine Image (AMI) that represents a predefined computer configuration, such as a big-data set-up designed specifically for emergency computing. There are two common approaches to create an AMI in Linux. The first approach is to start from an existing public AMI and modify it according to the users' requirements. The second approach is to build a fresh installation, either on a standalone machine or on an empty file system mounted by loopback [8]. Amazon also offers a choice between two types of storage services: Elastic Block Store (EBS) and Simple Storage Service (S3), along with management services such as checkpointing and security policies.

New file systems such as the Google File System (GFS, later renamed Colossus) [7] and Apache's open-source HDFS (Hadoop Distributed File System[11]) are

---

[9]https://aws.amazon.com/.

[10]https://docs.aws.amazon.com/AWSEC2/latest/UserGuide/concepts.html.

[11]See https://hadoop.apache.org/.

able to handle big-data volumes by distributing data storage across many computers, possibly in the tens of thousands. On these scales, data storage (and computing) must be fault-tolerant because failing components become the norm rather than the exception. Each big-data file (possibly of tera- or petabyte size) is therefore split into blocks (e.g., 128 Mb each) that are stored on different computers, called data nodes in HDFS. To achieve fault tolerance, the same block is replicated on several data nodes (*sharding*). Inside a data centre, the nodes are grouped into racks that correspond to physically co-located sub-networks of computing nodes served by the same router. HDFS attempts to shard each block across nodes that belong to different racks so that, if a rack becomes unavailable due to router failure or power outage, other copies of the blocks it stores will be available from other racks. A single name node handles client requests and keeps track of where the blocks in each file are stored. The name node thus makes HDFS appear as a single logical file store to client programs, although data is transmitted directly between clients and data nodes. Communication with clients and between HDFS nodes use TCP/IP, making it easy to include heterogeneous computing nodes in the same cluster (which is then often called a grid). To avoid making the name node a single-point of failure, other data nodes are continuously monitoring their name node and are always ready to step up should it lose connection. As with many big-data technologies, HDFS is optimised for mostly immutable files: the initial write and the subsequent reads of a file are much faster and use less resources than updating the file after it has been created.

The new distributed file systems quickly inspired similarly distributed database management systems (DDBMS), designed to accommodate big-data collections (tera- and petabytes) in a flexible way. In addition to supporting higher numbers of data items of the same type (*vertical scaling* in volume), new big-database systems also emphasise supporting rapidly evolving information needs of different types (*horizontal scaling* in variety). To achieve this, they deviate in several ways from traditional relational and SQL-based data models, giving them the name Not Only SQL (NOSQL) databases. MongoDB uses the JavaScript Object Model (JSON) as its data model for both storage and interaction. Google's Bigtable [4] organises data as sparsely populated tables, called wide-column stores, and has inspired both Apache HBase, which runs on top of HDFS, and Apache Cassandra [10]. The latter has become one of the most widely used big-data stores. Initially developed to support Facebook's messaging system, Cassandra combines features from key-value pairs and wide-column stores. Like most NOSQL databases, Cassandra is designed to support data replication, resilience towards failure, and ease of adding more machines to the cluster/grid. It offers flexibility, scalability and read-orientation: like HDFS, it is optimised for writing new data once and reading it many times, whereas updating existing data is more costly. Unlike HDFS, however, all Cassandra nodes are equal: they can both store data and answer client requests.

Like data storage, processing has become distributed and duplicated across computing nodes and centres too. The original Google MapReduce [6] and Apache's open-source Hadoop[12] support a massively parallel three-step model of computation called *map-reduce*. In the first step (*map*), each computer, called a worker (or slave) node in Hadoop, sorts the input data into local files according to a key. In the second step (*shuffle*), the nodes transfer temporary files between them, so that all data items with the same key end up in the same worker node. In the third and final step (*reduce*), each worker node processes the data for its keys, possibly combining its own results with results from its neighbour nodes. For example, to rapidly identify duplicates in a set of merged library catalogues, the map step sorts each item locally by title, the shuffle step moves all items with the same title to the same worker, and the reduce step decides whether pairs of items that happen to have the same title are actually duplicates. A Hadoop worker node can be the same computer that is also a data node in HDFS or database node in Cassandra, so that the node works on locally stored input data in the initial map step. Otherwise, a costly input split has to be carried out before first.

A Hadoop master node handles client requests and distributes tasks to the workers, ensuring that redundantly stored blocks are only processed by one worker each. Hence, in Hadoop, as in most other big-data processing frameworks, the tasks are moved to the data. This is a shift from conventional ("small-data") computing, where the data was moved to the task processor. In addition, the master node is responsible for balancing tasks between workers, taking into account their varying processing capacities, and for reallocating tasks when a worker is slow or becomes unavailable. Many extensions and variations of the basic map-shuffle-reduce model have been proposed, and multiple Hadoop computations are often chained. Because it has been so successful, Hadoop's subsystem for resource management and job scheduling and monitoring has been turned into a separate framework, called YARN (Yet Another Resource Negotiator) that can be used by other big-data processing tools as well.

These tools and their successors share a model of computing that is both highly distributed and highly redundant, so that each computation is carried out and each piece of data stored in several places simultaneously. On top of node-level replication, whole data centres can be replicated (or mirrored) across continents. Data-centre replication improves service availability and can also be used as a content delivery network (CDN) that improves responsiveness and communication cost by distributing services geospatially according to user locations: requests from Chinese users can be served by a replicated data centre in Guangzhou, European requests can be routed to Frankfurt, and so on.

In recent years, more specialised big-data technologies and tools have emerged, many of them growing out of the HDFS/YARN/Hadoop stack. Apache Hive is a data warehousing tool that offers an SQL-like query language on top of HDFS and converts the queries to Hadoop, Spark (see below), or other types of big-data jobs. Apache Kafka and Amazon Kinesis specialise in processing and storing big streams of data, which can be produced internally in an organisation or harvested externally

---

[12]https://hadoop.apache.org/.

from the social web or the Internet of Things. Google's Pregel [11] and Apache Giraph[13] specialise in processing and storing big graph-structured data. They have been used, respectively, to drive Google's PageRank algorithm [12] and Facebook's social network analyses. And many very large-scale applications still use good-old SQL databases. Alongside these and many other specialised technologies, a preferred tool for general big-data processing has emerged: Apache Spark, which we will present in the next section.

5   General Engine for Big Data Processing: Spark

The usefulness and power of Google's MapReduce and its successors surpassed many expectations. But this first generation of big-data processing engines also had severe limitations. They were batch-oriented, with jobs that could take days because they were heavily disk-based, copying their intermediate results repeatedly to and from disks. Their computation model was also rigid, restricted to chaining jobs that were composed of minor variants of the map, shuffle, and reduce operations.

In the early 2010s researchers therefore sought to develop big-data processing tools that were more interactive; that reduced disk load by relying on in-memory data storage; and that offered a broader variety of computing primitives. The most widely used among them is Spark [14], which is part of Apache's big-data ecosystem. In addition to Hadoop's map, shuffle, and reduce operations and their variants, Spark offers more than 80 different high-level processing operations, which can be detailed with functions written in standard programming languages such as Python, Java, Scala, and R. There are also Spark libraries for: connecting to Cassandra and SQL databases; analysing large graphs (GraphX); processing live data streams (DStream); and machine learning (MLib). Like in Hadoop, worker nodes do most of the computing. A driver node communicates with the client and distributes tasks to workers, whereas a cluster manager (either Spark's own built-in one, YARN, or another) allocates processing capacity.

A Spark computation is organised as a dataflow (or pipeline). The dataflow can be thought of as a directed acyclic graph (DAG) where each node represents data at some stage of processing and each edge represents a processing operation. The data in each node is treated as a Resilient Distributed Dataset (RDD) [13], which may contain anything from a single boolean variable to a petabyte collection of videos: the data in an RDD can be structured like key-value pairs (maps), tables, and graphs or unstructured like text and multimedia. But all data items in the same RDD must have the same type, which is written RDD[*type*]. Because of its size, an RDD is usually split into partitions that can be distributed across thousands of computing nodes, where they are stored in memory and normally not copied to disk, unless memory fills up or the user specifically requests a checkpoint to be saved.

---

[13]http://giraph.apache.org/.

Importantly, RDDs are immutable meaning, that once they have been created by a computing operation, they never change (more about that below).

Spark operations take input from one or more nodes and may produce output to a single node. They are divided into transformations, which take one or more RDDs and generate a new RDD, and actions, which take one or more input RDDs and produce either an output (that is not an RDD) or a side effect. For example, Spark *transformations* are available for mapping, filtering, reducing, sampling, and sorting RDDs in various ways, and for combining multiple RDDs using operations such as intersection, union, and join. After each transformation, the result is always a new RDD. Spark *actions* are available for counting, sampling, looping through, or otherwise reducing large RDDs into outputs that are easier for humans to interpret and for simpler software tools to process. Other actions are used for their side effects, for example to cache or checkpoint an RDD or save it to a (distributed) file system. Spark evaluation is lazy, so that a transformation in a dataflow will not be executed until the RDDs they produce are needed, either directly or indirectly, as input to an action.

Spark processing is resilient because both data storage and processing is highly redundant: each part of an RDD and of a computation can be stored and processed on several cluster nodes simultaneously. Whenever a node fails during computation, and that part of the computation is duplicated, the computation can just go on. Whenever a node fails that is not redundantly processed, the Spark engine instead relies on *lineage*. It automatically enforces recomputation of the necessary data from the last available checkpoints, perhaps even going back to the original inputs. Recomputation is possible exactly because the RDDs are immutable: once created they never change, so each later processing step can be recomputed safely.

To program using Spark, we can use languages like Python, Java, Scala, and R along with libraries that make Spark operations and RDDs available from inside these languages. We can also program interactively using Spark's built-in shells for Python and Scala. The following example is written in Scala using the spark-shell, but the code in other languages would not be much different.

To filter Twitter data with Spark in an emergency, we first import Spark's DStream library and its Twitter extensions:[14]

```
import org.apache.spark._
import org.apache.spark.streaming._
import org.apache.spark.streaming.twitter._
```

We also need to specify the credentials for our Twitter account and app, with lines like:[15]

```
System.setProperty( "twitter4j.oauth.consumerKey", "..." )
System.setProperty( "twitter4j.oauth.consumerSecret", "..." )
System.setProperty( "twitter4j.oauth.accessToken", "..." )
System.setProperty( "twitter4j.oauth.accessTokenSecret", "...")
```

---

[14]See the Apache Spark DStream and Bahir-Twitter projects. The Twitter4j library is also needed.
[15]To register and get credentials for a Twitter App, go to apps.twitter.com.

We are now ready to define a dataflow that harvests tweets from Spark (although nothing will be executed until we start the stream and specify an action):

```
sc.setLogLevel( "ERROR" )
val ssc = new StreamingContext( sc, Seconds( 5 ))
val stream = TwitterUtils.createStream( ssc, None )
```

The first line states that the running Spark engine, represented by the built-in Spark Context (sc) object, should only report serious errors. The second line states that Spark should run in streaming mode, collecting a new batch of input data every 5 s. The third line states that this data should come from the Twitter account we have already specified.

The stream variable represents the series of RDDs that are input to our pipeline, one every 5 s. Each RDD in it has the Scala type RDD[*Status*], meaning that it is an RDD that contains Status objects. The Status class is defined in the Twitter4j library to represent and process a single tweet along with its (quite extensive) metadata.[16]

We can easily add more operations to our dataflow. First, we use a map transformation to pick out the message texts from each tweet:

```
val texts = stream.map( status => status.getText )
```

This creates a new stream of RDDs of strings (type RDD[*String*]), which we can loop through and output (an action):

```
texts.foreachRDD( _.foreach( text => println( text )))
```

or split (a transformation) into a stream of RDDs of single words (again of RDD[*String*]):

```
val words = texts.flatMap( text => text.split( `` '' ))
```

which we then filter (another transformation) for hashtags:

```
val hashtags = words.filter( _.startsWith( "#" ))
```

We can easily add further operations that may extend, split or merge processing paths. When we are finished, we can start the flow of tweets and inspect the outputs:

```
ssc.start
```

In the example, this will start extracting message texts from live Twitter messages and output them to the console. But it will not start splitting texts into words and filter out the hashtags, because Spark evaluation is lazy and we have not yet used the hashtags in an action.

Finally, we stop the Spark streaming pipeline, making it clear that we want to wait until all data in the pipeline has been processed and that we do not want to close the Spark context permanently:

---

[16]See the introduction to Tweet JSON at developer.twitter.com and the twitter4j.Status interface in the Twitter4j API, which Bahir-Twitter wraps around.

```
ssc.stop( stopSparkContext=false, stopGracefully=true )
```

Of course, this small example barely scratches the surface of what a powerful big-data framework like Spark can do. But it illustrates how just a few lines of Spark code is enough to process social media data in ways that are potentially useful in emergency situations. In addition to its high-level processing operations, much of the power of Spark lies in its scaling: the above example can be run both on a single computer on a filtered stream of tweets and, without modifications, on a cluster of hundreds or thousands of nodes processing a fire hose of data. Of course, the Spark configuration would have to be changed, but there are many abstract machine images for distributed Spark freely available in the cloud, and instantiating one of them only takes minutes.

6 Ethical and Societal Issues

The previous sections have shown that big-data analytics offer many benefits in all phases of emergency management. New possibilities for large-scale yet precise surveillance on demand can save lives and property in emergency situations. But if the same surveillance is misused in everyday life, it can pose threats to individual privacy and to society in general. Use of big data during emergencies must therefore be carefully conducted and monitored, and a fine line must be tread between specific emergency needs and wider ethical and societal concerns [9].

Among the ethical concerns, privacy is central. *Personal information* refers to information that can be attributed to a physical person. This includes data that contains unambiguous identifiers such as personal id numbers, names, addresses, and birth dates, but also data that is sufficiently detailed to be indirectly attributable to a person. A study of mobile phone-users [5] showed that knowing only four spatio-temporal data points was enough to identify 95% of the users uniquely, and coarser datasets did not offer much stronger anonymity. Hence, when data sets about individuals are recombined in an emergency situation, the combined data items can become attributable to individuals, even when the original data were not. Privacy concerns are accentuated when the personal information is also *sensitive* because it covers: age, criminal records, ethnicity, gender, health, marital status, political opinions, race, religion, sexuality, or trade-union membership. The many dangers of personal data in the wrong hands are well known: it can be used for blackmail, coercion, social-engineering scams, personality theft, or sold to advertising and insurance companies. Live personal data can even be used by organised criminals who want to commit theft or kidnapping or by terrorist organisations for targeted attacks.

Personal information is not the only type of information that can be sensitive. Information about critical infrastructures is also likely to be collected and recombined as part of emergency computation. Such information can be valuable to criminals, potential terrorists, and foreign powers. Although many of the data sets used will be in the open, their potential value for adversaries increase when they are recombined and augmented with temporal information that can be used, for example, by criminals or terrorists to estimate police and other response times.

Finding the right balance between emergency needs and ethical/societal concerns requires an appropriate combination of organisational, informational, and technical measures. On the *organisational side*, sensitive data should only be made accessible to trusted agencies with clear procedures in place for screening personnel etc. For every data set that includes sensitive information, a steward should be appointed with clearly-defined responsibilities. As much as possible, data should be collected only from trusted sources, but this is not always an option—and certainly not in the case of socially generated data. And, of course, data should only be shared with trusted partners.

On the *informational side*, sensitive data should only be collected and recombined in response to concrete and carefully prioritised operational and tactical needs, even when it goes against the opportunistic tendency of big-data practice, which stores data opportunistically—exhaustively, historically, and in full detail—because it can potentially become valuable in the future. Data tables should be projected to remove unneeded attributes whenever they are shared. Whenever possible, anonymisation and pseudonymisation should be used to increase privacy, although they cannot be considered sufficient privacy measures in their own right.

On the *technical side*, only screened and trusted data processing organisations should be allowed to store and process the data. This applies in particular to cloud computing providers. The processing organisations should be transparent when it comes to where in the world—and thus under which jurisdiction—the data is stored and processed. Techniques such as secret sharing and watermarking should be considered to make the data more difficult to obtain and leave it traceable should it come into the wrong hands.

Exercises

1. What are the three V's of big data?
2. Some people talk about two more V's in addition to the three. Which ones?
3. What does it mean that big data are: exhaustive, fine grained, indexical, relational, extendible, historical, and opportunistic.
4. What is a data-driven organisation (or business)? Give examples?
5. Explain the four phases of emergency management. How can big data help in each of them?
6. Which big data sources can be leveraged in each phase of emergency management and how?
7. Name the most central big-data technologies for: file management, database management, and data processing.
8. What are the main improvements of Spark over Google's MapReduce and Apache Hadoop?

9. What is an RDD and what is lineage in Spark?
10. What are the most pressing ethical and societal dangers of big data?
11. In the Spark example, change the code to output Named Entities (names of individual things like people, places, organisations, and works) instead of hashtags, assuming that named entities are always written as a sequence of words with capital initial letters.

References

1. Atzori, L., Iera, A., Morabito, G.: The Internet of Things: a survey. Comput. Netw. **54**(15), 2787–2805 (2010). https://doi.org/10.1016/j.comnet.2010.05.010. http://linkinghub.elsevier.com/retrieve/pii/S1389128610001568
2. Berners-Lee, T., Hendler, J., Lassila, O.: The semantic web. Sci. Am. **284**(5), 34–43 (2001)
3. Castillo, C.: Big Crisis Data: Social Media in Disasters and Time-Critical Situations. Cambridge University Press, Cambridge (2016)
4. Chang, F., Dean, J., Ghemawat, S., Hsieh, W.C., Wallach, D.A., Burrows, M., Chandra, T., Fikes, A., Gruber, R.E.: Bigtable: a distributed storage system for structured data. ACM Trans. Comput. Syst. **26**(2), 4 (2008)
5. De Montjoye, Y.A., Hidalgo, C.A., Verleysen, M., Blondel, V.D.: Unique in the crowd: the privacy bounds of human mobility. Sci. Rep. **3**, 1376 (2013)
6. Dean, J., Ghemawat, S.: MapReduce: simplified data processing on large clusters. Commun. ACM **51**(1), 107 (2008). https://doi.org/10.1145/1327452.1327492. http://portal.acm.org/citation.cfm?doid=1327452.1327492
7. Ghemawat, S., Gobioff, H., Leung, S.T.: The Google File System, vol. 37. ACM, New York (2003)
8. Huang, Q., Yang, C., Nebert, D., Liu, K., Wu, H.: Cloud computing for geosciences: deployment of GEOSS clearinghouse on Amazon's EC2. In: Proceedings of the ACM SIGSPATIAL International Workshop on High Performance and Distributed Geographic Information Systems, HPDGIS '10, pp. 35–38. ACM, New York (2010). http://doi.acm.org/10.1145/1869692.1869699
9. Kitchin, R: The Data Revolution: Big Data, Open Data, Data Infrastructures and Their Consequences. Sage, Thousand Oaks (2014)
10. Lakshman, A., Malik, P.: Cassandra: a decentralized structured storage system. ACM SIGOPS Oper. Syst. Rev. **44**(2), 35–40 (2010)
11. Malewicz, G., Austern, M.H., Bik, A.J., Dehnert, J.C., Horn, I., Leiser, N., Czajkowski, G.: Pregel: a system for large-scale graph processing. In: Proceedings of the 2010 ACM SIGMOD International Conference on Management of Data, pp. 135–146. ACM, New York (2010)
12. Page, L., Brin, S., Motwani, R., Winograd, T.: The pagerank citation ranking: bringing order to the web. Tech. rep., Stanford InfoLab (1999)
13. Zaharia, M., Chowdhury, M., Das, T., Dave, A., Ma, J., McCauley, M., Franklin, M.J., Shenker, S., Stoica, I.: Resilient distributed datasets: a fault-tolerant abstraction for in-memory cluster computing. In: Proceedings of the 9th USENIX Conference on Networked Systems Design and Implementation, p. 14. USENIX Association, Berkeley (2012)
14. Zaharia, M., Xin, R.S., Wendell, P., Das, T., Armbrust, M., Dave, A., Meng, X., Rosen, J., Venkataraman, S., Franklin, M.J.: Apache spark: a unified engine for big data processing. Commun. ACM **59**(11), 56–65 (2016)

Learning Algorithms for Emergency Management

Minsung Hong and Rajendra Akerkar

1 Machine Learning and Emergency Management

1.1 Preliminaries

Machine learning is based on algorithms that can learn from data without relying on rules-based programming. There are many different types of machine learning algorithms, and they are commonly grouped by either learning style (i.e. supervised learning, unsupervised learning, semi-supervised learning, reinforcement learning) or by similarity in form or function (i.e. classification, regression, decision tree, clustering, deep learning, etc.). While machine learning algorithms have been around for decades, they have attained new popularity as artificial intelligence (AI) has grown in prominence. Specifically, deep learning models power latest advanced AI applications.

ML has been broadly utilised to create value and insight in various fields [2], from laboratory curiosity to a practical technology in widespread commercial use [22]. Even though ML and Data Mining (DM) are often overlapped and use the same methods, ML focuses on prediction while DM concentrates on discovering unknown properties from data. ML algorithms are categorised as shown in Fig. 1.

- **Supervised learning** predict a class of future instances using externally supplied instances that consists of data and a label (i.e., class). It's objective is to model the class distribution of the supplied instances (i.e., training set), and a classifier based on the model is then used to predict class to a test set [27].
- **Unsupervised learning** directly infers the properties of this probability density without the help of externally provided instances giving correct label or degree-

M. Hong · R. Akerkar (✉)
Big Data Research Group, Western Norway Research Institute, Sogndal, Norway
e-mail: msh@vestforsk.no; rak@vestforsk.no

© Springer Nature Switzerland AG 2020
R. Akerkar (ed.), *Big Data in Emergency Management: Exploitation Techniques for Social and Mobile Data*, https://doi.org/10.1007/978-3-030-48099-8_3

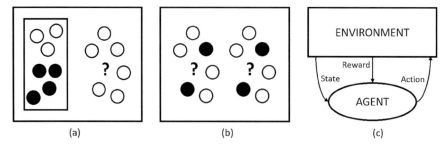

Fig. 1 Category of machine learning. An empty circle indicates an unlabelled instance while a filled circle presents an instance with (**a**) label. The rectangle of (**a**) means instances which are used for model training. (**a**) Supervised learning. (**b**) Unsupervised learning. (**c**) Reinforcement learning

of-error for each observation [19]. Therefore, with unsupervised learning, it is possible to learn larger and more complex models than with supervised learning. There are representative methods like Apriori algorithm, k-means, and so on.

– **Reinforcement learning** deduces labels of instances with a dynamic environment. In other words, it uses experience gained through interacting with the an agent in the environment state and actions' feedback (i.e., reward), to improve a system's ability [2]. There are two strategies: one is to search in the space of behaviours to find one that performs well in the environment such as genetic algorithms, and other relies on statistical techniques and dynamic programming methods to estimate the utility of taking actions in states [24].

1.2 Learning Algorithms and Its Usage

The objective of this chapter is to provide a broad and basic understanding about utilises of ML in the EM, we describe the basic concepts and usage cases of ML technologies by following its sub-categories such as clustering, neural networks, deep learning and so on. Such structure may help to comprehensively look through and easily compare between usage precedents of a specific ML technique for different tasks of EM. We start with decision tree which belongs to the family of supervised learning algorithms.

1.2.1 Decision Tree

Fundamental Concept

Decision tree is a powerful and popular tool for classification and prediction. It is usually working top-down, by choosing a variable at each step that best splits the set of items. The beauty of decision tree methods is the fact that they express

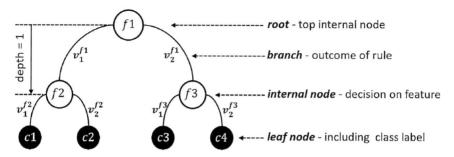

Fig. 2 Overview of a decision tree

rules which are able to be readily understand by human [2]. Given input $X = x_1, x_2, \ldots, x_n$, the goal is to predict a response or output variable Y. Each member of the set is called an input variable, and the input values of a decision tree can be categorical or continuous [16]. As shown in Fig. 2, The prediction can be achieved by constructing a decision tree with features/rules as nodes and branches as arcs. At each node, a decision is made to pick a specific branch and traverse down the tree. A node without further branches is called a leaf node which represents a class label, in some implementations, it returns a probability score. The depth of a node is the minimum number of steps required to reach the node from the root. The path from the root to a leaf involves a series of decisions made at various internal nodes.

Decision trees have two varieties: classification trees and regression trees. The former tree usually apply to output variables that are categorical—often binary—in nature, such as yes or no, purchase or not purchase and so on. On the other hand the later tree can be used for output variables that are numeric or continuous, such as the predicted price of a consumer good or the likelihood a subscription will be purchased.

The objective of decision tree algorithm is to construct a tree T from a training data set D. If all the data records in D belong to some class C, or if D is sufficiently pure (i.e., greater than a present threshold), then that node is generated as a leaf node and assigned the label C. The purity of a node is defined as its probability of the corresponding class, for instance proportion of the number of nodes corresponding a class by the number of total nodes. In contrast, if not all the records in D belong to class C or if D is not sufficiently pure, the algorithm selects the next most informative feature/attribute F and partitions D according to F's values. The algorithm constructs sub-trees for the subsets of D recursively unit one of the following criteria is satisfied:

- All the leaf nodes in the tree meet the minimum purity threshold.
- The tree cannot be further split with the present minimum purity threshold.
- Any other stopping criterion is satisfied such as the maximum depth of the tree.

The first step for constructing a decision tree is to choose a most informative feature. Identifying the feature usually uses entropy-based methods which are applied to decision tree learning algorithms such as ID3 (or Iterative Dichotomiser 3) [36] and C4.5 [37]. The entropy methods select the most informative feature according to two basic measures: entropy which indicates the impurity of a feature and information gain which presents the purity of a feature.

By limiting the number of splits, a short tree can be generated. Short trees are often combined as components (also called weak learners or base learners) into ensemble methods. Ensemble methods use multiple predictive models to vote, and decisions can be made based on the combination of the votes. Recently, some ensemble methods including random forest [34, 51], bagging and boosting [23] which are mixed with decision trees have been used for EM. The simplest short tree is called a decision stump, which is a decision tree with the root immediately connected to the leaf nodes. A decision stump makes a prediction based on the value of just a single input variable. Given a class C and its label $c \in C$, let $P(c)$ be the probability of c. The entropy H_c of C is defined by

$$H_c = - \sum_{\forall c \in C} P(c) log_2 P(c) \tag{1}$$

It means that entropy H_c becomes 0 when all $P(c)$ is 0 or 1. For a binary classification, H_c is zero if the probability $P(c)$ of each label c is either zero or one. On the other hand, H_c achieves the maximum entropy when all the class labels are equally probable. The maximum entropy increases as the number of possible outcomes increases. The next step if to calculate the conditional entropy for each feature. Given an feature F, its value f, its outcome Y and its value y, conditional entropy $H_{Y|F}$ is the remaining entropy of Y given F, formally defined as

$$H_{Y|F} = \sum_f P(f) H(Y|F = f) = - \sum_{\forall f \in F} P(f) \sum_{\forall y \in Y} P(y|f) log_2 P(y|f) \tag{2}$$

And the conditional entropy is always less than or equal to the base entropy ($H_{Y|F} \leq H_Y$). The conditional entropy is smaller then the base entropy when the feature and the outcome are correlated. In the worst case, when the feature is uncorrelated with the outcome, the conditional entropy sames with the base entropy. In this regard, the information gain $I_{F,Y}$ of an feature F for its outcome Y is defined as the difference between the base entropy and the conditional entropy of the feature as follows:

$$I_{F,Y} = H_Y - H_{Y|F} \tag{3}$$

Splits are determined using the information gain which compares the purity degree of the parent node before a split with the purity degree of the child node after a split. At each split, an feature which can obtain the greatest information gain is considered the most informative feature. In this regard, the information gain indicates the purity of an feature.

Usages for Emergency Management

Until now decision tree algorithms such as ID3, C4.5, CART and ADTree have been proposed for feature selection, tree pruning and data structure to improve the generalisation capability and scalability of decision trees. Similarly, various techniques of decision tree have been broadly applied to EM tasks such as event prediction [13, 29, 52], early warning [6] and emergency evaluation [11, 34, 51].

Zmazek et al. applied regression and model trees to earthquake prediction, by using radon concentration which is measured as a numeric variable within soil gas [52]. The regression trees were implemented with WEKA which is a DM toolkit. Inner nodes of that tree include such as temperature, barometric, pressure and so on, while leaf nodes indicates the radon concentration in soil gas. The model tree outperformed other regression methods such as linear regression and instance based regression in terms of accuracy of forecasting radon concentration for earthquake prediction. Regression tree based on M5P and association rules technique was proposed to help in earthquakes prediction [29]. The association rules mining was used to obtain quantitative association rules, and the M5P algorithm was used to discover patterns which model the behaviour of seismic temporal data. It was implemented by using WEKA. Data set including current earthquake magnitude, occurrence time, associated b-value and magnitude of the previously occurred earthquake are used to get four linear models, and the models then are applied to inner nodes of model tree M5P. The leaf nodes of the tree present three non-overlapped intervals for earthquake magnitudes. Chen et al. proposed a GIS-based vulnerability modelling which respectively utilises Naïve Bayes tree, alternating decision tree and the kernel logistic regression, to predict the landslide [13]. They considered 12 landslide conditioning factors such as slope aspect, slope angle, altitude, profile curvature, plan curvature, NDVI, landuse, lithological unit, distance to rivers, distance to roads, distance to faults and mean annual precipitation in modelling. The kernel logistic regression classifies the data in a high-dimensional space, and Naïve Bayes tree includes Naïve Bayes categorizers as leaf nodes. Alternating decision tree combining boosting algorithm and decision tree replace the each decision node by two nodes: a splitter node and a prediction node. Although the goodness-of-fits and the validations of three susceptibility models were good in the case of using all the factors, A model base on Naïve Bayes tree had the highest classification accuracy.

A binary decision tree was used to predict whether flooded or not in the pixel of various image data in order to assess damage [11]. The results are also combined with additional data harvested from social media. First they identify the flooded and non-flooded regions by using graphics software, and these regions then are used for learning a binary decision tree. The inner nodes are selected among nine spectral bands such as coastal aerosol, optical, near-IR, shortwave-IR, cirrus, and so on. And leaf nodes involve labels presenting whether water or not water. Pham et al. compared spatial predictions of Random Forest (RF), Logistic Model Trees (LMT), Best First Decision Tree (BFDT) and Classification and Regression Tree (CART) for landslide susceptibility assessment [34]. Sixteen conditioning factors

Table 1 Summarising decision tree for emergency management

EM task/ citation No.	ML technique	Inner node	Leaf node
Prediction/ [52]	Model tree M5	Various data related to radon	Radon concentration
Prediction/ [29]	Regression tree based on M5P	Location and magnitude of earthquake (linear models)	Earthquake magnitude
Prediction/ [13]	Naïve Bayes tree (and alternating decision tree)	12 landslide conditioning factors	Predictive capabilities of conditioning factors
Evaluation/ [11]	Binary decision tree	Nine spectral bands	Binary representing flooded and non-flooded
Evaluation/ [34]	Logistic model trees, best first decision tree and classification and regression tree	16 landslide conditioning factors	Five susceptible categories

including slope angle, elevation, slope aspect, profile curvature, land cover, and so on were considered. Although the RF model has the highest predictive capability, followed by the LMT, BFDT and CART models, respectively, the experimental results indicate that all four methods are good for susceptibility assessment.

Table 1 summarises the decision trees which have been applied to EM tasks. We believe that use cases listed below help to easily understand usages of decision tree in EM.

1.2.2   Clustering

Fundamental Concept

As one of the popular unsupervised learning, clustering analysis divides data into homogeneous clusters that have maximal intra-class similarity and minimal inter-class similarity. There are two main approaches to clustering, namely—hierarchical clustering and partitioning clustering. The former do a sequence of partitions, in which each partition is nested into the next partition in the sequence. In other words, it creates a hierarchy of clusters from small to big (agglomerate) or big to small (divisive). The later approach partitions the data set into a predefined number of clusters. Figure 3 illustrates the two major approaches to clustering. Clustering is a very useful technique when there is no pre-classified data (i.e., labelled data), therefore it is usually performed in the pre-processing phase to generate compressed representative of raw data for large, complex data set[12]. Since the k-means clustering method of cluster detection is the most commonly used in practice and is one of the oldest and simplest clustering algorithms which may still produce good results, we describe this method here. It involves with randomly choosing k

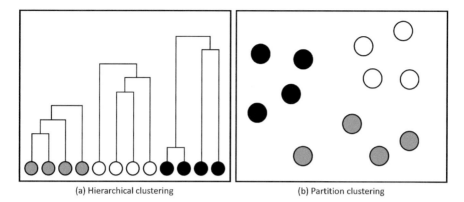

(a) Hierarchical clustering   (b) Partition clustering

Fig. 3 Overview of two clustering approaches. (**a**) indicates a division clustering and (**b**) presents
k-means clusters ($k = 3$) as one of main techniques for a partition clustering

Table 2 Basic steps of k-means clustering algorithm	
	1. Randomly select k points to be starting points for the centroids of the k clusters
	2. Assign each instance to the centroid closest, forming k exclusive clusters
	3. Recalculate new centroid of each cluster by taking the average of all attribute values of the instances belonging to the same cluster
	4. Check if the cluster centroids have changed their coordinates
	– If yes, repeat from the Step 2
	– If no, cluster detection is finished and all instances have their cluster memberships

points to be the centroids of clusters, and grouping instances around centroids based on proximity. The centroids then are iteratively recomputed for each cluster, and instances regrouped until there is sufficiently little change in centroid positions [2]. This algorithm depends heavily on the choice of k (which may not be obvious at all for a particular application) and the initial positioning of centroids [1].

k-means clustering algorithm starts with an input of predefined number of clusters, which is called k. "Means" stands for an average location of all the members within a single cluster. To use aforesaid geometry proximity, the values in the data set must all be numeric. If they are categorical one, they then should be normalised in order to obtain adequate results of the overall distances in a multi-attribute space. The k-means algorithm is a straightforward iterative procedure, in which a vital notion is centroid. A centroid indicates a point that represent an average position of a single cluster. That means, the coordinates of this point are the averages of attribute values of all instances that belong to the cluster. Table 2 describes the iterative process of redefining centroids and reassigning data instances into clusters which a small number of iterations for converge is generally needed.

Now, we discuss the partitioning technique in detail. The purpose of clustering is to obtain each subset whose much more similar instances belong to a same cluster. A partition $P_1, P_2, \ldots, P_k$ is represented by the centroids $z_1, z_2, \ldots, z_k$ such that

$$x \in P_i \leftrightarrow \rho(x, z_i) \leq \rho(x, z_j), i, j = 1, \ldots, k, \tag{4}$$

where the *rho* function means some metrics (e.g., Euclidean, Minkowski, Cosine or Manhattan) to measure the similarity or dissimilarity between instances. In order to recalculate new centroids, in the k-means algorithm, the mean of the real-values instances in the cluster P_i is calculated as:

$$z_i = \frac{1}{N_i} \sum_{x^{(j)} \in P_i} x^{(j)}, \tag{5}$$

where N_i indicates the number of data points in P_i. The iterative process works till z_i do not change. With the preceding algorithm, k clusters can be identified in a given data set, but what value of k is proper for the initial step? The value of k can be chosen based on a reasonable guess or some predefined requirement. However, even then, it would be good to know how much better of worse having k clusters versus $k - 1$ or $k + 1$ clusters would be in explaining the structure of the data [16]. In this regards, we can determine a reasonably optimal value of k with a heuristic using the Within Sum of Squares (WSS) metric which means "impurity measure" that is estimated as follows using centroids:

$$J(z_1, z_2, \ldots, z_k) = \frac{1}{N} \sum_{i=1}^{k} \sum_{x^{(j)} \in P_i} \rho(x^{(j)}, z_i) = \frac{1}{N} \sum_{j=1}^{N} \min_{1 \leq i \leq k} \rho(x^{(j)}, z_i), \tag{6}$$

where N denotes the total number of instances. If the points are relatively close to their respective centroids, the WSS is relatively small. Therefore if $k + 1$ clusters do not greatly reduce the WSS than the case with only k clusters, there may be little benefit to adding another cluster.

Usages for Emergency Management

In EM, clustering techniques mainly concentrate on the high quality information acquisition from a mass of raw data with redundancy and noise. Clustering is conducted by multiple approaches such as partitional clustering, hierarchical clustering, density-based clustering, grid clustering, concept clustering, self-organising map and so on. These approaches [18, 35, 47, 49, 50] have been widely used for various tasks in EM than decision trees.

Zhang et al. applied the particle swarm optimisation clustering algorithm to make a earthquake prediction model, with the characteristics of abnormally high-dimensional data [50]. The model analyses the relationship between earthquake precursor data and earthquake magnitude. In addition the average distance between points in clusters is set as the evaluation function. The inputs are 14 abnormal indexes such as belt, seismic gap and short levelling, and output is earthquake magnitude. They compared the algorithm with the k-means clustering, and experimental result showed that the proposed algorithm was superior than the k-means clustering.

Based on data collected from social media (i.e. Flickr and YouTube), self-organizing maps and agglomerative clustering was used to detect sub-events of emergencies by Pohl et al. [35]. They more focus on metadata than its content by considering time limitation which can be happened in real situation (e.g., it is often not possible to see an entire video to judge about the content in a stressful situation like an emergency). Consequently annotations (title, description, and tags) being established in vector space model, the GPS coordinates and the time (milliseconds) data were used as input of the two clustering algorithms whose outputs are sub-events. They combined Euclidean distance with the WARD link measure[1] shows good performance for our data sets. The experimental results shown that the algorithms can be used for a fast overview than the base methods.

In order to detect and track emergency events and to provides decision support for authorities and EM services, Xu et al. proposed an emergency event detection and opinion mining method using cross-media analytics [47]. Herein, a clustering algorithm by fast search and find of density peaks [39] was adopted to detect emergency events according to basic assumption that every cluster centre has a long distance to higher density points and is surrounded by lower density points. With comparing with k-means clustering, the clustering algorithm used by the authors can perform better even for relatively small emergency events.

Yin et al. developed an online incremental clustering algorithm by extending the single-pass algorithm [48] due to the fact that the conventional clustering algorithms such as partitional and hierarchical clustering algorithms are not suitable, when tweet contents are constantly evolving over time [49]. Their algorithm automatically groups similar tweets into topic clusters, so that each cluster corresponds to an event-specific topic. The topics are used for enhancing emergency situation awareness. Their results showed that usage of Jaccard similarity achieves higher clustering accuracy than that of cosine similarity.

Harris and Anitha utilised the fast k-means clustering to ensure the credibility of the crowdsourced information which social media users generate along with GIS annotation [18]. The algorithm aims to find subsets of data set for minimising the Euclidean squared distance between initial cluster centres and current centres, It works until to achieve to minimise within-cluster sum of squares which is a measure of the variability of the data points within each cluster. The fast k-means algorithm [42], the randomised cluster centres that are eliminated in the initial selection, effectively reduce the number of iterations and time of execution.

Table 3 summarises the clustering techniques for the various tasks in EM tasks.

---

[1]Wards distance between clusters C_i and C_j is the difference between the total within cluster sum of squares for the two clusters separately, and the within cluster sum of squares resulting from merging the two clusters in cluster C_{ij}.

Table 3 Summarising clustering techniques for emergency management

EM task/ citation No.	ML technique	Basic measure	Input	Output
Prediction/ [50]	Particle swarm optimization algorithm	Euclidean distance	14 abnormal indexes	Earthquake magnitude
Event detection/ [35]	Self-organizing maps and agglomerative clustering	Euclidean distance and WARD distance	Vector space model for term, GPS coordinates, time	Sub-event
Event detection/ [47]	Clustering algorithm by fast search and find of density peaks	Local density in clusters	Keywords on documents	Events
Situation Awareness/ [49]	Online incremental clustering algorithm	Cosine and Jaccard similarities	Terms in tweet stream	Topics
Crowd-sourcing/ [18]	Fast k-means clustering	Euclidean squared distance	Latitude and longitude of crowdsourced data	Incident location

1.2.3 Support Vector Machine

Fundamental Concept

Support vector machine (SVM) is a classification and regression prediction tool that uses ML theory to maximise predictive accuracy while automatically avoiding over-fit to the data. The foundations of SVM have been developed by Cortes and Vapnik [14], and have gained popularity due to many promising features such as better empirical performance.

Although the SVM can be utilised in various optimisation problems such as regression, the classic problem is mainly that of data classification. The SVM can be used when a classification needs are straightforward. Figure 4 shows the basic idea of the SVM, as the two-dimensional example where the data points are linearly separable.

The data points (samples) are identified as being positive or negative, and the problem is to find an optimal boundary (i.e. hyperplane) that separates the data points by a maximal margin. A location of this boundary is determined by a subset of the data points, known as support vectors, which are overlapped with the boundary. The two-class classification problem to be solved is the following:

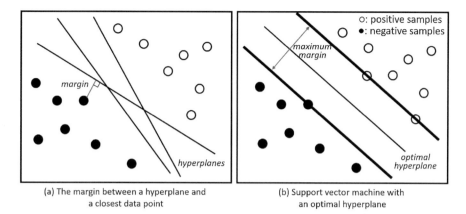

(a) The margin between a hyperplane and   (b) Support vector machine with
        a closest data point   an optimal hyperplane

Fig. 4 Overview of a support vector machine The margin is defined as the perpendicular distance between the decision boundary (i.e. hyperplane) and the closest of the data points, as shown on (**a**). Maximising the margin leads to a particular choice of decision boundary (i.e. optimal hyperplane), as shown on (**b**)

$$\min_{\vec{w},b} \frac{1}{2}\|w\|,$$

$$s,t \quad y_i = +1 \Rightarrow \vec{w} \cdot \vec{x_i} + b \geq +1$$

$$y_i = -1 \Rightarrow \vec{w} \cdot \vec{x_i} - b \leq -1 \tag{7}$$

$$s,t \quad y_i(\vec{w} \cdot \vec{x_i}) \geq 1, \forall i$$

where w and b indicate a weight vector and a bias. The identification of the each data point x_i is y_i, which can take a value of $+1$ or -1 (representing positive or negative, respectively). In this regard, the solution hyperplane present as follows:

$$u = \vec{w} \cdot \vec{x_i} + b. \tag{8}$$

As aforementioned, SVMs can be used for classification and regression problems.

- **Classification** in SVMs is contained in supervised learning. Known labels points to a desired response, validating the accuracy of the algorithm, or is used for learning to act correctly. In this regard, a step as called feature selection identifies which features are intimately connected to the known classes. Feature selection and SVM classification together can also be used to identify key sets that are involved in processes distinguish the classes.
- In linear and non-linear **regression** problems, SVMs can also be used by the introduction of an alternative loss function which is modified to include a distance measure. Similarly to classification, a non-linear model is generally

required to pertinently model data. Since, a non-linear mapping can be used to map the data into a high dimensional feature space where linear regression is performed, SVM is again employed to address the curse of dimensionality [40].

Usages for Emergency Management

SVMs have shown significant generalisation performance when the underlying data is nonlinear and non-stationary. Therefore the technique has attracted wide popularity in solving both regression and classification tasks. It is designed for binary classification in nature, but they can also solve the multi-class classification problems through one-against-one or one-against-all strategy. SVMs were found effective to classify topics and relevancy of data for the EM in various researches [4, 10, 20, 30, 41, 44].

To use a real-time nature as an important characteristic of Twitter for earthquake event detection, an algorithm to monitor tweets and to detect a target event was proposed [41]. It starts with a SVM-based semantic analysis on tweet to discriminate whether a tweet is truly referring to an actual earthquake occurrence. The statistical, keyword and word context features as input are respectively transferred into the SVM in order to classify the emergency tweet or not, such as keywords on a tweet, the number of words, the position of the query word and the words before and after the query word (i.e. word context) in tweets. From experiments with two query words earthquake and shaking, the SVM based on statistical features (the number of words in a tweet message, and the position of the query word within a tweet) outperforms the others.

In order to classify tweets and text messages automatically for understanding the emergency situation better, a reusable information technology infrastructure was developed based on the SVM which uses a sign function [10]. Its components are (1) an iPhone application, (2) a Twitter crawler component, (3) machine translation and (4) automatic message classification. For the fourth component, two classifiers by keywords and SVM were implemented and compared, based on four techniques such as the bag of word approach, feature abstraction, feature selection and latent Dirichlet allocation. The classification via SVM based on the feature abstraction significantly outperformed other combinations for distinguishing topics of text messages.

To improve high reliability of judging emergency of rescue evacuation support system which reduces the number of victims by supporting real-time evacuation in the critical situation immediately after emergency outbreak, a new method by buffering judgement results of SVM was introduced [20, 30]. The SVM with a radial function uses the maximum acceleration of mobile terminal for the behaviour analysis and emergency recognition. From the results of experiments about the emergency evacuation with more than 200 examples, it revealed that the approach by performing a final judgement using accumulation of a judgement result can improve the reliability of emergency recognition.

Table 4 Summarising SVM techniques for emergency management

EM task/ citation No.	ML technique(kernal function)	Input feature(s)	Output
Event detection/ [41]	SVMs (polynomial and RBF)	statistical, keyword and word context features	Positive and negative classes
Event detection/ [10]	SVM (sign function)	Four representation types of bag of words	Topics
Event detection/ [20, 30]	Buffering-SVM (radial function)	Maximum acceleration of mobile terminal	Running or not
Crowdsourcing/ [4]	SSVM (linear function)	Tweets	Emergency severity labelled by human
Situation awareness/ [44]	SVM (radial function)	Messages of tweets including locations	Emergency and non-emergency

A system performing the collection of emergency tweets based on trending emergency hash tags and classifying the emergency severity based on the structured support vector machine (SSVM) using the tweets was proposed [4]. First, initial model parameters of learning is developed by combining feature vectors as set and pattern-label pairs are taken as input with linear kernel functions. Then the label related to most violated constraint for the pattern is obtained and a model is created for the classification. As a result, it is observed relatively high detection rate using SSVM classifier comparing with Naïve Bayse classifier. Table 4 summarises the SVM techniques for various EM tasks.

1.2.4 Bayesian

Fundamental Concept

Bayesian learning applies Bayes' rule to problems such as classification and regression. The rule gives a relationship between the posterior probability and the prior probability. Let D be the data record (or case) whose class label is unknown and H be some hypothesis, such as "data record D belongs to a specified class C." In this case, our purpose is finding $P(H|D)$ for classification, and $P(H|D)$ is the posterior probability of H conditioned on D. In contrast, $P(H)$ is the prior probability of H. For instance, $P(H)$ is the probability that any given data record is a class C, regardless of how the data record looks. Given $P(H)$, $P(D)$ and $P(D|H)$, the posterior probability $P(H|D)$ is calculated by using the Bayes' rule as follows:

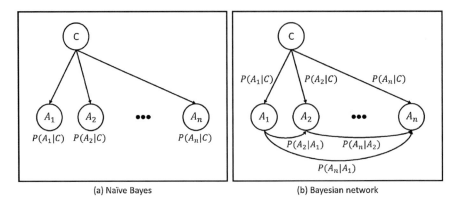

(a) Naïve Bayes

(b) Bayesian network

Fig. 5 Overview of two Bayesian approaches It shows the Naïve Bayes classifier, with conditional probabilities $P(A_i|C)$ depicted as arcs from a class variable C to an attribute A_i. The dependencies between attributes, which are missing in Naïve Bayes (**a**), are added in the Bayesian network in (**b**)

$$P(H|D) = P(D|H) * P(H)/P(D) \qquad (9)$$

As shown in Fig. 5, there are two popular approaches, which use the Bayes' rule, such as Naïve Bayes and Bayesian networks.

- A Naïve classifier considers all properties to contribute independently to the probability that a data record belongs to a class. Although the conditional independence assumption is almost always violated in practice, a long history of application shows that Naïve Bayes tends to work remarkably well even when the assumption is violated [40]. The input variables are generally categorical data, but variations of the algorithm can work with continuous variables. The output typically includes a class label and its corresponding probability score. The probabilities of prior and conditional are all normally estimated on the basis of their frequency in a training set.
- Bayesian networks consist of nodes that indicate random variables, and vertices denoting conditional probabilities between nodes. Their purpose is to provide a computationally feasible and graphically representable way about dependencies between attributes whose dependencies have an strong enough impact on the solution to a particular problem, under constraints that ensure the correctness and feasibility of computation. It can be done manually, by supplying the structure of the network, and then training a Bayesian network is similar to training the Naïve Bayes classifier with conditionals being estimated from the data set. Learning structure of the network presents a bigger challenge, and active researches are still going on.

Usages for Emergency Management

In order to distinguish "informational" from "conversational" tweets, a Bayesian approach to the classification of tweets (posts on Twitter) during Hurricane Sandy was introduced [46]. It is designed an effective set of features and used them as input to Naïve Bayes classifiers. Nine extracted features (i.e. "has hash tag," "abrupt sentence," "multiple sentences," "informative URL," "has phone number," "has emoticon," "has retweet," "has keyword" and "has curse word." And the features then are listed in descending order based on Information Gain Ranking from the Weka DM toolkit[2] to be applied the Naïve Bayes classifier. The proposed feature set provides similar results in the classification of tweets comparing with a "bag of words" approach.

In the EmerGent project[3] which aimed to develop a tool that collects, analyses and presents emergency relevant information, they used Naïve Bayes based on a bag of words to discriminate two sets as "spam" (not relevant) and "not spam" (relevant) [45]. Experimental results showed that 76.1% of tweet data set were correctly labelled. In addition the Naïve Bayes was performed using the statistical analysis programme R^4 to classify three types: 'safety warning,' 'flood warning' and 'update.' As a result, appeared that in particular case that has the high prior probability of one type of content, the Naïve Bayes classifier was not applicable.

When an earthquake occurs, a huge amount of data is generated by social media users and social networks play therefore a fundamental role, like a crowdsourcing, in the development of decision support systems that could help both government and citizens [17]. In this regard, to effectively extract and organise knowledge from online social media data, a decision support system for earthquake management based on Bayesian model averaging and natural language processing techniques was proposed. The system identifies messages related to (real) earthquakes and critical tremors, highlights those posts provided by spontaneous users and containing any actionable knowledge about damages, magnitude, location and time references. In this system Bayesian model averaging was utilised to identify the probability of the labels related to emergencies, magnitude (or damages) and authors of tweets.

To address the difficulty which is not readily available for an emerging target disaster of conventional supervised learning algorithms relying on labelled data, Li et al. utilised the Naïve Bayes based on a multivariate Bernoulli model, which is an iterative self-training strategy, to classify hard and soft-labels and to make a cleaner decision boundary [28]. Experimental results on the task of identifying tweets relevant to a disaster of interest showed that the domain adaptation classifiers are better as compared to the supervised classifiers learned only from labelled source data. Table 5 summarises the Bayesian-based ML techniques for various EM tasks.

---

[2]http://www.cs.waikato.ac.nz/ml/weka/.

[3]http://www.fp7-emergent.eu/.

Table 5 Summarising Bayesian-based ML techniques for emergency management

EM task/ citation No.	ML technique	Input	Output
Crowdsourcing/ [46]	Naïve Bayes	Nine extracted features	"informational" and "conversational"
Crowdsourcing/ [45]	Naïve Bayes	A bag of words in tweets	Emergency and non-emergency
Early warning/ [17]	Bayesian model averaging	Tweets	Probability of the labels related to emergencies, magnitude (or damages) and authors of tweets
Situation awareness/ [28]	Naïve Bayes based on a multivariate Bernoulli model	A set of words in tweets	Hard-label and soft-label

1.2.5   Neural Networks

Fundamental Concept

Artificial Neural Network (ANN) simulates the natural intelligence of biological brain and nervous system in human. The human brain and nervous system are consist of a huge number of processing units called neurons interconnected with each other. Even though each neuron is having a limited processing power and contributes very little in decision making and solution providing, intelligence is generated from the parallel functioning and distributed asynchronous control of neurons in the network. In other words, simple solutions from different neurons can be worked out in parallel and contributed into a global solution. By mimicking of ANN toward the biological neural network, it generates human-like intelligence.

Simple functionality that comprises hardware and/or software (programming constructs), which mimic the properties of biological neurons, is called artificial neuron as shown like the (a) of Fig. 6. A biological neuron has cell body, nucleus and axon in right upper of (a), similarly the artificial neuron has functionality in its nucleus (here $\sum(W_i X_i)$) and n number of sensory inputs along with their weights. The aggregated and processed input with weight is compared with a threshold value provided with the artificial neuron (here F). If the processed input is substantial in comparison with the threshold value provided, the output is generated. Since there are many real-life problems that cannot be solved with a single neuron, the use of multiple neurons working in parallel fashion is required. These multiple neurons can be arranged in systematic architectures (e.g., multilayer perceptron, Kohonen and Hopfield network) to solve complex problems and intelligent decision making. The (b) of Fig. 6 shows the multilayer perceptron architecture which contains neurons that are arranged in various layers such as input layer, hidden layer and output layer. Neurons of the input layer directly take normalised environmental values

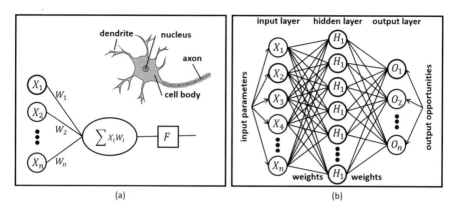

Fig. 6 Overview of an artificial neural network. (**a**) Artificial and biological neuron. (**b**) Multilayer architecture of neural network

Table 6 Operating of a multilayer ANN

1. Determine parameters with sufficient number of neurons/nodes to accommodate these parameters
2. Determine all output opportunities (i.e., the number of neurons in the output layer)
3. Take one hidden layers containing average number (average of total input plus total output neurons) of nodes
4. Connect the network architecture properly and randomly provide weights to every connections for an initial step
5. Collect training data sets containing input values as well as output values
6. Repeat the following steps for all training data sets
– Provide input from the environment and actual output in the training data, as a forward pass
– Compare the calculated output with actual output in the training data and find out the error (i.e., difference between them) according to the well-known back-propagation algorithm. Propagate the error back for a backward pass to generalise the weights of the network
– Adjust the weights and recalculate til you get correct according to the training data. As the generalised weights according to the training set, the network is able to give meaningful output
7. Use the architecture for the real input values for which output is required

without processing function. In the case of output layer, neurons are enriched with application-specific output functions. Similarly neurons of a hidden layer have appropriate activation functions. Each neuron from a given layer is connected with every neuron of its adjacent layer in forward direction. Table 6 shows the simplified steps how the architecture operates.

This learning algorithm transfers the input values into forward direction (i.e. forward pass), compares the calculated outputs with the actual outputs in training set, calculates the error value and propagates the error back (i.e. backward pass).

Quality of the network generally depends on the quality of the sample data. To test the network, similar data called validation set is used.

Usages for Emergency Management

As aforesaid, ANN as an information processing paradigm inspired from the biological neural network to deal with nonlinear complex problems that are difficult for conventional computations. ANNs with different architectures [25, 26, 31, 38] have been used in various tasks of the EM.

For predicting earthquakes occurring in the region of Greece with the use of different types of input data, a multilayer feed-forward network and back-propagation was studied [31]. The authors considered two different case studies: the prediction of the earthquake magnitude of the following day and the prediction of the magnitude of the impending seismic event following the occurrence of pre-seismic signals. The signals called as Seismic Electric Signals (SES), that are believed to occur prior to an earthquake. Three network models were presented based on the SES's flowing directions (i.e., North-south and East-west) and an average magnitudes for the previous 30 days as input for the network. These models make outputs such as earthquake magnitudes (and time lag) by passing through hidden layers that consist of five or ten neurons. The accuracy rate of the magnitude prediction as 84.01% was high, and the corresponding rates from the prediction of both magnitude and time lag were 83.56% for magnitude and 92.96% for time lag.

Similarly, to predict earthquake in Chile region, Reyes et al used the feed-forward neural network with back-propagation [38]. Their method receives five b-values from Gutenberg-Richter and Omori/Utsu laws that are strongly correlated with seismicity, as inputs, and it passes the input into hidden layers containing fifteen neurons to predict a maximum magnitude. It also provides the probability that an earthquake of magnitude larger than a threshold value happens, and the probability that an earthquake of a limited magnitude interval might occur, both during the next 5 days in the areas analysed. By means of statistical tests and compared with well-known ML classifiers such as K-nearest neighbors, SVM and k-means clustering, the proposed method has showed the high success rate.

Kim et al. proposed a time-dependent surrogate model of storm surge based on an multilayer feed-forward network and backpropagation with synthetic simulations of hurricanes [25]. The ANN pass six input hurricane parameters (Longitude, latitude, central pressure, moving speed of storm, heading direction and radius of exponential scale pressure) into a hidden layer which consists of 16 25 neurons to predict a normalised surge water level. Experiment results showed that the developed surrogate model is validated with measured data and high-fidelity simulations of two historical hurricanes at four points in southern Louisiana.

A seismic system based on an ANN was introduced to collect data from personal/private smart-phone sensors and analyse earthquakes using the collected data [26]. Sensor data such as the acceleration vector sum, the maximum zero crossing rate and the cumulative absolute velocity of the acceleration vector sum are

Table 7 Summarising ANN techniques for emergency management

EM task/ citation No.	ML technique	Input layer	Hidden layer	Output layer
Prediction/ [31]	Multilayer feed-forward network and backpropagation	SES-NS, SES-EW and average magnitudes for the previous 30 days	Five or ten neurons	Earthquake magnitude
Prediction/ [38]	Feed-forward neural network with backpropagation	Five b-value of Gutenberg-Richter and Omori/Utsu laws	Fifteen neurons	Earthquake magnitude
Prediction/ [25]	Multilayer feed-forward network and backpropagation	Six hurricane parameters	From 16 to 25 neurons	Normalised surge water level
Early warning/ [26]	ANN	Acceleration sensor data from smart phones	Five neurons	Earthquake and non-earthquake

carried into a hidden layer consisting of five neurons to predict whether earthquake occurrence or not. It showed that smart-phones can record magnitude 5 earthquakes at distances of 10 km or less. Table 7 summarises the ANN techniques for various EM tasks.

1.2.6 Deep Learning

Fundamental Concept

Since 2006 [21], deep learning or hierarchical learning has emerged as a new area of ML research [8]. Although there are various definitions or high-level descriptions of deep learning, common among them are two key aspects: (1) models involving multiple layers of nonlinear information processing; and (2) supervised or unsupervised learning methods of feature representation at successively higher, more abstract layers.

The popularity of deep learning today are the drastically increased by following three import reasons:

– the drastically increased chip processing abilities (e.g. GPGPUs)
– the significantly increased size of training data
– the recent advances in ML and information processing research.

Before appearing deep learning, most ML techniques had exploited shallow-structured architectures which typically include at most one or two layers of nonlinear feature transformations. Even though the shallow architectures have been

Fig. 7 Overview of a deep
neural network

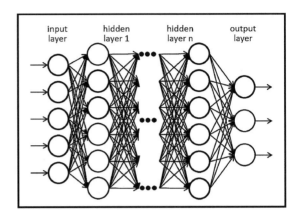

shown effectiveness in solving many simple or well-constrained problems, their
limited modelling and representational power can lead to difficulties to deal with
more complicated real-world applications such as human speech, natural image etc.

In a same vein with ANN, deep learning techniques mimic the human information processing mechanisms which suggest the need of deep architectures for
extracting complex structure and building internal representation. Historically, the
concept of deep learning originated from ANN research. As shown in Fig. 7, deep
learning refers to a rather wide class of ML techniques and architectures using the
many layers of non-linear information processing [15]. Therefore, a deep learning
significantly improves the modelling power and creates many closely optimal
configurations. Even if parameter learning is converged in a local optimum, the
resulting deep learning can still perform well since the probability of having a poor
local optimum is lower than the case of using a small number of neurons in the
network. By using deep and wide neural networks, however, deep learning costs
great demand to the computational power during the training process.

Depending on how the architectures and techniques are intended for use, deep
learning can broadly be categorise most of the work into three major classes [15]:

- **Deep networks for unsupervised learning** are intended to capture high-order
  correlation of the observed data for pattern analysis (or synthesis purposes) when
  no information about target class labels is available. Unsupervised feature or
  representation learning is involved in this category.
- **Deep networks for supervised learning** directly provide discriminative power
  for pattern classification purposes by characterising the posterior distributions
  of classes conditioned on the observed data. They are also called discriminative
  deep networks.
- **Hybrid deep networks** whose a goal is discrimination provide outcomes of
  generative or unsupervised deep networks. It can often be achieved by better
  optimisation or/and regularisation of the deep networks in the second category.
  The goal can also be accomplished when discriminative criteria for supervised

learning are used to estimate the parameters in the unsupervised deep networks of the first category.

Usages for Emergency Management

In the EM domain, most of deep learning techniques distinguishing images such as the post from social media and the imagery from unmanned aerial vehicles have been exploited the task of the emergency evaluation (e.g., damage and informative level) [3, 5, 7, 32, 33].

A VGG16 technique as the convolutional neural networks (CNNs) was used in order to improve the capability of the evaluation task from a large proportion of web crawling images including irrelevant or redundant [32, 33]. A proposed image processing pipeline based on the deep learning automatically detect and filter out images that are not relevant or do not convey significant information for crisis response and management. The 224×224 RGB images from social media are inputted for the deep neural network and pass through the hidden layer which consists of 13 convolutional and three (and two) fully connected layers. As a result, three damage levels (i.e. severe, mild and none) as the output are annotated for the images. Their experimentation indicated the utility of the proposed pipeline based on the deep learning technique, in a number of real-world emergency datasets from social media and web service (i.e. Google image data).

Attari et al. proposed Nazr-CNN, a deep learning pipeline for object (i.e. building) detection and fine-grained classification in images acquired from unmanned aerial vehicles for damage assessment and monitoring [5]. In order to discriminate between different levels (i.e. mild, medium and severe) of damage, the pipeline comprises of two components: (1) the object localisation by carrying out a pixel-level classification and (2) the hidden layer of CNN consisting of 14 convolutional and three fully connected layers for encoding fisher vectors[4] of the segments generated from the first component. Experimental results presented that Nazr-CNN performs relatively better and improves on mild and severe classes than the baseline semantic segmentation.

In order to filter the redundant or irrelevant of an overwhelming amounts of imagery content on social networks within minutes of a disaster hit generated by people, a real-time social media image processing pipeline that combines human and machine intelligence was proposed by Alam et al. [3]. The CNN technique based on VGG16 as the machine intelligence are utilised to capture and filter the relevancy of the social media imagery content, for emergencies. Some their experiments showed that the deep learning technique provide almost perfect performance for the binary classifier stemming from the fact that relevant and irrelevant images.

---

[4]In Computer Vision, a Fisher Vector is used to describe an entire image for image classification [43].

Table 8 Summarising deep learning techniques for emergency management

EM task/ citation No.	ML technique	Input	Hidden layer	Output
Evaluation/ [32, 33]	CNN (VGG16 and VGG16-fine-turned)	224×224 RGB image from social media	13 convolutional and three (two) fully connected layers	Damage level (severe, mild and none)
Evaluation/ [5]	Nazr-CNN (VGG16)	Images from unmanned aerial vehicles	14 convolutional and three fully connected layers	Damage level (mild, medium and severe)
Evaluation/ [3]	CNN (VGG-16)	224×224 RGB image from social media	13 convolutional and three fully connected layers	Events
Evaluation/ [7]	CNN (SqueezeNet)	64×64 pixels images from radar Earth observation satellite	nine convolutional and two fully connected layers	Damage level (washed away, collapsed and slightly damaged regions)

For real-time decision making in disaster relief using building damage mapping, One of CNN techniques was introduced [7]. First a selection algorithm is based on the SqueezeNet[5] network to swiftly distinguish between built-up and nonbuilt-up regions, and a recognition algorithm with a modified wide residual network then classify the built-up regions into wash away, collapsed and slightly damaged regions. The deep network involves the nine convolutional and two fully connected layers as a hidden part. Experiments on data sets about the 2011 Tohoku earthquake and tsunami area showed that the proposed framework based on the deep learning technique is operational and fast in training and prediction calculations.

Table 8 summarises the deep learning techniques for evaluation task in EM.

2 Practices of Learning Techniques in Emergency Management

2.1 Data Sets

In order to practice learning techniques in EM, we use social media data collected in August 2017, when Hurricane Harvey hit the United States. Hurricane Harvey is a category 4 storm that hit Texas on August 26, 2017. According to the National Hurricane Center (NHC), it had caused a total estimated economic cost of $125

---

[5]SqueezeNet: https://github.com/DeepScale/SqueezeNet.

billion and death estimates between 68–89 as reported by the NHC and National Oceanic and Atmospheric Administration.[6] Analysis of the Kinder Institute showed that almost 30% of Houston's population has been impacted by the storm.[7] The social media dataset used for these practices consists of over 8.5 million tweets that were extracted using the keywords "Harvey" and "hurricane Harvey." These tweets data covers a period of three days August 27th through the 29th, 2017. Since, most of the tweets in the data set has not geo-tag, we had implicitly encoded their geographic using relevant messages and their physical addresses. It can be find on and downloaded from the website of the BDEM project.[8] In addition, data sets extracted and filtered for following practices also are shared. There are five R programming examples of learning techniques for EM on this section. We hope these examples can help to more easily understand the theoretical descriptions aforementioned and applying them to real situations. An usage way of R[9] language and Rstudio[10] are not described in here, since it is out of scope of this book.

2.2 Decision Trees in R

In R, *rpart* is for modeling decision trees, and an optional package *rpart.plot* enables the plotting of a tree. The rest of this section shows an example of how to use decision trees in R with *rpart.plot* to predict whether a tweet related to demand of people in emergency. Data set[11] used here includes one relevance column and three factors such as topic of tweets, release data of the tweets and the number of retweet. We start with initialising the used packages.

```
# Load libraries
library(rpart)
library(rpart.plot)
```

The working directory contains a comma-separated-value (CSV) file named DTdata.csv. The file has a header row consisting of four attributes such as *Topic*, *TWDate*, *RTNumber* and *Demand*, and 27 rows of training data. *Demand* would be the output variable as the predicted class, and the others would be the input variables. In R, read the data from the CSV file in the working directory and display the content.

---

[6]https://www.nhc.noaa.gov/data/tcr/AL092017_Harvey.pdf, accessed on July 27th, 2018.

[7]https://ricegis.maps.arcgis.com/apps/Cascade/index.html?appid= 6ea5082d69484c7a922bd18705afbf85, accessed on July 27, 2018.

[8]https://www.bigdata.vestforsk.no/.

[9]Download-link:https://www.r-project.org/.

[10]Download-link:https://www.rstudio.com/products/rstudio/download/.

[11]https://bdem.squarespace.com/links/#links-home.

```
demand_decision <- read.table("C:/DTdata.csv", header=TRUE, sep=",")
demand_decision[1:10,]
```

```
> demand_decision[1:10,]
      Topic    TWDate RTNumber Demand
1  Damage 8/27/2017        3     No
2  Damage 8/27/2017        1     No
3  Damage 8/27/2017        2     No
4  Damage 8/27/2017        2     No
5  Damage 8/27/2017        1     No
6  Damage 8/28/2017        2     No
7  Damage 8/28/2017        1     No
8  Damage 8/28/2017        1     No
9  Damage 8/28/2017        1     No
10 Damage 8/28/2017        1     No
```

Display a summary of *demand_decision*.

```
> summary(demand_decision)
     Topic          TWDate          RTNumber        Demand
 Clothes: 2   8/27/2017: 5   Min.   : 1.00      No :17
 Damage :14   8/28/2017: 8   1st Qu.: 1.00      Yes:10
 Food   : 4   8/29/2017:14   Median : 1.00
 Power  : 2                  Mean   : 4.63
 Water  : 5                  3rd Qu.: 2.50
                             Max.   :76.00
```

The *rpart* function models recursive partitioning and regression trees[9]. The following code shows how to use the *rpart* function to construct a decision tree.

```
fit <- rpart(Demand ~ Topic + TWDate + RTNumber,
             method = "class",
             data = demand_decision,
             control = rpart.control(minsplit = 1),
             parms = list(split = 'information'))
```

The *rpart* function has four parameters. The first parameter is the model indicating that attribute Demand an be predicted based on the others such as *Topic*, *TWDate* and *RTNumber*. The second parameter, method, is set to "class" telling R it is building a classification tree. The third control parameter is optional and controls the tree growth. In the preceding example, control=rpart.control (minsplit = 1) means that each node should have at least one observation before splitting nodes. The minsplit = 1 marks sense for the small dataset, but for larger dataset minsplit could be set to 10% of the dataset size to combat over-fitting. Besides minsplit, other parameters are available to control the construction of the decision tree. For instance, repart.control (maxdepth = 10, cp = 0.001) limits the depth of the tree to no more than 10, and a split must decrease the overall lack of fit by a factor of 0.001 before being attempted. The last parameter (i.e. parms) indicates the purity measure being used for the splits. The value of split can be either information (for using the information gain) or gini (for using the Gini index).

Enter summary(fit) to produce a summary of the model built from *rpart*.

```
> summary(fit)
call:
rpart(formula = Demand ~ Topic + TwDate + RTNumber, data = demand_decision,
    method = "class", parms = list(split = "information"), control = rpart.cont
rol(minsplit = 1))
  n= 27

          CP nsplit rel error xerror       xstd
1 0.70000000      0       1.0    1.0 0.2509242
2 0.06666667      1       0.3    0.4 0.1845916
3 0.01000000      4       0.1    0.4 0.1845916

Variable importance
  Topic    TwDate RTNumber
     48        34       18

Node number 1: 27 observations,    complexity param=0.7
  predicted class=No    expected loss=0.3703704  P(node) =1
    class counts:    17    10
   probabilities: 0.630 0.370



     left son=2 (14 obs) right son=3 (13 obs)
     Primary splits:
         Topic     splits as  RLRRR,    improve=10.774460, (0 missing)
         TwDate    splits as  LLR,      improve= 9.421343, (0 missing)
         RTNumber  < 41  to the left,   improve= 1.026256, (0 missing)
     Surrogate splits:
         TwDate    splits as  LLR,      agree=0.889, adj=0.769, (0 split)
         RTNumber  < 4.5 to the left,   agree=0.630, adj=0.231, (0 split)

Node number 2: 14 observations
  predicted class=No    expected loss=0  P(node) =0.5185185
    class counts:    14     0
   probabilities: 1.000 0.000

Node number 3: 13 observations,    complexity param=0.06666667
  predicted class=Yes   expected loss=0.2307692  P(node) =0.4814815
    class counts:     3    10
   probabilities: 0.231 0.769
   left son=6 (7 obs) right son=7 (6 obs)
   Primary splits:
```

```
        Topic    splits as  R-RLL,   improve=2.242297, (0 missing)
        TWDate   splits as  -LR,     improve=1.615919, (0 missing)
        RTNumber < 5.5 to the right, improve=0.420827, (0 missing)
    Surrogate splits:
        RTNumber < 1.5 to the right, agree=0.615, adj=0.167, (0 split)

Node number 6: 7 observations,    complexity param=0.06666667
    predicted class=Yes  expected loss=0.4285714  P(node) =0.2592593
        class counts:     3     4
      probabilities: 0.429 0.571
    left son=12 (1 obs) right son=13 (6 obs)
    Primary splits:
        TWDate   splits as  -LR,     improve=0.96127170, (0 missing)
        RTNumber < 5.5 to the right, improve=0.96127170, (0 missing)
        Topic    splits as  ---LR,   improve=0.02900404, (0 missing)

Node number 7: 6 observations
    predicted class=Yes  expected loss=0  P(node) =0.2222222
        class counts:     0     6
      probabilities: 0.000 1.000

Node number 12: 1 observations
    predicted class=No   expected loss=0  P(node) =0.03703704
        class counts:     1     0
      probabilities: 1.000 0.000

Node number 13: 6 observations,    complexity param=0.06666667
    predicted class=Yes  expected loss=0.3333333  P(node) =0.2222222
        class counts:     2     4
      probabilities: 0.333 0.667
    left son=26 (3 obs) right son=27 (3 obs)
    Primary splits:
        RTNumber < 1.5 to the left,  improve=1.9095430, (0 missing)
        Topic    splits as  ---LR,   improve=0.1834501, (0 missing)

Node number 26: 3 observations
    predicted class=No   expected loss=0.3333333  P(node) =0.1111111
        class counts:     2     1
      probabilities: 0.667 0.333

Node number 27: 3 observations

        predicted class=Yes  expected loss=0  P(node) =0.1111111
            class counts:     0     3
          probabilities: 0.000 1.000
```

The output summarise every node of the constructed decision tree. If a node is a leaf, the output includes both the predicted class labels (*Yes* or *No* for *Demand*) and the class probabilities. Whereas, if a node is internal, the output in addition displays the number of observations that lead to each child node and the improvement that each attribute may bring for the next split. These outputs are difficult to read and comprehend. The **rpart.plot()** function from the *rpart.plot* package can visually present the output of a decision tree.

Enter the following R code to plot the tree based on the model being built.

```
rpart.plot(fit, type = 4,
           extra = 2,
           clip.right.labs = FALSE)
```

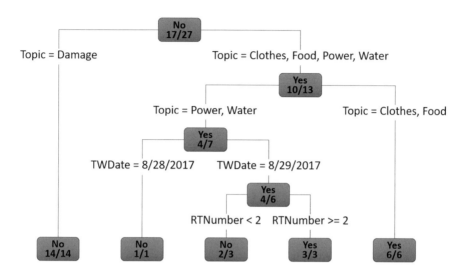

The decision tree can be used to predict outcomes with the following record. The goal is to predict the relevance of the tweet information for demand in Hurricane Harvey. The following code loads the data into R as a data frame *newdata*. Note that the training set does not contain this case.

```
newdata <- data.frame(Topic = "Clothes", TWDate = "8/29/2017", RTNumber = 70)
newdata
    Topic    TWDate RTNumber
Clothes 8/29/2017       70
```

Next, use the *predict* function to generate predictions from the fitted decision tree. The code of the prediction function follows. Parameter *type* denotes the type of the predicted value. Set it to either **prob** or **class** to predict and receive the result as either the class probabilities or just the class.

```
predict(fit, newdata = newdata, type = "prob")
predict(fit, newdata = newdata, type = "class")
```

The output shows that one instance is classified as *Demand=*Yes, and zero instances are classified as *Demand=*No. Therefore, in both cases, the decision tree predicts that the demand decision of the testing tweet data is related to demand of a person in emergency.

```
> predict(fit, newdata = newdata, type = "prob")
  No Yes
1  0   1
> predict(fit, newdata = newdata, type = "class")
  1
Yes
Levels: No Yes
```

2.3 Naïve Bayes in R

In this section, we practice the Naïve Bayes as one of the Bayesian methods. The data set[12] is same with that of decision trees, except for the number of retweet. The *RTNumber* column containing numerical numbers is transformed to categorical values for easy calculating the probabilities. In addition, the data set contains one record as test data. Here the *e1071* package are used for the *naiveBayes* function. The data set are included in a CSV file (NBdata.csv). The file has 27 rows of training data and one other row as testing data. From the CSV file, last ten records of data set generated by following codes is shown next. Two data frame objects called *trainData* and *testData* are created for the Naïve Bayes classifier.

```
tweetsample <- read.table("C:/NBdata.csv", header = TRUE, sep = ",")
trainData <- as.data.frame(tweetsample[1:27,])
testData <- as.data.frame(tweetsample[28,])
trainData[19:27,]
testData
```

```
> trainData[19:27,]
      Topic    TWDate RTNumber Demand
19    Power 8/29/2017       <5     No
20   Damage 8/29/2017       <5     No
21  Clothes 8/29/2017      >10    Yes
22    Water 8/29/2017       <5    Yes
23    Water 8/29/2017  3 to 10    Yes
24     Food 8/29/2017       <5    Yes
25     Food 8/29/2017       <5    Yes
26     Food 8/29/2017       <5    Yes
27   Damage 8/29/2017  3 to 10     No
> testData
      Topic    TWDate RTNumber Demand
28    Water 8/29/2017  3 to 10
```

The first method shown here is to build a Naïve Bayes classifier from scratch by manually computing the probability scores. The first step is to compute the prior probabilities of each attribute, such as *Topic*, *TWDate* and *RTNumber*. According

---

[12]https://bdem.squarespace.com/links/#links-home.

to the Naïve Bayes classifier, these attributes are conditional independent. The dependent variable is *Demand*. Compute the prior probabilities $P(c_i)$ for Demand, where $c_i \in C$ and $C = \{Yes, No\}$.

```
> tprior <- table(trainData$Demand)
> tprior

   No Yes
 0  17  10
> tprior <- tprior/sum(tprior)
> tprior

           No        Yes
0.0000000 0.6296296 0.3703704
```

The next step is to compute conditional probabilities $P(A|C)$, where $A = \{Topic, TWDate, RTNumber\}$ and $C = \{Yes, No\}$. Count the number of "Yes" and "No" entries for each group, and normalise by the total number of "Yes" and "No" entries to get the conditional probabilities.

```
> topicCounts <- table(trainData[,c("Demand", "Topic")])
> topicCounts <- topicCounts/rowSums(topicCounts)
> topicCounts
        Topic
Demand     Clothes       Damage         Food        Power        Water

  No    0.00000000  0.82352941  0.00000000  0.05882353  0.11764706
  Yes   0.20000000  0.00000000  0.40000000  0.10000000  0.30000000
```

```
> twdateCounts <- table(trainData[,c("Demand", "TWDate")])
> twdateCounts <- twdateCounts/rowSums(twdateCounts)
> twdateCounts
        TWDate
Demand 8/27/2017 8/28/2017 8/29/2017

  No   0.2941176 0.4705882 0.2352941
  Yes  0.0000000 0.0000000 1.0000000
```

```
> rtnoCounts <- table(trainData[,c("Demand", "RTNumber")])
> rtnoCounts <- rtnoCounts/rowSums(rtnoCounts)
> rtnoCounts
        RTNumber
Demand        <5       >10   3 to 10

  No   0.7647059 0.0000000 0.2352941
  Yes  0.7000000 0.1000000 0.2000000
```

According to Eq. 9, probability $P(c_i|A)$ is determined by the product of $P(a_j|c_j)$ times the (c_i) where $c_1 = Yes$ and $c_2 = No$. The predicted result of the output is determined by the larger value of $P(Yes|A)$ and $P(No|A)$. Given the test data, use the following code to predict the *Demand*.

```
prob_yes <- topicCounts["Yes", testData[,c("Topic")]] *
    twdateCounts["Yes", testData[,c("TWDate")]] *
    rtnoCounts["Yes", testData[,c("RTNumber")]] *
    tprior["Yes"]

prob_no <- topicCounts["No", testData[,c("Topic")]] *
    twdateCounts["No", testData[,c("TWDate")]] *
    rtnoCounts["No", testData[,c("RTNumber")]] *
    tprior["No"]
```

The predicted results of the test data is *Demand*= Yes.

```
> prob_yes
           Yes
0.02222222
> prob_no
            No
0.004100987
> max(prob_yes, prob_no)
[1] 0.02222222
```

Exercise the *naiveBayes* Function in R Until now, we manually calculated the probabilities and predicted the result of the *testData* using the Bayes' rule. The *e1071* package in R has a built-in *naiveBayes* function that can compute the conditional probabilities of a categorical class variable given independent categorical predictor variables using the Bayes' rule. The function takes the form of naiveBayes(formula, data, ...), where the data denotes a data frame of factors x1, x2, ..., when the formula of the form class x̃1 + x2 + ... assuming x1, x2, ... are conditionally independent.

Exercise Develop a model using naiveBayes function and display results.

2.4 k-Means Clustering in R

In this section, we illustrate how to use the WSS mentioned in Sect. 1.2.2 to determine an appropriate number k of clusters we practice the k-means clustering. The task is to group 161 tweets based on their location data (i.e. GPS coordinates).[13] Note that we created the latitude and longitude of extracted physical addresses from the collected tweets by performing a geocoding procedure, and negative values of the west longitudes were changed into positive values to fulfil the k-means

---

[13] https://bdem.squarespace.com/links/#links-home.

clustering. The following R code establishes the necessary libraries and imports the CSV file containing the locations.

```
library(plyr)
library(cluster)
library(lattice)
library(graphics)
library(factoextra)

location_input = as.data.frame(read.csv("C:/KMdata.csv"))
```

The data file includes three columns such as a tweet identification (ID) number, a latitude and a longitude. The identification is excluded from the k-means input matrix *KMdata_orig* like the results according to following codes, since the tweets ID is not used in the clustering.

```
> KMdata_orig = as.matrix(location_input[,c("TWNumber", "Latitude", "Longitude")])
> KMdata <- KMdata_orig[,2:3]
> KMdata[1:5,]
        Latitude  Longitude
[1,]  32.88086   96.83910
[2,]  29.99964   97.14612
[3,]  29.52301   95.08167
[4,]  32.78050   96.80186
[5,]  30.04932   94.08202
```

If we use mixed numerical data, where each attribute is something entirely different (say, shoe size and weight), the data can be standardised by following scale function. Here the latitude and longitude should avoid to apply the scale function, because it causes distortion.

```
KMdata.scaled <- scale(KMdata_orig[,2:3])
summary(KMdata.scaled)
KMdata[1:10,]
```

To determine an appropriate value for k, the k-means algorithm is used to identify clusters for $k = 1, 2, 3, \ldots, 10$. For each value, the WSS is calculated. If an additional cluster provides a better partitioning of the data points, the WSS should be smaller without the additional cluster. The following R code loops through several k-means analyses for the number of centroids, k, varying from 1 to 10. For each k, the option nstart = 30 specifics that the k-means algorithm will be repeated 30 times, each starting with k random initial centroids. The corresponding value of WSS for each k-means analysis is stored in the *wss* vector. The results can be showed using the basic R plot function.

The k-means clustering will be conducted for $k = 2$, since the WSS is greatly reduced when k increases from one to two.

The showed contents of the variable *KMresult* include the following:

```
wss <- numeric(10)
for(k in 1:10) wss[k] <- sum(kmeans(KMdata, centers=k, nstart=30)$withinss)
plot(1:10, wss, type = "b", xlab = "Number of Clusters", ylab = "Within Sum of
Wquares")
```

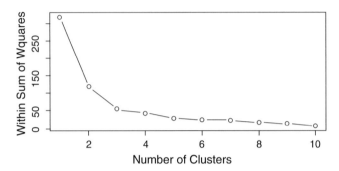

Fig. 8 WSS of the tweet location data

```
> KMresult=kmeans(KMdata, 2, nstart = 10)
> KMresult
K-means clustering with 2 clusters of sizes 26, 135

Cluster means:
   Latitude Longitude
1 31.85976  97.54729
2 29.75015  95.39149

Clustering vector:
  [1] 1 2 2 1 2 2 2 2 2 2 1 2 2 2 2 2 2 2 2 1 2 2 1 2 1 1 2 2 2 2 2 2 1 2 2 2 2 2
 [39] 2 2 1 1 2 1 2 2 2 2 2 2 2 2 2 2 2 2 2 2 2 1 1 2 2 2 2 1 2 2 2 2 2 2 2 2
 [77] 2 2 2 2 2 2 1 2 2 2 2 2 2 2 2 2 2 2 2 1 1 1 2 2 2 2 2 2 2 2 2 2 1 2 2 2 2 2
[115] 2 1 2 2 2 1 2 2 2 2 2 2 2 2 2 2 2 2 2 2 2 2 2 2 2 1 1 2 2 2 2 1 2 2 2 2 2 2
[153] 2 2 2 1 2 2 1 2 2

Within cluster sum of squares by cluster:
[1] 72.89125 46.27130
 (between_SS / total_SS =  62.5 %)

Available components:

[1] "cluster"        "centers"        "totss"          "withinss"        "tot.withinss"
[6] "betweenss"      "size"           "iter"           "ifault"
```

- The location of the cluster means
- A clustering vector that defines the membership of each tweet to a corresponding cluster 1 or 2
- The WSS of each cluster
- A list of all the available *k*-means components

The reader may wonder whether the *k*-means results stored in *KMresult* are same as the WSS results obtained earlier in generating the plot in Fig. 8. The following code and result show that the results are indeed equivalent.

```
> c(wss[2], sum(KMresult$withinss))
[1] 119.1626 119.1626
```

The data scientist should visualize the data and assigned clusters, when the value of k is determined. In the following code, the *fviz_cluster* function on the *factoextra* package is used to visualise the distinguished tweet clusters and centroids. The function can include many parameters for various visualisation.[14]

```
fviz_cluster(KMresult, KMdata, ellipse.type = "norm")
```

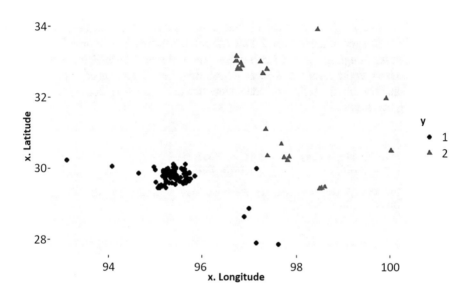

Exercise The *k*-Means Clustering in R Until now, we separated the tweet location data into two clusters according to the WSS values in Fig. 8. On the one hand, the improvement in WSS is also fairly linear for $k > 3$. The process of identifying the appropriate value of k is referred to as finding the "elbow" of the WSS curve. Clustering techniques belong to unsupervised learning, while SVM introducing in the next section is supervised learning. The example and practice results of the *k*-means clustering can be used for the SVM. Therefore, generate other dataset for the next section using the following code.

Exercise Cluster tweet data into three groups and compare its result with that of the upper example. Generate two CSV files about the results.

---

[14]factoextra: https://cran.r-project.org/web/packages/factoextra/factoextra.pdf.

```
exportData <- cbind(KMdata_orig, ClusterValue=(KMresult$cluster))
exportData[1:3,]

write.csv(exportData, "C:/SVMdata.csv")
```

```
> exportData[1:3,]
      TWNumber Latitude Longitude ClusterValue
[1,]         1 32.88086  96.83910            2
[2,]         2 29.99964  97.14612            1
[3,]         3 29.52301  95.08167            1
```

2.5 Support Vector Machine in R

In this section, we will leverage the *tidyverse* package to perform data manipulation, the *e1071* packages to execute calculations and produce visualizations related to SVMs. Data sets generated in Sect. 2.4 are used.[15] It contains four column *TWNumber*, *Latitude*, *Longitude* and *ClusterValue*. The column *ClusterValue* indicates group numbers as the results of *k*-means clustering. Let's import needed packages and the data set using the following code. Note that our exercise (practice) uses data set having two classes.

```
# Attach Packages
library(tidyverse)    # data manipulation
library(e1071)        # SVM methodology

location_input = as.data.frame(read.csv("C:/SVMdata1.csv"))
location_input[1:5,]
```

```
> location_input[1:5,]
  X TWNumber Latitude Longitude ClusterValue
1 1        1 32.88086  96.83910            2
2 2        2 29.99964  97.14612            1
3 3        3 29.52301  95.08167            1
4 4        4 32.78050  96.80186            2
5 5        5 30.04932  94.08202            1
```

First the data set should be manipulated for the SVM practice. The *TWNumber* is eliminated, and input variables (i.e. *Latitude* and *Longitude*) and one class factor (i.e. *ClusterValue*) are separated into x and y variables for dot plot visualisation. Execute the following code to regulate the data and to see the clustering result.

In addition, from the last line in the above code, the data set converted into a data frame to use for the *svm* function. As mentioned in Sect. 1.2.3, the goal of the maximal margin classifier is to identify the linear boundary that maximizes the total

---

[15]https://bdem.squarespace.com/links/#links-home.

```
# Manipulate data
SVMdata <- SVMdata_orig[,2:4]
x=SVMdata[,1:2]
y=as.character(SVMdata_orig[,4])
df <- data.frame(x=x, y=as.factor(y))

# Plot data
ggplot(data = df, aes(x = x.Longitude, y = x.Latitude, color = y, shape = y))
+   geom_point(size = 2) +
  scale_color_manual(values=c("#000000", "#FF0000")) +
  theme(legend.position = "right")
```

distance between the line and the closest point in each class. We can use the *svm* function in the *e1071* package to find this boundary.

```
# Fit Support Vector Machine model to data set
SVMfit_linear = svm(y~., data = df, kernel = "linear", scale = FALSE)
plot(SVMfit_linear, df)
```

In the plot, points being represented by an "X" indicate the support vectors, or the points that directly affect the classification line. The points marked with an "o" denote the other points which don't affect the calculation of the line. In the *svm* function, kernel = "linear" means using the linear kernel, and it can be set as radial like the following code.

Exercise the SVM Classification in R So far we performed the SVM classification with the data set including two groups.

Exercise Build a SVM classification for another data set containing three groups, using various kernel functions such as "linear", "polynomial" and "radial ". In addition analyse between previous results in Sect. 2.4.

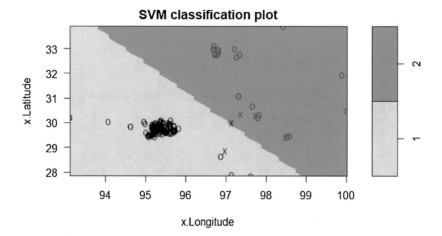

```
SVMfit_radial = svm(y~., data = df, kernel = "radial", gamma = 1, cost = 10,
scale = FALSE)
plot(SVMfit_radial, df)
```

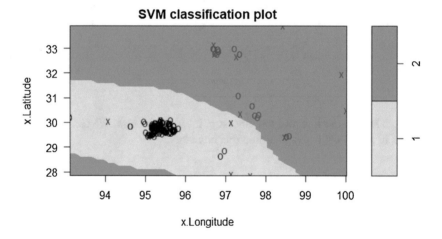

2.6   Artificial Neural Networks in R

In this section we will fit a neural network model in R. A data set[16] used here is manipulated from an original data set and consequently contains five columns such as *TWDate*, *RTNumber* as integer, Latitude, *Longitude* and *Demand*. The *TWDate* was modified as generation days (i.e. 27, 28 and 29), and the Demand was distinguished into three values (i.e. 0, 0.5 and 1). The values denotes the relevance degree of tweets for demand, in other words "0" and "1" respectively represent "no relevance for demand" and "related to demand."

Let's start with importing packages using the following code. The *neuralnet* package is providing a nice tool to plot the ANN model which is used for the analysis of a neural network. Also we use the *matrixStats* package for operating on rows and columns of a matrix.

```
library(neuralnet)
library(matrixStats)
```

To validate the ANN model developed in this experiment, we divide the data into training (60% of the data set) and test set (the remained data set). Training set is used to find the relationship between dependent and independent variables while the test set assesses the performance of the model. The assignment of the data to training and test set is done using random sampling. We perform random sampling on R using the *sample* function. The *set.seed* function is used to generate same random sample every time and maintain consistency, and the index variable while fitting neural network will be used to create training and test data sets. Let's use the following R script to do these tasks.

```
## Creating index variable
# Read the Data
data = read.csv("C:/ANNdata.csv", header=T)

# Random sampling
samplesize = 0.60 * nrow(data)
set.seed(80)
index = sample( seq_len ( nrow ( data ) ), size = samplesize )

# Create training and test set
datatrain = data[ index, ]
datatest = data[ -index, ]
datatrain[1:5,]
datatest[1:5,]
```

---

[16]https://bdem.squarespace.com/links/#links-home.

```
> datatrain[1:5,]
     TWDate RTNumber Latitude Longitude Demand
71       28        1       30        95      0
90       28        6       29        97      1
125      29        2       30        96      0
12       27        6       30        96      0
95       28        1       30        95      0
> datatest[1:5,]
     TWDate RTNumber Latitude Longitude Demand
4        27        1       33        97      1
6        27        1       30        95      0
9        27        5       30        95      0
10       27        1       30        95      0
15       27        2       30        95      0
```

The first step is to scale the tweet data set. The scaling of data is essential because otherwise a variable may have large impact on the prediction variable only because of its scale. Here we use the min-max normalisation as one of common techniques to scale the data using the following script.

```
## Scale data for neural network
max = apply(data , 2 , max)
min = apply(data, 2 , min)
scaled = as.data.frame(scale(data, center = min, scale = max - min))
```

The scaled data is used to fit the neural network. Visualize the neural network with weights for each of the variable as follows.

```
## Fit neural network
# creating training and test set
trainNN = scaled[index , ]
testNN = scaled[-index , ]

# fit neural network
set.seed(2)
NN = neuralnet(Demand ~ TWDate + RTNumber + Latitude + Longitude, trainNN,
hidden = 3 , linear.output = T )

# plot neural network
plot(NN)
```

Figure 9 shows the computed neural network. The generated model has three neurons in its hidden layer. The black lines show the connections with weights which are calculated using the back propagation algorithm explained earlier. The blue line is the displays the bias term.

Evaluation of the neural network model is performed through the k-fold cross-validation. In this method, the overall data is divided into k equal subsets, and each time a subset is assigned as test set while others used as training set. Every data gets a chance to be in test set and training set, thus the k-fold cross validation is able to reduce the dependence of performance on test-training split and to decrease the

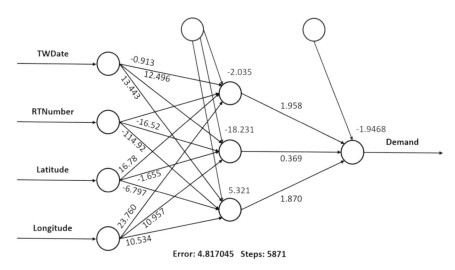

Fig. 9 Neural network model

variance of performance metrics. Let set the number of elements in the training set as from 10 to 60 (i.e. for(j in 10:60)) and to select 80 samples from the dataset (i.e. k = 80). The rest of the elements are assigned to test set. The model is trained on each of the 4000 training datasets and then tested on the corresponding test sets. RMSE of each of the test set is calculated. The RMSE values for each of the set is stored in a 80 × 50 matrix *Matrix.RMSE*. This method ensures that our results are free of any sample bias and checks for the robustness of our model. The R script is as follows:

Since the size of the matrix (i.e. *Matrix.RMSE*) is large, visualise the RMSE using a *boxplot* function like the following code and result.

The boxplot in Fig. 10 shows that the median RMSE across 80 samples when length of training set is fixed to 60 is 0.437. In the next visualization, Let us look at the variation of RMSE with the length of training set. We calculate the median RMSE for each of the training set length and plot them using the following R script.

Figure 11 shows that the median RMSE of the model decreases as the length of the training the set. This is an important result. Note that the model accuracy is dependent on the length of training set. The performance of neural network model is sensitive to training-test split.

```
## Cross validation of neural network model
# Initialize variables
set.seed(50)
k = 80
RMSE.NN = NULL

List = list( )

# Fit neural network model within nested for loop
for(j in 10:60){
  for (i in 1:k) {
    index = sample(1:nrow(data),j )

    trainNN = scaled[index,]
    testNN = scaled[-index,]
    datatest = data[-index,]

    NN = neuralnet(Demand ~ TWDate + RTNumber + Latitude + Longitude,
                   trainNN, hidden = 3, linear.output= T)
    predict_testNN = compute(NN,testNN[,c(1:4)])
    predict_testNN = (predict_testNN$net.result
                     *(max(data$Demand)-min(data$Demand)))+min(data$Demand)

    RMSE.NN [i]<- (sum((datatest$Demand-predict_testNN)^2)/nrow(datatest))^0.5
  }
  List[[j]] = RMSE.NN
}
Matrix.RMSE = do.call(cbind, List)


        ## Variation of median RMSE
        med = colMedians(Matrix.RMSE)
        X = seq(10,30)

        plot (med~X, type = "l",
              xlab = "length of training set",
              ylab = "median RMSE",
              main = "Variation of RMSE with length of training set")
```

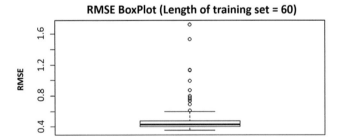

Fig. 10 Boxplot for RMSE of ANN model

```
## Variation of median RMSE
med = colMedians(Matrix.RMSE)
X = seq(10,60)

plot (med~X, type = "l",
      xlab = "length of training set",
      ylab = "median RMSE",
      main = "Variation of RMSE with length of training set")
```

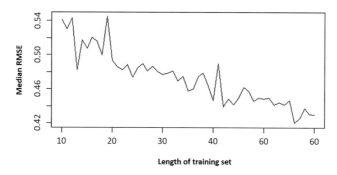

Fig. 11 Variation of RMSE of ANN model

Acknowledgments The work is funded from the Research Council of Norway (RCN) and the Norwegian Agency for International Cooperation and Quality Enhancement in Higher Education (Diku) grant through INTPART programme.

References

1. Akerkar, R., Lingras, P.: Building an Intelligent Web - Theory and Practice Jones and Bartlett Publishers, Burlington (2008)
2. Akerkar, R., Sajja, P.S.: Intelligent Techniques for Data Science. Springer, Berlin (2016)
3. Alam, F., Ofli, F., Imran, M.: Processing social media images by combining human and machine computing during crises. Int. J. Hum. Comput. Int. **34**(4), 311–327 (2018)
4. Anbalagan, B., Valliyammai, C.: # chennaifloods: Leveraging human and machine learning for crisis mapping during disasters using social media. In: Proceedings of the IEEE 23rd International Conference on High Performance Computing Workshops (HiPCW), pp. 50–59. IEEE, Piscataway (2016)
5. Attari, N., Ofli, F., Awad, M., Lucas, J., Chawla, S.: Nazr-CNN: Fine-grained classification of UAV imagery for damage assessment. In: Proceedings of the 2017 IEEE International Conference on Data Science and Advanced Analytics, DSAA 2017, pp. 50–59. IEEE, Tokyo (2017)
6. Bahrepour, M., Meratnia, N., Poel, M., Taghikhaki, Z., Havinga, P.J.: Use of wireless sensor networks for distributed event detection in disaster management applications. Int. J. Space-Based Situated Comput. **2**(1), 58–69 (2012)

7. Bai, Y., Gao, C., Singh, S., Koch, M., Adriano, B., Mas, E., Koshimura, S.: A framework of rapid regional tsunami damage recognition from post-event terrasar-X imagery using deep neural networks. IEEE Geoscience Remote Sens. Lett. **15**(1), 43–47 (2018)
8. Bengio, Y.: Learning deep architectures for AI. Found. Trends Mach. Learn. **2**(1), 1–127 (2009)
9. Breiman, L., Friedman, J.H., Olshen, R.A., Stone, C.J.: Classification and Regression Trees. Wadsworth, Belmont (1984)
10. Caragea, C., McNeese, N., Jaiswal, A., Traylor, G., Kim, H.W., Mitra, P., Wu, D., Tapia, A.H., Giles, L., Jansen, B.J., et al.: Classifying text messages for the haiti earthquake. In: Proceedings of the 8th International Conference on Information Systems for Crisis Response and Management (ISCRAM2011). CiteSeer (2011)
11. Cervone, G., Sava, E., Huang, Q., Schnebele, E., Harrison, J., Waters, N.: Using twitter for tasking remote-sensing data collection and damage assessment: 2013 boulder flood case study. Int. J. Remote Sens. **37**(1), 100–124 (2016)
12. Chen, N., Wenjing, L., Ruizhen, B., Chen, A.: Application of computational intelligence technologies in emergency management: a literature review. Artif. Intell. Rev. **52**, 1–38 (2017)
13. Chen, W., Xie, X., Peng, J., Wang, J., Duan, Z., Hong, H.: Gis-based landslide susceptibility modelling: a comparative assessment of Kernel logistic regression, naïve-bayes tree, and alternating decision tree models. Geomat. Nat. Haz. Risk **8**(2), 950–973 (2017)
14. Cortes, C., Vapnik, V.: Support-vector networks. Mach. Learn. **20**(3), 273–297 (1995)
15. Deng, L., Yu, D.: Deep learning: methods and applications. Found. Trends Signal Process. **7**(3–4), 197–387 (2014)
16. Dietrich, D., Heller, B., Yang, B.: Data Science and Big Data Analytics: Discovering, Analyzing, Visualizing and Presenting Data. EMC Education Services, Saint Paul (2015)
17. Fersini, E., Messina, E., Pozzi, F.A.: Earthquake management: a decision support system based on natural language processing. J. Ambient. Intell. Humaniz. Comput. **8**(1), 37–45 (2017)
18. Harris, P., Anitha, J.: Post earthquake disaster awareness to emergency task force using crowdsourced data. In: Proceedings of the IEEE International Conference on Industrial and Information Systems (ICIIS), pp. 1–6. IEEE, Piscataway (2017)
19. Hastie, T., Tibshirani, R., Friedman, J.: Unsupervised learning. In: The Elements of Statistical Learning, pp. 485–585. Springer, Berlin (2009)
20. Higuchi, H., Fujimura, J., Nakamura, T., Kogo, K., Tsudaka, K., Wada, T., Okada, H., Ohtsuki, K.: Disaster detection by statistics and SVM for emergency rescue evacuation support system. In: Proceedings of the 43th International Conference on Parallel Processing Workshops (ICCPW), pp. 349–354. IEEE, Piscataway (2014)
21. Hinton, G.E., Osindero, S., Teh, Y.W.: A fast learning algorithm for deep belief nets. Neural Comput. **18**(7), 1527–1554 (2006). https://doi.org/10.1162/neco.2006.18.7.1527
22. Jordan, M.I., Mitchell, T.M.: Machine learning: trends, perspectives, and prospects. Science **349**(6245), 255–260 (2015)
23. Joshi, A.R., Tarte, I., Suresh, S., Koolagudi, S.G.: Damage identification and assessment using image processing on post-disaster satellite imagery. In: IEEE Transaction on Global Humanitarian Technology Conference (GHTC), pp. 1–7. IEEE, Piscataway (2017)
24. Kaelbling, L.P., Littman, M.L., Moore, A.W.: Reinforcement learning: a survey. J. Artif. Intell. Res. **4**, 237–285 (1996)
25. Kim, S.W., Melby, J.A., Nadal-Caraballo, N.C., Ratcliff, J.: A time-dependent surrogate model for storm surge prediction based on an artificial neural network using high-fidelity synthetic hurricane modeling. Nat. Hazards **76**(1), 565–585 (2015)
26. Kong, Q., Allen, R.M., Schreier, L., Kwon, Y.W.: Myshake: a smartphone seismic network for earthquake early warning and beyond. Sci. Adv. **2**(2), e1501,055 (2016)
27. Kotsiantis, S.B., Zaharakis, I., Pintelas, P.: Supervised machine learning: a review of classification techniques. Emerg. Artif. Intell. Appl. Comput. Eng. **160**, 3–24 (2007)
28. Li, H., Caragea, D., Caragea, C., Herndon, N.: Disaster response aided by tweet classification with a domain adaptation approach. J. Conting. Crisis Manag. **26**(1), 16–27 (2018)

29. Martínez-Álvarez, F., Lora, A.T., Morales-Esteban, A., Riquelme, J.C.: Computational intelligence techniques for predicting earthquakes. In: Corchado, E., Kurzynski, M., Wozniak, M. (eds.) Hybrid Artificial Intelligent Systems - 6th International Conference, HAIS 2011, Wroclaw, May 23–25, 2011, Proceedings, Part II. Lecture Notes in Computer Science, vol. 6679, pp. 287–294. Springer, Berlin (2011)

30. Mori, K., Nakamura, T., Fujimura, J., Tsudaka, K., Wada, T., Okada, H., Ohtsuki, K.: Development of ERESS in panic-type disasters: Disaster recognition algorithm by buffering-SVM. In: Proceedings of the 13th International Conference on ITS Telecommunications (ITST), pp. 337–343. IEEE, Piscataway (2013)

31. Moustra, M., Avraamides, M., Christodoulou, C.: Artificial neural networks for earthquake prediction using time series magnitude data or seismic electric signals. Expert Syst. Appl. **38**(12), 15032–15039 (2011)

32. Nguyen, D.T., Alam, F., Ofli, F., Imran, M.: Automatic image filtering on social networks using deep learning and perceptual hashing during crises. Comput. Res. Repo. abs/1704.02602 (2017)

33. Nguyen, D.T., Ofli, F., Imran, M., Mitra, P.: Damage assessment from social media imagery data during disasters. In: Proceedings of the 2017 IEEE/ACM International Conference on Advances in Social Networks Analysis and Mining 2017, pp. 569–576. ACM, New York (2017)

34. Pham, B.T., Khosravi, K., Prakash, I.: Application and comparison of decision tree-based machine learning methods in landside susceptibility assessment at Pauri Garhwal area, Uttarakhand, India. Environ. Process. **4**(3), 711–730 (2017)

35. Pohl, D., Bouchachia, A., Hellwagner, H.: Social media for crisis management: clustering approaches for sub-event detection. Multimedia Tools Appl. **74**(11), 3901–3932 (2015)

36. Quinlan, J.R.: Induction of decision trees. Mach. Learn. **1**(1), 81–106 (1986)

37. Quinlan, J.R.: C4.5: Programs for Machine Learning. Morgan Kaufmann, Burlington (1993)

38. Reyes, J., Morales-Esteban, A., Martínez-Álvarez, F.: Neural networks to predict earthquakes in Chile. Appl. Soft Comput. **13**(2), 1314–1328 (2013)

39. Rodriguez, A., Laio, A.: Clustering by fast search and find of density peaks. Science **344**(6191), 1492–1496 (2014)

40. Sajja, P.S., Akerkar, R.: Intelligent Technologies for Web Applications. Chapman and Hall/CRC, Boca Raton (2016)

41. Sakaki, T., Okazaki, M., Matsuo, Y.: Earthquake shakes twitter users: Real-time event detection by social sensors. In: Proceedings of the 19th International Conference on World Wide Web, pp. 851–860. ACM, New York (2010)

42. Salman, R., Kecman, V., Li, Q., Strack, R., Test, E.: Fast k-means algorithm clustering. CoRR abs/1108.1351 (2011)

43. Sánchez, J., Perronnin, F., Mensink, T., Verbeek, J.J.: Image classification with the fisher vector: theory and practice. Int. J. Comput. Vis. **105**(3), 222–245 (2013)

44. Shen, S., Murzintcev, N., Song, C., Cheng, C.: Information retrieval of a disaster event from cross-platform social media. Inf. Discovery Deliv. **45**(4), 220–226 (2017)

45. Spielhofer, T., Greenlaw, R., Markham, D., Hahne, A.: Data mining twitter during the UK floods: Investigating the potential use of social media in emergency management. In: Proceedings of the 3rd International Conference on Information and Communication Technologies for Disaster Management (ICT-DM), pp. 1–6. IEEE, Piscataway (2016)

46. Truong, B., Caragea, C., Squicciarini, A., Tapia, A.H.: Identifying valuable information from twitter during natural disasters. Proc. Assoc. Inf. Sci. Technol. **51**(1), 1–4 (2014)

47. Xu, W., Liu, L., Shang, W.: Leveraging cross-media analytics to detect events and mine opinions for emergency management. Online Inf. Rev. **41**(4), 487–506 (2017)

48. Yang, Y., Pierce, T., Carbonell, J.: A study of retrospective and on-line event detection. In: Proceedings of the 21st Annual International ACM SIGIR Conference on Research and Development in Information Retrieval, pp. 28–36. ACM, New York (1998)

49. Yin, J., Lampert, A., Cameron, M., Robinson, B., Power, R.: Using social media to enhance emergency situation awareness. IEEE Intell. Syst. **27**(6), 52–59 (2012)

50. Zhang, X.Y., Li, X., Lin, X.: The data mining technology of particle swarm optimization algorithm in earthquake prediction. In: Advanced Materials Research, vol. 989, pp. 1570–1573. Trans Tech Publications, Zürich (2014)
51. Zhang, Y., Burton, H.V., Sun, H., Shokrabadi, M.: A machine learning framework for assessing post-earthquake structural safety. Struct. Saf. **72**, 1–16 (2018)
52. Zmazek, B., Todorovski, L., Džeroski, S., Vaupotič, J., Kobal, I.: Application of decision trees to the analysis of soil radon data for earthquake prediction. Appl. Radiat. Isot. **58**(6), 697–706 (2003)

Knowledge Graphs and Natural-Language Processing

Andreas L. Opdahl

1 What Are Knowledge Graphs?

Knowledge graphs originate from Tim Berners-Lee's vision of a *machine-processable* web of data that would augment the original web of *human-readable* documents [5, 23]. A central idea is to represent data as graphs, with nodes that represent concrete objects, information, or concepts and with edges that represent semantic relations [1].

The most central standard is the Resource Description Framework (RDF[1]), which is the standard way of representing knowledge graphs. An RDF graph consists of *triples*, each expressing that a semantic *resource* (the *subject*) has a particular semantic relation (the *predicate* or *property*) to either a *literal value* or another semantic resource (the *object*). Resources and properties are identified using Internationalized Resource Names (IRN[2]), and literals are typically expressed using XML Schema Definition (XSD) datatypes. A special `rdf:type` property can be used to state that one resource is the type of another, such as in the triple `dbpedia:Tim_Berners-Lee rdf:type foaf:Person` (where we have used standard prefixes `dbpedia:`, `rdf:`, and `foaf:` to shorten the IRNs). Standard formats are available for exchanging RDF files, and the new JSON-LD[3]

---

[1] https://www.w3.org/TR/rdf11-primer/.

[2] Here, we use IRN about Uniform Resource Names (URN) that are extended to the Unicode character set, although it remains more common to use the initialism URN even when Unicode is allowed.

[3] http://json-ld.org.

A. L. Opdahl (✉)
Department of Information Science and Media Studies, University of Bergen, Bergen, Norway
e-mail: Andreas.Opdahl@uib.no

© Springer Nature Switzerland AG 2020
R. Akerkar (ed.), *Big Data in Emergency Management: Exploitation Techniques for Social and Mobile Data*, https://doi.org/10.1007/978-3-030-48099-8_4

standard extends JavaScript Object Notation (JSON) with semantic tags so that RDF data as can be easily exchanged through web APIs.

RDF Schema (RDFS[4]) extends RDF with terms—represented as IRNs—that make knowledge graphs richer and more precise. For example, RDFS defines resource types and properties for expressing that one resource type is a subtype of another (i.e., that toxic fume is a kind of pollution), that one property is a subtype of another (i.e., that being a nurse is a form of being a healthcare worker), and that some property is always used with subjects and objects of specific types (i.e., that only living things can be poisoned). The meaning of RDFS terms is defined through axioms and entailment rules. The Web Ontology Language (OWL[5]) offers even more precise semantics and automated reasoning on top of RDFS, but computational complexity grows quickly when datasets become large. Therefore, OWL is most effective for smaller and more specific semantic datasets, called *ontologies*. One important use of ontologies is to precisely define and interrelate the resource types and properties that are used to organise and give meaning to larger knowledge graphs. Such ontologies—even when they are expressed less formally in RDFS—are often called *vocabularies* (more about that later).

SPARQL (Simple Protocol and RDF Query Language[6]) lets users and programs extract information from knowledge graphs. The result can be tables of information, yes/no answers, or new knowledge graphs. SPARQL Update also lets users and programs modify knowledge graphs by adding or removing triples. SPARQL is supported both by native RDF database management systems, called *triple stores*, and by wrappers that expose tabular and other data in legacy databases as knowledge graphs—whether as downloadable RDF files, through online *SPARQL endpoints*, or by other means.

The Linked Open Data (LOD) principles offer further advice for creating and sharing knowledge graphs [6]. The four central principles are:

1. sharing graphs using standard formats and protocols such as RDF, RDFS, OWL, and SPARQL;
2. using Internationalized Resource Names (IRNs) to name resources (nodes) and properties (edges);
3. making these IRNs into dereferencable Internationalized Resource Identifiers (IRIs[7]) that can be accessed on the web to provide further information about the resource in RDF format; and
4. using standard IRNs that are defined in vocabularies as types and properties in graphs.

---

[4]https://www.w3.org/TR/rdf-schema/.

[5]https://www.w3.org/OWL/.

[6]https://www.w3.org/TR/sparql11-overview/.

[7]IRIs are Uniform Resource Identifiers (URIs) that are extended to the Unicode character set. They both *name* a resource uniquely and specify its *location* on the web.

Today, more than 1200 datasets that adhere to these principles are openly available in the LOD cloud [13], adding up to almost 150 trillion triples. Much-used datasets we will mention later (such as DBpedia, GeoNames, LinkedGeoData, and Wikidata) act as hubs that tie these linked open datasets even more tightly together by offering standard names (again IRNs) for individual people, organisations, places, works, and so on.

Knowledge graphs can also be stored and processed using property graph databases and other technologies outside the semantic standard but, even for such graphs, RDF and SPARQL are commonly used for information exchange.

2 Benefits and Challenges

In an emergency situation, diverse data sources must be recombined and used to support complex querying, processing, and reasoning in unforeseeable ways. This is exactly the type of situation where knowledge graphs shine, because they leverage an interoperable set of semantic technologies and tools for quickly and easily interpreting, combining, analysing, and presenting potentially related datasets from different sources.

2.1 Benefits

Given that the right competencies, tools, and infrastructure are in place, knowledge graphs building on semantic technologies and tools have the potential to simplify and speed up all stages of emergency data processing. *Identifying* data sources is made easier by semantic search engines and semantically searchable registries of open data (such as http://lod-cloud.net). *Harvesting* semantic data is made easier by standard data-exchange formats such as Turtle, NT and OWL/XML for downloading files, JSON-LD for web APIs, and SPARQL for database endpoints. *Lifting* non-semantic data to RDF format is supported by tools such as Karma,[8] and JSON data from web APIs can be easily lifted to JSON-LD by adding simple semantic metadata. A wide range of wrappers, such as D2RQ,[9] provide SPARQL access to relational and other DBMSs that do not natively support SPARQL. *Identifying vocabularies* to use for lifting is made easier by semantically searchable registries such as Linked Open Vocabularies (LOV[10] [25] and LODstats [9]). *Understanding* data becomes easier for humans when the data attributes are marked up with semantically precise tags from well-defined vocabularies. *Alignment* of related

---

[8]http://usc-isi-i2.github.io/karma/.

[9]http://d2rq.org/.

[10]https://lov.linkeddata.es/dataset/lov.

terms from different vocabularies (and other kinds of ontologies) is supported by techniques and tools that use term and structural similarity as indicators of term equivalence and of other semantic relations between terms. *Recombining* data from different data sets is the most central strength of knowledge graphs: as soon as their vocabularies have been aligned, knowledge graphs can be recombined simply by loading them into the same triple store or through SPARQL, using federated queries that combine partial results from multiple endpoints. *Enriching* data means to recombine a dataset with reference data, for example from the Linked Open Data (LOD) cloud. *Contextualising* and *validating* data is thus simplified further by openly available semantic datasets that can be used to make data even easier to understand and to control its validity. *Reasoning* over data is supported to some extent by the description logic (DL) subset of OWL, although computational effort may grow quickly for large ontologies if they are not carefully designed. Rule-based reasoning is therefore more applicable to large datasets than DL reasoning. *Visualising* semantic data, e.g., in dashboards, is also well supported. In all these processing stages, the strength of knowledge graphs and semantic technologies lies in the same set of ideas and practices: expressing knowledge uniformly in a standard format (RDF or OWL) that is annotated semantically using well-defined terms (IRIs) defined as part of semantically interlinked vocabularies that are expressed in the same standard formats (RDFS or OWL).

2.2   Challenges

A full stack of semantic technologies for knowledge graphs is already available for simplifying and speeding up information processing in an emergency situation. The challenge is to have the right combinations of competencies, capacities, and tools already in place when disaster strikes.

On the *competence side*, it is critical to recruit and train staff and volunteers with the right combination of semantic-technology competence and collaboration and communication skills. To have maximal impact in an emergency, a semantic technologist must not only be expert in the use of their tools and techniques, but also be able to communicate well with emergency workers and perhaps directly with the people affected. Communicating in an emergency situation is particularly challenging, because the people involved: may be scared, fatigued. and otherwise working in stressful situations; will have a broad variety and levels of other competencies and skills; may come from different cultures, use different languages and perhaps operate in different climates and time zones; may not be knowledgeable and skilled in ICT; may experience low-quality transmission and delays due to long distances and perhaps compromised infrastructures.

On the *capacity side*, most of the semantic interpretation, lifting, combining, and analysing can take place in the cloud in a distributed fashion that makes it highly suitable for volunteer work. Cloud computing platforms such as Amazon's EC2 and others make it possible to set up collaborative computing infrastructures on-demand quickly. The basic tools needed for handling knowledge graphs can be downloaded and installed quickly, and some cloud providers even offer pre-configured virtual hosts (such as Amazon's Machine Images, AMIs) that can be instantiated on demand. Hence, dedicated emergency machine images can be defined in advance where important and trusted reference datasets have already been loaded into a running triple store, along with ready-to-use tools such as data scrapers and lifters, ontology editors, programming tools and APIs, visualisers, dashboard generators, and various types of social emergency software. Training to create, use, and curate such advance-prepared infrastructures is therefore a useful emergency-preparation activity, and mastering management and use of virtual hosts and other cloud infrastructures is a useful competence.

On the *tool side*, for all types of non-semantic data, precise semantic lifting is essential to avoid information loss. We have already mentioned the computational complexity of OWL reasoning. Indeed, computational complexity is a challenge for graph-based reasoning and pattern matching in general, and it is an important consideration both for native RDF programming and when providing and querying SPARQL endpoints. Although triple-store technologies have been used to store more than a trillion triples in benchmarks, most existing technologies do not scale to the biggest data sizes. An important future challenge is therefore to extend current big-data technologies to also handle semantic data. Finally, knowledge graphs and semantic technologies need to become seamlessly integrated with mainstream machine-learning techniques.

A final challenge is *textual data*, which must be lifted to semantic form before they can be represented in knowledge graphs. This issue is so central that we will discuss it in a separate section below.

3   Vocabularies for Emergency Response

Semantic technologies, LOD, and knowledge graphs rely heavily on vocabularies, expressed either in RDFS or more precisely and formally as OWL ontologies. Vocabularies define terms that can be used to make the meaning of knowledge graphs explicit, precise, and easier to understand. The terms in a vocabulary provide standard IRNs for the most important resource types and properties in a domain. For example, an organisation vocabulary can define resource types for *Person* and *Project* and a *currentProject* property to relate them. We have already mentioned Linked Open Vocabularies (LOV[11]), a web site that offers a searchable overview over and entry point into the most used vocabularies. Precisely defined and interlinked vocabularies also make it easier to combine knowledge graphs that use different vocabularies.

---

[11] https://lov.linkeddata.es/dataset/lov.

There is no all-encompassing and widely accepted ontology that covers all of emergency management. But many data-exchange standards have been proposed for specific concerns, such as people, organisations, resources, infrastructure, processes, disaster description, damage assessment, geography, hydrology, meteorology, and topography. Unfortunately, most standards are defined in plain XML or proprietary formats, and some of them are not even publicly available.

Among the vocabularies that are both open and semantic, MOAC (Management of a Crisis[12]) combines three types of crisis information used by: (a) traditional humanitarian agencies, (b) disaster affected communities, and (c) volunteer and technical committees for humanitarian data exchange. Accordingly, MOAC is divided into three sections that offer terms (IRNs) for: emergency types, security incidents, and affected populations (emergency management); shelters, water, sanitation, food, health, logistics, and telecommunications (emergency cluster); and who/what/where/when, needs, and responses (who-what-where). Parts of MOAC are supported by the Ushahidi web platform[13] for emergency management.

HXL (Humanitarian eXchange Language[14]) aims to improve information sharing during humanitarian crises without adding extra reporting burdens. It defines hashtags for describing: places, such as geolocations, populated places and administrative units in countries; people and households, such as affected populations, their needs and characteristics; responses and other operations, such as their capacities and operations; crises, incidents and events, including their causes, impacts and severity; and general metadata, such as data provenance, approvals, and timestamps. It offers a broader infrastructure that also comprises training, tools and other materials, including a semantic version of the vocabulary.

EDXL-RESCUER is an attempt to make the XML-based Emergency Data Exchange Language (EDXL[15]) standard available as an OWL ontology. EDXL facilitates sharing of emergency information between government agencies and other involved organisations. It offers terms for: alerts, information about events, affected areas, and additional image or audio resources (the common alerting protocol); requesting, responding to, and committing resources (resource messaging); field observations, causality, illness, and management reporting (situation reporting); hospitals, their statuses, bed capacities, facilities, resources, and services (hospital availability exchange); emergency patients (emergency patients tracking); and high-level information modelling (reference information model).

Other examples of domain ontologies or vocabularies that can be relevant in emergency situations are: km4city (city data), Linked Datex II (traffic), Semantic Sensor Network Ontology (sensors), Ordnance Survey Hydrology Ontology (hydrology), Weather Ontology (meteorology), USGS CEGIS (topography), Ordnance Survey Building and Places Ontology, E-response Building Pathology Ontol-

---

[12]http://observedchange.com/moac/ns/.

[13]https://www.ushahidi.com.

[14]http://hxlstandard.org/.

[15]http://docs.oasis-open.org/emergency/edxl-de/v2.0/edxl-de-v2.0.html.

ogy, and E-response Building Internal Layout Ontology. These vocabularies can be used alongside general vocabularies for, e.g., time and duration (OWL-Time), locations (geo, GeoNames, LinkedGeoData), people (FOAF, bio), organisations (org, InteLLEO), events (the Event Ontology), provenance (PROV-O), and data rights (CC).

4 Semantic Datasets for Emergency Management

The chapter on Big Data has already reviewed many data sources that are relevant for emergency management. Some of them are also available in semantic formats or, at least, have semantic counterparts.

The LOD Cloud[16] [13] is a searchable portal of more than 1200 interrelated datasets available as knowledge graphs. It contains both general datasets and sets that are specific to emergency-related domains such as geography, government, social networking, and user-generated content. DBpedia [3, 7] is an automated extraction of structured data from Wikipedia (in particular, its fact boxes) into RDF. It describes more than 14 million resources and is available in over a hundred languages. It is one of the most central hubs in the LOD cloud, where it has been standard practice to name people, organisations, works, and so on using their (dereferencable) DBpedia IRIs. Wikidata[17] is Wikipedia's sister project for crowdsourcing structured factual information. The idea is that the information in Wikipedia's fact boxes will be extracted from and maintained by the Wikidata project. Hence, whereas DBpedia extracts its data *from* Wikipedia, Wikidata is a supplier of information *to* Wikipedia. It currently contains around 50 million items with unique IRIs, similar to RDF resources. Although Wikidata's knowledge graph is not natively stored and maintained in RDF, the data is available through a SPARQL endpoint and downloadable as RDF files. GeoNames[18] is a crowdsourced open repository of more than 10 million geotagged toponyms (geographical names) categorised using a three-level taxonomy with nine letter-coded top-level categories and more than 600 sub-categories. The nine top-level categories are: countries, states, regions... (A); streams, lakes... (H); parks, areas... (L); cities, villages... (P); roads, railways... (R); spots, buildings, farms... (S); mountains, hills, rocks... (T); undersea... (U); and forests, heaths... (V). GeoNames can be browsed online through a map interface. It is also available as RDF and SPARQL and has a web API. It is common in the LOD cloud to name places using their (dereferencable) GeoNames IRIs. LinkedGeoData [4, 24] is an automated extraction of structured data from OpenStreetMap, much as DBpedia is an extraction from Wikipedia.

---

[16]http://lod-cloud.net.

[17]https://www.wikidata.org/wiki/Wikidata:Introduction.

[18]http://www.geonames.org/about.html.

BabelNet[19] is a multi-lingual word net [16]. LODstats[20] [9] has been used to index an even larger body of semantic datasets and endpoints and can be used to search for datasets that use specific RDF types, properties, vocabularies, etc.

The big internet-companies like Google, Facebook, and Amazon also maintain large internal knowledge graphs, although the information is not in general open or always represented using standard semantic formats and protocols. In some cases, commercial data can be sampled or shared in an emergency situation, either pro bono or paid. Google's Emergency Map service and Person Finder[21] are examples of such services, although they are not exposed through semantic interfaces.

Google also supports the GDELT project,[22] which continuously harvests and analyses media in print, broadcast, and web formats in over 100 languages. The GDELT Event Database represents and codifies physical events reported in the world news, whereas the GDELT Global Knowledge graph represents the reported people, places, organisations, themes, and emotions. Both databases are open to the public and incremental updates are available every 15 min. Although the graphs are distributed in tabular form with unique identifiers and well-defined columns, the data are not represented in standard semantic format with IRNs and XSD-typed literals. GDELT does not target emergency management specifically, but offers an open-data firehose about human society that can be used to monitor unstable situations and escalating crises.

The new JSON-LD[23] format extends basic JSON in a simple way with semantic tags taken from standard vocabularies. JSON-LD makes it easy to lift JSON-based APIs to a semantic format, so the responses can be inserted directly into knowledge graphs as soon as a suitable vocabulary has been found or created and interlinked. Data represented in XML-based or other formats, such as from Google Person Finder, can easily be converted to JSON before lifting to JSON-LD by adding simple semantic metadata.

Semantic web APIs also make it much easier to connect the rapidly growing number of more or less smart things available on the internet. Networks of sensors, actuators and other networked devices on the Internet of Things [2] can thereby be identified, integrated, and leveraged much more quickly and easily in an emergency situation, and the information they provide becomes easier to recombine with semantic data from other sources. Smart semantic things can describe, gain access to, and reason about their own context, They can describe themselves and their services semantically in graph form, making them more self-contained and easier to find, for example using the new Semantic Sensor Network Ontology.

---

[19]https://babelnet.org/.

[20]http://lodstats.aksw.org/.

[21]http://www.google.org/crisismap, http://www.google.org/personfinder.

[22]https://www.gdeltproject.org/.

[23]http://json-ld.org.

Regular datasets that are available as spreadsheets or in SQL databases can also be lifted easily to semantic format. We have already mentioned Karma,[24] which is one of several semantic lifting tools that can generate RDF from structured (tabular or hierarchical) data and D2RQ,[25] which is a much-used wrapper for creating SPARQL endpoints and RDF interfaces on top of SQL databases. Automatic semantic annotation of images, video, and audio is an emerging area. In particular, deep neural convolution networks have made image analysis much more precise in recent years [11].

Nevertheless, some of the most important information during an emergency will be available as text, in particular as messages harvested from social media in real time. The next section therefore discusses natural-language processing and lifting of texts into semantic form as knowledge graphs.

5 Analysing Natural-Language Texts

5.1 Pre-processing

Natural-language processing (NLP) use AI and ML techniques to make the semantic content of written texts processable by computers. Central challenges are to identify: which topics and things a text is about; how the topics and things are related; as well as which attitudes and emotions the text expresses. Conventionally, NLP has built on a pre-processing pipeline that combines all or some of the following steps [8, chapter 3]:

1. *Character decoding and tokenisation* breaks the text into a list of words, word pieces, or even single characters, called *tokens*, that are represented using a standard character set such as Unicode.
2. *Normalisation* standardises use of abbreviations, accents, emoticons, shorthands, slang, upper- versus lower-case characters, etc.
3. *Stopword removal* eliminates words that are too common to convey much meaning, such as "of", "the", and "or". One much-used stopword list contains around 300 words but, for some types of analyses, aggressively eliminating as much as the 20% most frequent words produce the best results. Removing little used words is also common.
4. *Stemming or lemmatisation* are two alternative ways of handling words such as "build", "builds", "built", "builder", and "building" that are grammatical forms of the same word (and stem) "build". The difference is that stemming uses simple pattern-based string substitutions (typically based on regular expressions), whereas lemmatisation embeds more lexical and grammatical knowledge,

---

[24] http://usc-isi-i2.github.io/karma/.
[25] http://d2rq.org/.

including exception lists. For example, a hypothetical and very simple stemmer might treat the word "was" as the plural form of (the non-word) "wa", whereas a lemmatiser would look up its exception list and identify "was" correctly as the past tense of "is".

5. *Part of Speech (PoS) tagging* parses sentences to assign words to classes such as nouns, verbs, adjectives, and adverbs. Lemmatisation can sometimes benefit from PoS tags, so the order of steps does not have to be strict. For example, a grammatically-informed lemmatiser would recognise "building" as a form of "build" when it is used as a verb, but retain the form "building" when it is used as a noun.

6. *Dependency parsing* detects how the words and phrases in a sentence are related, for example which noun (phrase) that an adjective modifies, which earlier noun phrase that a pronoun refers to, and which noun phrases that are the subject and object of a verb phrase.

While pre-processing has often relied on hand-crafted algorithms and rules, pre-processing with neural networks and other machine-learning techniques has become more common.

5.2 Word Embeddings

Natural-language processing techniques are developing rapidly. Google's *word2vec* has trained a neural network to predict which words that occur in which contexts in a 1.6 billion-word corpus [10, 15]. The result is a set of *word vectors*, each of which represents the semantics of a word as a few hundred real numbers. *GloVe* has generated a similar set of word vectors using statistical techniques instead of a neural network [20]. The vectors generated by word2vec and GloVe can describe word meanings on a very precise level that opens up for new modes of analysis and reasoning. For example, when the vector for the word "France" is subtracted from the vector for "Paris" and the vector for "Germany" is added, the sum turns out to be close to the vector for "Berlin". Similar additive relations exist between different grammatical forms of the same stem, so that "biggest"—"big" + "small" produces a vector similar to the one for "smallest" [15]. But word-vector addition and subtraction does not work equally well for all kinds of relations.

Word-embedding techniques have also been used to generate vectors that approximate the meaning of sentences, paragraphs, and documents [12] and even the nodes (resources) and edges (properties) in knowledge graphs [21], so that the semantic distance between a word or paragraph and a LOD resource can be approximated by the distance (Euclidian or other) between their vector representations. Vector representations of words, sentences, paragraphs, documents, LOD resources, and other semantic phenomena are paving the way for research that may increase the quality of NL processing as word embedding becomes better understood and more widely used.

Word-embedding approaches often skip all but the first step of the conventional pre-processing pipeline, treating even misspellings and punctuation signs as meaning-bearing tokens. Skipping stemming or normalisation can also improve accuracy because grammatical forms carry semantic information.

5.3 Analysis Problems

Sentiment analysis, sometimes known as opinion mining, attempts to identify whether a text (or its parts) expresses a positive or negative attitude [18, 19]. Most sentiment analysers are implemented using supervised machine-learning algorithms. For example, a collection of movie reviews where each text is associated with a numerical ranking can be used to train a regression algorithm [17]. Emotion analysis uses similar techniques to identify more specific feelings such as joy, anger, disgust, sadness, and fear, both for the text as a whole and for the keywords and phrases it contains.

Negation analysis attempts to identify negated parts of a text. Otherwise a sentence like "I did not find the jokes entertaining." could easily be scored as a positive statement: the words "joke" and "entertain" are both positive, and the rest are neutral or stop words.

Keyword extraction attempts to find the most important words and phrases in a text. Conventional keyword analysis uses a bag of words that results from pre-processing steps 1–4. Extraction proceeds by comparing this bag to a large corpus of other pre-processed texts (for example news articles or Wikipedia pages). Good keywords are ones that occur many times in the input text, but are rare elsewhere in the corpus. A suitable measure is term frequency-inverse document frequency (TF-IDF). Word phrases can be extracted in much the same way as keywords, but comparing bags of two- and three-word sequences (called 2- and 3-grams) instead of single words [22].

Topic identification is used to identify topics or themes that are related to a text, but that may not be explicitly mentioned in it. For example, a newspaper article may be related to the Summer Olympic Games although the text does not contain that exact phrase nor a synonym. Machine-learning techniques are much used for this purpose [17]. Latent Dirichlet Allocation (LDA) is a statistical technique that identifies groups of words that tend to occur together in a corpus of texts, under the assumption that each such word group marks a topic or theme that a text can be about. Word-embedding techniques are increasingly being used to identify and represent the topics of sentences, paragraphs, and documents [12].

Classification is similar to topic identification but, whereas topic identification is open, text classification relies on a closed taxonomy of labels. Standard machine-learning approaches are available for single-label or multi-label classification [17], and standard clustering algorithms can be used to establish the initial taxonomy structure. Afterwards, other NL techniques can be used to suggest class labels, although manual curation and labelling is also common.

Named entity recognition (NER) attempts to identify the individuals that are mentioned in a text, such as people, companies, organisations, cities, geographic features, etc., usually along with their types. Conventionally, this has been treated as a three-step task. First, the words or phrases that name an individual are identified. Common techniques are gazetteer lists (of known names) and typesetting conventions (such as capital initials) in combination with PoS analysis that identifies nouns. Next, the identified names are disambiguated: does the name "Bergen" refer to an American actress, a college football team, or a city in the Netherlands, New Jersey, or Norway? Statistical techniques like LDA can be used here, because each meaning of a name like "Bergen" will tend to co-occur with different groups of words. Finally, when the meaning of a name is clear, it is represented in some standard way, preferably linked by an IRN defined in a common Linked Open Data resource. Examples of LOD sets that can be used to define IRNs are the English WordNet (its RDF version), the multi-lingual BabelNet, DBpedia, Wikidata, GeoNames, and LinkedGeoData. Keywords and phrases, concepts, and categories/labels can also be semantically linked with IRNs using similar techniques. Recently, neural networks have been applied to all three sub-problems, both separately and in combination.

Relation extraction is a challenging area that attempts to identify precise semantic relations between the keywords, phrases, concepts, labels, and named entities that are extracted from a text [26]. For example, when a text mentions a "hurricane" near the name of a town, does it mean that the hurricane is approaching, hitting, or passing by? Supervised machine learning has been used to extract specific relations in narrow domains, such as sports results. But general relation extraction using deeper PoS tagging and dependency analysis is an open research area. A new generation of neural-network and word-embedding based joint entity and relation extractors and linkers are producing increasingly accurate (complete and precise) results, often surpassing specialised entity recognisers-linkers and specialised relation extractors-linkers.

Literal extraction is a two-step task: first identifying data that constitutes a literal such as a phone number, web address, date or time, and then representing its meaning in a standard way, for example as an IRN or XSD-typed literal string.

5.4   Discussion

With the advent of statistical NL analysers trained on large text corpora, the area of natural-language processing is currently progressing rapidly. But not even advanced machine learning and deep neural networks will be able to handle the more difficult problems of natural-language understanding anytime soon. Such problems include irony, sarcasm, and metaphorical speech that presume a shared pragmatic and social understanding between sender and receiver. Current narrow NL and ML techniques have not yet dealt with these higher levels of communication, which approach the so far unsolved problem of general artificial intelligence. On the other hand, emergencies—in particular when broken down into particular emergency types (avalanche, derailing, fire, terrorism)—deal with highly specific domains for which precise NL processors can be trained specifically. Also, during emergencies, people can be expected to use simple and straightforward language that makes NLP easier, with limited use of sarcasm, irony, and metaphor.

In the foreseeable future, general NLP will remain useful but inaccurate. In situations where lives, health, property, and the environment are at stake, we cannot fully trust the results of even the most accurate NL analysers on the single-text level. This applies even more strongly to the kind of short and context-dependent messages people write on social media. Nevertheless, NLP techniques will remain useful in emergency situations in at least two ways:

- They can *provide strategic overviews* by aggregating analysis results over collections of many messages, for example by averaging sentiment and emotion scores and by eliminating concepts and named entities that are not repeated across messages. They can offer answers to questions like: "In a disaster area, how does the sentiment of tweets that mention food change over time in different locations?" The hope is that aggregation of many messages will cancel or straighten out single-text analysis errors, but some bias may always remain.
- They can *suggest potentially actionable insights* by identifying single messages or groups of messages that may contain important tactical information, such as a rapidly approaching fire front, a gas leak, or an entrapment. Semantically categorising a single message as a distress call may not alone justify directing a rescuer or medical worker to a dangerous spot. But it can act as a trigger for further information gathering by automatic or manual means. And it can act as one of several indicators that aid tactical operation leaders in making the best possible decisions based on the available information.

6   Using a Sentiment Analyser

A wide range of tools support both sentiment analysis and other NLP techniques. They are available as online services, as downloadable programs, or as APIs that can be used from programming languages such as Python, Java, Scala, and R. Most of them bundle several different analysis techniques together in a single interface.

We will look more closely at the NLP component of IBM's Watson platform.[26] Through a web interface, the user enters either a plain text or the URL of a web page. In response, the following features are returned:

- *Keywords and phrases*, ranked by their relevance.
- *Sentiment* of the text as a whole and for the specific keywords and phrases it contains.

---

[26]IBM Watson offers a free online demo at http://natural-language-understanding-demo.ng. bluemix.net/, but you must register with IBM Watson to get your own API key.

- *Emotions*, such as joy, anger, disgust, sadness, and fear, both for the text as a whole and for specific keywords and phrases.
- *Named entities*, such as people, companies, organisations, cities, and geographic features, along with their types, relevance, and occurrence counts.
- *Concepts* that are related to the text, but that may not be explicitly mentioned in it, ranked by their relevance scores.
- *Categories* selected from a fixed taxonomy and ranked by their relevance scores: IBM Watson's taxonomy is up to five levels deep with more than a thousand leaf nodes and 23 top categories, such as education, finance, news, science, shopping, and sports.
- *Semantic roles* that break sentences down into their grammatical and semantic parts.

Overall sentiment is scored in the $[-1, 1]$ range, whereas emotions and relevance are $[0, 1]$-scored. The results are returned in a human-readable web page or as machine-readable JSON. For example, the results of sentiment and emotion analysis may look like this in JSON format:

```
{
  "sentiment": {
    "document": {
      "score": 0,
      "label": "neutral"
    }
  },
  "emotion": {
    "document": {
      "emotion": {
        "sadness": 0.029943,
        "joy": 0.056795,
        "fear": 0.025568,
        "disgust": 0.034639,
        "anger": 0.549087
      }
    }
  }
}
```

Of course, the analyser can be accessed through API calls as well, e.g., from a Python program or from a terminal window using the command-line tool curl:

```
curl -X POST -u "apikey:{your-apikey}"                      \
     "https://{your-api}/analyze?version={your-version}}"   \
     --header "Content-Type: application/json"              \
     --data '{
              "text": "Wildfires rage in Arctic Circle as
                       Sweden calls for help",
              "features": {
                "sentiment": {},
                "concepts": {},
                "entities": {}
              }
            }'
```

This command will return JSON results about sentiments, concepts, and entities found in the given newspaper headline. If possible, it will also return a DBpedia IRI for each concept and entity. More specific results can be requested using additional arguments, but a single headline usually contains too little context information to be accurately lifted.

There is a wide range of similar natural language analysers available, differing mostly in precision and in the range of analyses, metrics, and languages they support. For example, DBpedia Spotlight[27] returns DBpedia IRIs for topics and named entities found in texts in 12 major languages [14]. The code is open and can be trained and tailored to other languages and more specific domains, such as particular types of emergency situations. The BabelNet[28] analyser returns IRIs for topics and named entities in BabelNet, a multi-lingual version of WordNet. NLP services that leverage next-generation NL analysers trained on large text corpora are also appearing. It is likely that the quality of NL analysis tools will continue to improve as word embedding becomes better understood and more neural-network based text-analysis APIs and services become available.

Exercises

1. What is RDF, RDFS, OWL, and SPARQL?
2. What is a knowledge graph (RDF graph)?
3. Outline the following knowledge graph: *Tim Berners-Lee is a person and an author. He has authored a book with title "Weaving the Web", published in 2001. Another person, Mark Fischetti is co-author of this book, which has ISBN 0756752310.*
4. What are the benefits of knowledge graphs in an emergency situation?
5. And what are the main challenges?
6. What is LOD? Give examples of LOD resources that can be useful for emergency management. Where can you go to find more?
7. What is a vocabulary in connection with RDFS and OWL? Why are vocabularies important?
8. Give examples of vocabularies that can be useful for emergency management. Where can you find more?
9. What is TF-IDF?
10. What is LDA?
11. What are the main steps in natural-language processing?
12. What is a sentiment analyser? Explain its typical outputs.

---

[27]A three-language demo is available at https://www.dbpedia-spotlight.org/demo/.
[28]http://live.babelnet.org/.

References

1. Allemang, D., Hendler, J.: Semantic Web for the Working Ontologist: Effective Modeling in RDFS and OWL. Elsevier, Amsterdam (2011)
2. Atzori, L., Iera, A., Morabito, G.: The Internet of Things: a survey. Comput. Netw. **54**(15), 2787–2805 (2010). https://doi.org/10.1016/j.comnet.2010.05.010. http://linkinghub.elsevier.com/retrieve/pii/S1389128610001568
3. Auer, S., Bizer, C., Kobilarov, G., Lehmann, J., Cyganiak, R., Ives, Z.: DBpedia: a nucleus for a web of open data. In: The Semantic Web, pp. 722–735. Springer, New York (2007)
4. Auer, S., Lehmann, J., Hellmann, S.: LinkedGeoData: Adding a Spatial Dimension to the Web of Data, pp. 731–746. Springer, New York (2009)
5. Berners-Lee, T., Hendler, J., Lassila, O.: The semantic web. Sci. Am. **284**(5), 34–43 (2001)
6. Bizer, C., Heath, T., Berners-Lee, T.: Linked data-the story so far. Int. J. Seman. Web Inf. Syst. **5**(3), 1–22 (2009)
7. Bizer, C., Lehmann, J., Kobilarov, G., Auer, S., Becker, C., Cyganiak, R., Hellmann, S.: DBpedia-a crystallization point for the Web of Data. Web Semantics: Science, Services and Agents on the World Wide Web **7**(3), 154–165 (2009)
8. Castillo, C.: Big Crisis Data: Social Media in Disasters and Time-Critical Situations. Cambridge University Press, Cambridge (2016)
9. Ermilov, I., Martin, M., Lehmann, J., Auer, S.: Linked open data statistics: collection and exploitation. In: Proceedings of the International Conference on Knowledge Engineering and the Semantic Web, pp. 242–249. Springer, New York (2013)
10. Goldberg, Y., Levy, O.: word2vec Explained: deriving Mikolov et al.'s negative-sampling word-embedding method (2014). arXiv:14023722 [cs, stat]. arXiv:1402.3722. http://arxiv.org/abs/1402.3722
11. Krizhevsky, A., Sutskever, I., Hinton, G.E.: Imagenet classification with deep convolutional neural networks. In: Advances in Neural Information Processing Systems, pp. 1097–1105
12. Le, Q., Mikolov, T.: Distributed representations of sentences and documents. In: International Conference on Machine Learning (2014), pp. 1188–1196
13. McCrae, J.P., Cyganiak, R., Bizer, C.: The Linked Open Data Cloud (2018). http://lod-cloud.net/
14. Mendes, P.N., Jakob, M., García-Silva, A., Bizer, C.: DBpedia spotlight: shedding light on the web of documents, pp. 1–8. ACM, New York (2011)
15. Mikolov, T., Chen, K., Corrado, G., Dean, J.: Efficient Estimation of Word Representations in Vector Space (2013) . arXiv:13013781 [cs]. arXiv: 1301.3781. http://arxiv.org/abs/1301.3781
16. Miller, G.A.: Wordnet: a lexical database for english. Commun. ACM **38**(11), 39–41 (1995)
17. Müller, A.C., Guido, S., et al.: Introduction to Machine Learning with Python: A Guide for Data Scientists. O'Reilly Media, Inc., Sebastopol (2016)
18. Pak, A., Paroubek, P.: Twitter as a corpus for sentiment analysis and opinion mining. Int. J. Adv. Res. Comput. Commun. Eng. **5**(12), 320–322 (2016). https://doi.org/10.17148/IJARCCE.2016.51274. http://ijarcce.com/upload/2016/december-16/IJARCCE%2074.pdf
19. Pang, B., Lee, L.: Opinion mining and sentiment analysis. Found. Trends Inf. Retr. **2**(1–2), 1–135 (2008)
20. Pennington, J., Socher, R., Manning, C.: Glove: Global vectors for word representation. In: Proceedings of the 2014 Conference on Empirical Methods in Natural Language Processing (EMNLP), pp. 1532–1543 (2014)
21. Ristoski, P., Paulheim, H.: Rdf2Vec: Rdf graph embeddings for data mining. In: International Semantic Web Conference, pp. 498–514. Springer, New York (2016)
22. Sebastiani, F.: Machine learning in automated text categorization. ACM Comput. Surv. **34**(1), 1–47 (2002)
23. Shadbolt, N., Berners-Lee, T., Hall, W.: The semantic web revisited. IEEE Intell. Syst. **21**(3), 96–101 (2006). https://doi.org/10.1109/MIS.2006.62. http://ieeexplore.ieee.org/document/1637364/

24. Stadler, C., Lehmann, J., Höffner, K., Auer, S.: LinkedGeoData: a core for a web of spatial open data. Seman. Web **3**(4), 333–354 (2012)
25. Vandenbussche, P.Y., Atemezing, G.A., Poveda-Villalón, M., Vatant, B.: Linked Open Vocabularies (LOV): a gateway to reusable semantic vocabularies on the Web. Seman. Web **8**(3), 437–452 (2017)
26. Wong, W., Liu, W., Bennamoun, M.: Ontology learning from text: a look back and into the future. ACM Comput. Surv. **44**(4), 1–36 (2012). https://doi.org/10.1145/2333112.2333115.

Social Media Mining for Disaster Management and Community Resilience

Hemant Purohit and Steve Peterson

1 Social Media and Disasters

The emergence of Internet or Web 2.0 and mobile technology has led to the widespread adoption of communication platforms for content generation and sharing. Social media refers to such platform applications, which enable computer-mediated communication among citizens to create and share a variety of information online [41], pursue topical interests via joining online communities as well as network with like-minded users [39]. For instance, as per Pew Research Center's social media fact-sheet [38], only 5% of Americans used some form of social media platforms in 2005 but the percentage has only grown over the years (Fig. 1), leading to 72% in 2019. Also, according to a 2018 survey, about two-thirds of American adults (68%) say they get news about real world events from social media [37].

Social media has created an opportunity for public to act as citizen sensors [57] and not just consumers of information. This phenomenon can be extremely valuable to timely sense and share useful observations during the times of emergencies. A citizen-driven information infrastructure has created a new information sourcing channel for the emergency management organizations, in order to continually enrich information for dynamic situational awareness and improve the response services [29]. The role of social media in disasters in helping the affected citizens has grown substantially over the past decade correlating to the rapid adoption rate of social media use in general by the public as shown in Fig. 1. Social media messages

H. Purohit (✉)
Department of Information Sciences and Technology, George Mason University, Fairfax, VA, USA
e-mail: hpurohit@gmu.edu

S. Peterson
National Institutes of Health, Bethesda, MD, USA
e-mail: steve.peterson@nih.gov

© Springer Nature Switzerland AG 2020
R. Akerkar (ed.), *Big Data in Emergency Management: Exploitation Techniques for Social and Mobile Data*, https://doi.org/10.1007/978-3-030-48099-8_5

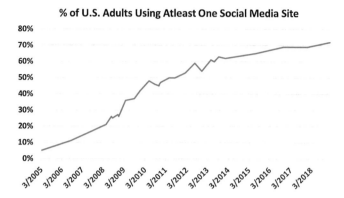

Fig. 1 Evidence for the rapid adoption rate of social media in our daily life indicating the greater need to incorporate social media channels for information sourcing during emergencies. Source: Pew Research Center [38]

during recent emergencies and disasters have included relevant information such as caution-advice and damage reports [14], requests and offers to help [42] as well as emotional support for the affected community [10]. However, the relevant information is often buried in the haystack of noisy, large-scale unstructured data on social media, which has a variety of multimodal (text, images, videos) data being generated at high velocity. Thus, addressing this *big crisis data* problem [6] is an important challenge for emergency services to achieve the goals of efficient disaster management and community resilience.

Social media during disasters is leveraged for both natural hazards or manmade disaster types. Table 1 highlights a variety of disasters and examples of social media use over a 10-year period. This table is not an all-inclusive list though, it is just for an illustrative purpose.

2   Scenarios of Using Social Media Mining

Social media has revolutionized both the public's and response agencies' ways of communication before, during, and after disasters. Following a disaster, the public will obtain information from any number of sources [61, 67, 68]. Specifically located within the disaster-affected area, the public will search for meaning as they are confronted with situations and problems outside their bounds of normal, everyday existence. Both the public in the disaster-affected area and the general public have a need for immediate information. Recent studies indicate social media is one of the most popular sources for receiving and collecting critical disaster information [6, 51]. Social media has expedited and fed our appetite of seeking and obtaining disaster-related information. When a response agency, or their communication procedures, do not adequately take into consideration the

Table 1 Illustration of social media usage during disasters in the last decade

Year	Country	Disaster	Type	Advance notice?	Social media usage
2018	Japan	Flooding and mud-flows	Natural	Some advance notice	Japan Floods: Social media was used to identify specific places where people were stuck, posting information on what to do, listing locations of running water, fund-raising, and updating road conditions [70]
2017	United States	Hurricane	Natural	Advance notice	Hurricane Harvey: Several social media platforms and apps were used to coordinate citizen volunteers and rescuers during the floods in Houston, Texas [60]
2016	Germany	Terrorist attack	Man-made	No notice	2016 Munich Shopping Mall Shooting: Dependency of the Munich population on the messages by police on both Facebook and Twitter drastically increased during and after the incident [3]
2015	France	Terrorist attack	Man- made	No notice	2015 Paris Attacks: Following the events, official accounts saw significant increases in Twitter followers, e.g., the Prefecture of Police of Paris (@prefpolice). Facebook was also heavily used; with 4.1 million users activating the SafetyCheck feature [35]
2014	India	Flooding	Natural	Some advance notice	Jammu & Kashmir Floods: Digital volunteer teams identified need categories based on information communicated on social media by the affected communities, such as rescue calls for help, hazard impact, transportation conditions, and relief distribution [47]
2013	Kenya	Terrorist attack	Man-made	No notice	Westgate Mall Attack: Governmental officials and first responders tweeted information concerning the terrorist attack. Kenya Police tweeted 569 times on Twitter and the public expressed emotional support and also, requested to volunteer [59]

(continued)

Table 1 (continued)

Year	Country	Disaster	Type	Advance notice?	Social media usage
2012	United States	Hurricane	Natural	Advance notice	Hurricane Sandy: Water, power, and transportation agencies shared information on the status and availability of their resources through various social media platforms [72]
2011	Japan	Earthquake	Natural	No notice	Japan Earthquake: Initial social media platform usage served to send and receive breaking information from a variety of official and unofficial sources, including eyewitness accounts. As time passed, platforms acted as an electronic bulletin board, sharing tips, and tracking loved ones [36]
2010	New Zealand	Earthquake	Natural	No notice	Christchurch Earthquake: Through the small beginnings of a Facebook event sent to 200 friends, thousands of student volunteers helped local residents most affected by the earthquake with non-life saving tasks. The group grew to become the Student Volunteer Army [66]
2009	United States	Flooding	Natural	Some advance notice	Red River Flooding: Local individuals used social media to communicate flood related issues once flood predictions and warnings appeared. Flooding, sandbagging, and evacuation information were posted [30]

value of rapidly disseminating disaster-related content via social media, the online information search will be more challenging.

The automated methods of artificial intelligence such as natural language processing and machine learning can help in designing tools for social media mining to identify and consolidate time-sensitive, relevant social media content. The classification, prioritization, and summarization of the relevant content into valuable information categories would benefit both the public (e.g., life/safety information) and response agencies (e.g., actionable intelligence for decision makers) before the content becomes obsolete as time passes.

We describe such potential benefits next and summarize in Fig. 2.

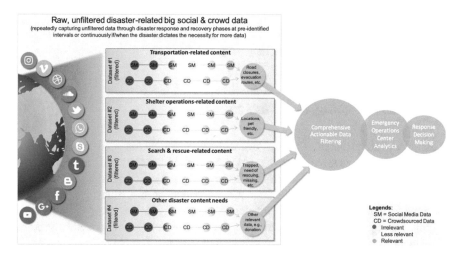

Fig. 2 A process overview of filtering, categorizing, extracting, and assigning actionable intelligence to respective Emergency Support Function (ESF) needs

2.1 Filtering Social Data for Actionable Intelligence

The information present in the social media messages can be valuable and sometimes redundant but complementary for the emergency management and response coordination. Therefore, the challenge is to extract timely, actionable intelligence (c.f. Fig. 2) that can align with the operational needs of the emergency management, such as the *Emergency Support Functions* (ESF)[1] as follows:

- Search and Rescue (*ESF-9: Search & Rescue*): Social media messages with calls for help by the public [60]
- Situational Updates (*Multiple ESFs*): Social media posts providing reassurance and updates on disaster response efforts, and other pertinent information [75]
- Crisis Management (*ESF-15: External Affairs*): Social media mining to gauge atmosphere of public and identify and stop the spread of any rumors/ disinformation/ misinformation [64]
- Health/Medical (*ESF-8: Public Health & Medical Services*): Mine social media data for hospital statuses, potential post-disaster disease, injury updates, etc. [5]
- Shelter Operations (*ESF-6: Mass Care, Emergency Assistance, Housing, & Human Services*): Social media updates on shelter locations and availability [65]
- Road Closures (*ESF-1: Transportation*): Social media messages on road closures, contraflow, etc. [54]

---

[1]Overview of Emergency Support Functions: https://www.phe.gov/Preparedness/support/esf8/Pages/default.aspx.

The technical challenge is how to create efficient artificial intelligence techniques for transforming the unstructured social media content to structured information categories (e.g., types of resource help [42]) to inform *ESFs*.

2.2 Alert, Warning, and Notifications

Emergency management officials can author social media alert, warning, and notification messages and quickly disseminate time-sensitive information to the public via social media platforms at large scale [31]. The public recipients of the authoritative messages will be better informed of the situation. Public can become further information disseminators [43], amplifying the critical messages by simply sharing the actionable content to their social network. This behavior helps the emergency management expand its audience reach. The technical challenge is though how to maximize the spread of information for both response agencies and the public.

2.3 Leveraging Volunteer Networks for Virtual Operations

Collective behavior is a desire to understand and resolve disruptive, disorienting conditions [55]. The public will engage in collective behavior following a disaster that allows them to finding meaning for the current situation [62]. Social media provides a transparent avenue for the public to engage in collective behavior. They may also converge to form a collective intelligence where they begin to either help those in need or to support officials [22, 44]. This form of volunteering may come in either of two forms: a physical presence on-site at the disaster-affected area, or through a virtual presence of mining social media data for either victims or the response agencies, or both [47].

   In a study of emergency management practitioners, 75% of participants had identified limited resources as their reason for lacking social media monitoring services [76]. The collective behavior of volunteers through virtual organizations could address this staffing limitation challenge by leveraging their social media mining skills and easily connect and coordinate via social media platforms. For example, digital volunteers in Community Emergency Response Teams (CERTS) or Virtual Operations Support Teams (VOSTS) could be activated during times of disaster to assist the response agency in establishing and sustaining a social media presence [34]. In 2018, DHS released step-by-step guidance on developing a digital volunteer program to support response agencies [73]. The technical challenge here is how to efficiently identify emerging social media volunteers with help offering intent [46] to meet the needs of the response agency and classify the type of help the individual is offering to volunteer for. Similarly, another challenge is how to create adaptive information filtering tools for such volunteer teams that would align the automated filtering with the changing definition of content relevance for the emergency responders and their supporting volunteers.

Exercise 1 Create a survey of 10 news articles that report the use of social media during an emergency event and identify the category of the reported usage of social media across the set of Emergency Support Functions.

3   Collecting Data for Social Media Mining

Social media platforms (e.g., Twitter, Facebook) generally provide an Application Programming Interface (API) or web service to facilitate a channel for collecting data, either through free or paid subscription mechanism. An illustrative API is Twitter Streaming API,[2] which provides various subscription types for data collection. There are three popular approaches for collecting data from social media for disaster management. First, a keyword and hashtag-based method provides a mechanism to collect relevant social media messages that contain a term from a given set of relevant keywords and hashtags for an event (e.g., hurricane, flood, #sandy, etc. were used during hurricane sandy 2012 [42]). Second, a location-based method provides a mechanism to collect relevant social media messages that originate in a given bounding box region (e.g., New York city). Third, a user-based method provides a mechanism to collect relevant social media messages that are written by a given set of users (e.g., a Twitter account of influential and active user).

An analyst can collect and store all the relevant metadata with the returned responses such as message text, posting timestamp, message type such as 'retweet' or forwarded message on Twitter as well as authoring user's self-reported author profile information such as full name, and location. One requires a systematic processing pipeline to handle the big social data streams during disasters and therefore, recent advancement in social stream analytics systems with a focus on disaster informatics applications (e.g., CitizenHelper [32], AIDR [13], Twitris [58], CrisisTracker [52], Twitcident [2], TweetTracker [15]) become very useful.

For the early identification of the incidents to start the data collection, an analyst can take help of event detection methods [53, 77]; for instance, Sakaki et al. [53] showed efficacy of Twitter in detecting earthquake in realtime. After event detection, one needs a relevance criterion for information filtering such as relevant keyword set, in order to collect event-related social media messages, given the large amount of noisy, operationally irrelevant content shared on social media. Given that manual keyword set can be biased and outdated during the rapidly changing times of a disaster event, domain modelling and topic tracking are important techniques to employ. They allow us to adapt existing domain models or dynamically create

---

[2]Twitter   API: https://developer.twitter.com/en/docs/tweets/filter-realtime/api-reference/post-statuses-filter.html.

models for event relevance that help identify and filter relevant social data for analysis [25, 69].

Exercise 2 Collect a sample of tweets related to disasters using the keyword-based data collection approach. Implement a data collector by following the 'filter-track' method of Twitter Streaming API, with seed keywords as {flood,tornado,wildfire}.

4   Social Media Mining Techniques

There are several applications of mining social data for all phases of the emergency management cycle. In the past decade, with the rising adoption of social media, a variety of computational techniques in different areas including data mining, machine learning, natural language processing, and network sciences were developed given the easier access to data, such as public Twitter data streams [78].

Once the data is collected either in streaming mode or batch mode, processing large-scale social data requires a variety of techniques to meaningfully extract information to improve situational awareness and decision support (for comprehensive surveys, cf. [6, 14, 23]). These techniques can be primarily categorized into five types that we describe next: content-based, network-based, user-based, context-based, and lastly, visual analytics for the ultimate human-computer interaction.

4.1   Content Analytics

This type of approaches infer information categories across various content modalities of a social media message [75], such as classifying topics like caution-advice from text [14] and damage reports from images [17], extracting entities present in the message [18] such as location mentions, modeling behaviors such as requests and offers to help [33, 42, 74], quantifying serviceability characteristics for ranking messages [48], as well as detecting rumors [7, 11, 64]. For instance, the following message "got a bunch of clothes, I'd like to donate to #sandy victims. Anyone know where/how do that?" could be classified into clothing/logistics related category.

4.2   User Analytics

Such methods focus mainly on the identification of a variety of user categories [26], such as on-ground informants [63], emerging informants [43], influential users [16], real and virtual volunteers [50], and organizational users [28, 40] as well as measurement of user credibility [1, 71]. For instance, the Twitter user handle

@RedCross can be categorized as an organizational user that could help filter the highly-trusted source of information for a social media analytics system.

4.3   Network Analytics

These techniques primarily investigate information diffusion for message reachability [12, 30], community formation and evolution [19, 45]. In addition, simulation and agent-based modeling are useful methods to study social network behaviors before, during, and after disaster events [49, 56]. For instance, a network of 'retweet' interaction on Twitter can be constructed to study the cascades of specific messages posted by an emergency service and study the patterns of (non-)viral messages.

4.4   Context Analytics

These methods help enrich the metadata of the streaming data instances, such as geo-location of the information source, which is often present in the less than 2% of the records. Geo-tagging [4, 18, 21] and spatio-temporal analytics [8, 9] are some of the examples of this type of techniques to enhance modeling and analysis of social data. For instance, a location extraction technique could identify the mention of the Brooklyn entity, i.e. one of New York City's 5 boroughs, in the following message "Hey! this Brooklyn guy got a bunch of clothes, I'd like to donate to #sandy victims. Anyone know where/how do that?"

4.5   Visual Analytics

For easily understanding extracted information from social data visualization is the ultimate need to assist the emergency management teams as well as public. One popular approach is to create customized dashboard, such as shown in Fig. 3 [15, 32, 52, 58], which provides a spatio-temporal organization of the information for what is happening where and where are the needs. A key component of the dashboards is a geo-tagged data visualization and often used standalone as 'crisis map' [20], which has been used as an effective tool in various disasters in the last decade, for instance, check the crisis map created during Hurricane Harvey in 2017 by *@HarveyRelief*, a volunteer group [24].

Exercise 3 During an emergency, public can mention several types of entities such as locations and landmarks in the affected area. Use the dataset collected in Exercise 2 and apply a natural language processing technique of Named Entity

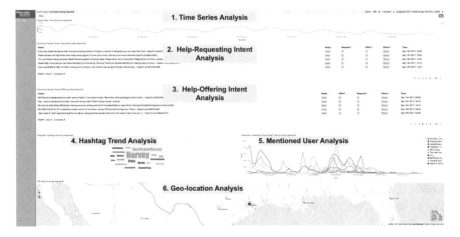

Fig. 3 Example of a customized dashboard *CitizenHelper* [32] during Hurricane Harvey to visually interact with relevant social media messages by selecting time (widget 1, numbered top to bottom) and location (widget 6), any trending hashtags (widget 4) or mentioned users (widget 5) as well as filtered messages of public or groups requesting and offering help (widgets 2 and 3), extracted by active learning techniques in the background that have an ability to take feedback (e.g., irrelevant request) from a viewer using buttons next to the tweet message

Recognition (NER) for location entities. Report the identified entities and analyze a random sample of those entities for reflecting on the accuracy.

5 Open Challenges for Social Media Mining During Disasters

While there have been a lot of technical research in the last decade on social media analytics for emergency management, there are problems still in existence, in order to actually integrate social media analytics as capabilities for the emergency management operations. Some of the existing problems include managing dynamic information overload of social media. It is still not efficient assistance to emergency managers in terms of providing complete and concise summarization of the key relevant information, where the relevance of information rapidly changes during the disaster times [32]. Other set of problems include the sampling bias and noise removal fallacy [78] for data collection as well as algorithmic biases in any data processing phase [27]. Among other open problems, real-time social analytics and integration of information in real-time for situational awareness and decision making are challenging issues, given the unstructured and non-standardized data sharing across different social platforms. Similarly, there is a need for mining social data across other phases of the emergency management cycle than the response phase, such as how to detect fake content and financial scammers with the malicious intent during the rebuilding and recovery phase after a disaster.

In summary, this chapter provided a systematic overview of the usage of social media mining, the data collection approaches, and the types of analytics techniques to meaningfully leverage the non-traditional data source of social media for disaster management and community resilience.

Exercise 4 Implement an automated text classifier for categorizing the messages in the dataset collected in Exercise 2. To train the model, use an existing crisis-relevant annotated dataset or create your own annotated dataset using the categories of the Emergency Support Functions.

Acknowledgments Purohit acknowledges U.S. National Science Foundation for partially supporting the related research on disaster informatics through grants IIS-1657379 and IIS-1815459.

References

1. Abbasi, M.A., Liu, H.: Measuring user credibility in social media. In: International Conference on Social Computing, Behavioral-Cultural Modeling, and Prediction, pp. 441–448. Springer, Berlin (2013)
2. Abel, F., Hauff, C., Houben, G.J., Stronkman, R., Tao, K.: Twitcident: fighting fire with information from social web streams. In: Proceedings of the 21st International Conference on World Wide Web, pp. 305–308. ACM, New York (2012)
3. Akkaya, C., Federowicz, J., Krcmar, H.: Use of social media by the German police: the case of munich. In: Proceedings of the 19th Annual International Conference on Digital Government Research: Governance in the Data Age, p. 116. ACM, New York (2018)
4. Al-Olimat, H., Thirunarayan, K., Shalin, V., Sheth, A.: Location name extraction from targeted text streams using gazetteer-based statistical language models. In: Proceedings of the 27th International Conference on Computational Linguistics, pp. 1986–1997 (2018)
5. Bennett, K.J., Olsen, J.M., Harris, S., Mekaru, S., Livinski, A.A., Brownstein, J.S.: The perfect storm of information: combining traditional and non-traditional data sources for public health situational awareness during hurricane response. PLoS Curr. **5** (2013). https://doi.org/10.1371/currents.dis.d2800aa4e536b9d6849e966e91488003
6. Castillo, C.: Big Crisis Data: Social Media in Disasters and Time-critical Situations. Cambridge University Press, Cambridge (2016)
7. Castillo, C., Mendoza, M., Poblete, B.: Information credibility on twitter. In: Proceedings of the 20th International Conference on World Wide Web, pp. 675–684. ACM, New York (2011)
8. Chae, J., Thom, D., Jang, Y., Kim, S., Ertl, T., Ebert, D.S.: Public behavior response analysis in disaster events utilizing visual analytics of microblog data. Comput. Graph. **38**, 51–60 (2014)
9. Crooks, A., Croitoru, A., Stefanidis, A., Radzikowski, J.: # earthquake: Twitter as a distributed sensor system. Trans. GIS **17**(1), 124–147 (2013)
10. Glasgow, K., Vitak, J., Tausczik, Y., Fink, C.: "with your help… we begin to heal": Social media expressions of gratitude in the aftermath of disaster. In: Social, Cultural, and Behavioral Modeling: 9th International Conference, SBP-BRiMS 2016, Washington, DC, June 28–July 1, 2016, Proceedings 9, pp. 226–236. Springer, Cham (2016)
11. Gupta, A., Lamba, H., Kumaraguru, P., Joshi, A.: Faking sandy: characterizing and identifying fake images on twitter during hurricane sandy. In: Proceedings of the 22nd International Conference on World Wide Web, pp. 729–736. ACM, New York (2013)
12. Hui, C., Tyshchuk, Y., Wallace, W.A., Magdon-Ismail, M., Goldberg, M.: Information cascades in social media in response to a crisis: a preliminary model and a case study. In: Proceedings of the 21st International Conference on World Wide Web, pp. 653–656. ACM, New York (2012)

13. Imran, M., Castillo, C., Lucas, J., Meier, P., Vieweg, S.: Aidr: Artificial intelligence for disaster response. In: Proceedings of the 23rd International Conference on World Wide Web, pp. 159–162. ACM, New York (2014)
14. Imran, M., Castillo, C., Diaz, F., Vieweg, S.: Processing social media messages in mass emergency: a survey. ACM Comput. Surv. (CSUR) **47**(4), 67 (2015)
15. Kumar, S., Barbier, G., Abbasi, M.A., Liu, H.: Tweettracker: an analysis tool for humanitarian and disaster relief. In: ICWSM, pp. 661–662 (2011)
16. Kumar, S., Morstatter, F., Zafarani, R., Liu, H.: Whom should I follow?: identifying relevant users during crises. In: Proceedings of the 24th ACM Conference on Hypertext and Social Media, pp. 139–147. ACM, New York (2013)
17. Li, X., Caragea, D., Zhang, H., Imran, M.: Localizing and quantifying infrastructure damage using class activation mapping approaches. Soc. Netw. Anal. Min. **9**(1), 44:1–44:15 (2019). https://doi.org/10.1007/s13278-019-0588-4
18. Lingad, J., Karimi, S., Yin, J.: Location extraction from disaster-related microblogs. In: Proceedings of the 22nd International Conference on World Wide Web, pp. 1017–1020. ACM, New York (2013)
19. Lu, X., Brelsford, C.: Network structure and community evolution on twitter: human behavior change in response to the 2011 Japanese earthquake and tsunami. Sci. Rep. **4**, 6773 (2014)
20. Meier, P.: Crisis mapping in action: How open source software and global volunteer networks are changing the world, one map at a time. J. Map Geogr. Libr. **8**(2), 89–100 (2012)
21. Middleton, S.E., Middleton, L., Modafferi, S.: Real-time crisis mapping of natural disasters using social media. IEEE Intell. Syst. **29**(2), 9–17 (2014)
22. Mirbabaie, M., Bunker, D., Deubel, A., Stieglitz, S.: Examining convergence behaviour during crisis situations in social media-a case study on the Manchester bombing 2017. In: International Working Conference on Transfer and Diffusion of IT, pp. 60–75. Springer, Cham (2018)
23. Nazer, T.H., Xue, G., Ji, Y., Liu, H.: Intelligent disaster response via social media analysis a survey. ACM SIGKDD Explor. Newsl. **19**(1), 46–59 (2017)
24. NBC News: Social media becomes a savior in Hurricane Harvey relief (2017). https://www.nbcnews.com/tech/social-media/social-media-becomes-savior-hurricane-harvey-relief-n796701. Accessed 12 Nov 2019
25. Olteanu, A., Castillo, C., Diaz, F., Vieweg, S.: Crisislex: a lexicon for collecting and filtering microblogged communications in crises. In: ICWSM, pp. 376–385 (2014)
26. Olteanu, A., Vieweg, S., Castillo, C.: What to expect when the unexpected happens: social media communications across crises. In: Proceedings of the 18th ACM Conference on Computer Supported Cooperative Work & Social Computing, pp. 994–1009. ACM, New York (2015)
27. Olteanu, A., Castillo, C., Diaz, F., Kiciman, E.: Social data: biases, methodological pitfalls, and ethical boundaries. Front. Big Data **2**, 13 (2019)
28. Opdyke, A., Javernick-Will, A.: Building coordination capacity: post-disaster organizational twitter networks. In: IEEE Global Humanitarian Technology Conference (GHTC 2014), pp. 86–92 (2014)
29. Palen, L., Anderson, K.M., Mark, G., Martin, J., Sicker, D., Palmer, M., Grunwald, D.: A vision for technology-mediated support for public participation & assistance in mass emergencies & disasters. In: Proceedings of the 2010 ACM-BCS Visions of Computer Science Conference, pp. 8:1–8:12. ACM-BCS '10. British Computer Society, Swinton (2010)
30. Palen, L., Starbird, K., Vieweg, S., Hughes, A.: Twitter-based information distribution during the 2009 red river valley flood threat. Bull. Am. Soc. Inf. Sci. Technol. **36**(5), 13–17 (2010)
31. Panagiotopoulos, P., Barnett, J., Bigdeli, A.Z., Sams, S.: Social media in emergency management: Twitter as a tool for communicating risks to the public. Technol. Forecast. Soc. Change **111**, 86–96 (2016)
32. Pandey, R., Purohit, H.: Citizenhelper-adaptive: expert-augmented streaming analytics system for emergency services and humanitarian organizations. In: 2018 IEEE/ACM International Conference on Advances in Social Networks Analysis and Mining (ASONAM), pp. 630–633. IEEE, Piscataway (2018)

33. Pedrood, B., Purohit, H.: Mining help intent on twitter during disasters via transfer learning with sparse coding. In: International Conference on Social Computing, Behavioral-Cultural Modeling and Prediction and Behavior Representation in Modeling and Simulation, pp. 141–153. Springer, Cham (2018)
34. Peterson, S.: Social media resources for emergency management. Int. Assoc. Emerg. Manag. Bull. **32**(6), 34–36 (2015)
35. Petersen, L., Fallou, L., Havarneanu, G., Reilly, P., Serafinelli, E., Bossu, R.: November 2015 Paris terrorist attacks and social media use: preliminary findings from authorities, critical infrastructure operators and journalists. In: ISCRAM, pp. 629–638 (2018)
36. Pew Research Center: Twitter responds to the Japanese disaster (2011, March). http://www.journalism.org/2011/03/17/twitter-responds-japanese-disaster/. Accessed 12 Nov 2019
37. Pew Research Center: News use across social media platforms 2018 (2018, Sept). http://www.journalism.org/2018/09/10/news-use-across-social-media-platforms-2018/. Accessed 12 Nov 2019
38. Pew Research Center: Social media fact sheet (2019). http://www.pewinternet.org/fact-sheet/social-media. Accessed 12 Nov 2019
39. Preece, J.: Online Communities: Designing Usability and Supporting Sociability, 1st edn. Wiley, New York (2000)
40. Purohit, H., Chan, J.: Classifying user types on social media to inform who-what-where coordination during crisis response. In: ISCRAM, pp. 656–665 (2017)
41. Purohit, H., Pandey, R.: Intent Mining for the Good, Bad, and Ugly Use of Social Web: Concepts, Methods, and Challenges, pp. 3–18. Springer International Publishing, Cham (2019)
42. Purohit, H., Castillo, C., Diaz, F., Sheth, A., Meier, P.: Emergency-relief coordination on social media: automatically matching resource requests and offers. First Monday **19**(1) (2013). https://doi.org/10.5210/fm.v19i1.4848
43. Purohit, H., Bhatt, S., Hampton, A., Shalin, V.L., Sheth, A.P., Flach, J.M.: With whom to coordinate, why and how in ad-hoc social media communications during crisis response. In: ISCRAM, pp. 787–791 (2014)
44. Purohit, H., Hampton, A., Bhatt, S., Shalin, V.L., Sheth, A.P., Flach, J.M.: Identifying seekers and suppliers in social media communities to support crisis coordination. Comput. Supported Coop. Work (CSCW) **23**(4–6), 513–545 (2014)
45. Purohit, H., Ruan, Y., Fuhry, D., Parthasarathy, S., Sheth, A.P.: On understanding the divergence of online social group discussion. In: Proceedings of the Eighth International AAAI Conference on Weblogs and Social Media, pp. 396–405. AAAI, Menlo Park (2014)
46. Purohit, H., Dong, G., Shalin, V., Thirunarayan, K., Sheth, A.: Intent classification of short-text on social media. In: 2015 IEEE International Conference on Smart City/SocialCom/Sustain-Com (SmartCity), pp. 222–228. IEEE, Piscataway (2015)
47. Purohit, H., Dalal, M., Singh, P., Nissima, B., Moorthy, V., Vemuri, A., Krishnan, V., Khursheed, R., Balachandran, S., Kushwah, H., et al.: Empowering crisis response-led citizen communities: lessons learned from jkfloodrelief.org initiative. In: Strategic Management and Leadership for Systems Development in Virtual Spaces, pp. 270–292. IGI Global, Pennsylvania (2016)
48. Purohit, H., Castillo, C., Imran, M., Pandey, R.: Social-eoc: serviceability model to rank social media requests for emergency operation centers. In: 2018 IEEE/ACM International Conference on Advances in Social Networks Analysis and Mining (ASONAM), pp. 119–126. IEEE, Piscataway (2018)
49. Rand, W., Herrmann, J., Schein, B., Vodopivec, N.: An agent-based model of urgent diffusion in social media. J. Artif. Soc. Soc. Simul. **18**(2), 1 (2015)
50. Reuter, C., Heger, O., Pipek, V.: Combining real and virtual volunteers through social media. In: Proceedings of 10th International Conference on Information Systems for Crisis Response and Management (2013)
51. Reuter, C., Hughes, A.L., Kaufhold, M.A.: Social media in crisis management: an evaluation and analysis of crisis informatics research. Int. J. Hum. Comput. Interact. **34**(4), 280–294 (2018)

52. Rogstadius, J., Vukovic, M., Teixeira, C., Kostakos, V., Karapanos, E., Laredo, J.A.: Crisis-tracker: crowdsourced social media curation for disaster awareness. IBM J. Res. Devel. **57**(5), 4–1 (2013)
53. Sakaki, T., Okazaki, M., Matsuo, Y.: Earthquake shakes twitter users: real-time event detection by social sensors. In: Proceedings of the 19th International Conference on World Wide Web, pp. 851–860. ACM, New York (2010)
54. Schnebele, E., Cervone, G., Waters, N.: Road assessment after flood events using non-authoritative data. Nat. Hazards Earth Syst. Sci. **14**(4), 1007–1015 (2014)
55. Schneider, S.K.: Governmental response to disasters: the conflict between bureaucratic procedures and emergent norms. Public Adm. Rev. **52**(2), 135–145 (1992)
56. Serrano, E., Iglesias, C.A., Garijo, M.: A survey of twitter rumor spreading simulations. In: Computational Collective Intelligence, pp. 113–122. Springer, Cham (2015)
57. Sheth, A.: Citizen sensing, social signals, and enriching human experience. IEEE Internet Comput. **13**(4), 87–92 (2009)
58. Sheth, A., Purohit, H., Smith, G.A., Brunn, J., Jadhav, A., Kapanipathi, P., Lu, C., Wang, W.: Twitris: A System for Collective Social Intelligence, pp. 1–23. Springer, New York (2017)
59. Simon, T., Goldberg, A., Aharonson-Daniel, L., Leykin, D., Adini, B.: Twitter in the cross fire – the use of social media in the westgate mall terror attack in kenya. PloS One **9**(8), e104136 (2014)
60. Smith, W.R., Robertson, B.W., Murthy, D., Stephens, K.K., Li, J.: Social media in citizen-led disaster response: rescuer roles, coordination challenges, and untapped potential. In: ISCRAM, pp. 639–648 (2018)
61. Sorensen, J.H., Sorensen, B.V.: Community processes: warning and evacuation. In: Handbook of Disaster Research, pp. 183–199. Springer, New York (2007)
62. Stallings, R.A., Quarantelli, E.L.: Emergent citizen groups and emergency management. Public Adm. Rev. **45**, 93–100 (1985)
63. Starbird, K., Muzny, G., Palen, L.: Learning from the crowd: collaborative filtering techniques for identifying on-the-ground Twitterers during mass disruptions. In: ISCRAM (2012)
64. Starbird, K., Maddock, J., Orand, M., Achterman, P., Mason, R.M.: Rumors, false flags, and digital vigilantes: misinformation on twitter after the 2013 Boston marathon bombing. In: iConference 2014 Proceedings (2014)
65. Stokes, C., Senkbeil, J.C.: Facebook and Twitter, communication and shelter, and the 2011 Tuscaloosa tornado. Disasters **41**(1), 194–208 (2017)
66. Student Volunteer Army: New Zealanders to give back to their communities (Nd). https://sva.org.nz/our-story/. Accessed 12 Nov 2019
67. Sutton, J.N., Palen, L., Shklovski, I.: Backchannels on the front lines: emergency uses of social media in the 2007 southern California wildfires. In: ISCRAM, pp. 624–632 (2008)
68. Taylor, J.G., Gillette, S.C., Hodgson, R.W., Downing, J.L.: Communicating with wildland interface communities during wildfire. Technical report, US Geological Survey (2005)
69. Temnikova, I.P., Castillo, C., Vieweg, S.: Emterms 1.0: a terminological resource for crisis tweets. In: ISCRAM, pp. 147–157 (2015)
70. The Japan Times: Recent flooding highlights power of social media in a disaster (2018, July). https://www.japantimes.co.jp/news/2018/07/14/national/media-national/recent-flooding-highlights-power-social-media-disaster/#.XGFnbBlKhTY. Accessed 12 Nov 2019
71. Thomson, R., Ito, N., Suda, H., Lin, F., Liu, Y., Hayasaka, R., Isochi, R., Wang, Z.: Trusting tweets: the Fukushima disaster and information source credibility on twitter. In: ISCRAM (2012)
72. U.S. Homeland Security: Using social media for enhanced situational awareness and decision support (2014). https://www.dhs.gov/publication/using-social-media-enhanced-situational-awareness-decision-support. Accessed 12 Nov 2019
73. U.S. Homeland Security: Digital volunteer program guide (2018). https://www.dhs.gov/sites/default/files/publications/1025_IAS_HSHQDC-17-C-B0013_Digital-Volunteer-Program-Guide_180814-508.pdf. Accessed 12 Nov 2019

74. Varga, I., Sano, M., Torisawa, K., Hashimoto, C., Ohtake, K., Kawai, T., Oh, J.H., De Saeger, S.: Aid is out there: looking for help from tweets during a large scale disaster. In: ACL, vol. 1, pp. 1619–1629 (2013)
75. Vieweg, S.E.: Situational awareness in mass emergency: a behavioral and linguistic analysis of microblogged communications. Ph.D. thesis, University of Colorado at Boulder (2012)
76. Yee San, S., Wardell III, C., Thorkildsen, Z.: Social media in the emergency management field: 2012 survey results (2013). CNA Analysis and Solutions. http://citeseerx.ist.psu.edu/viewdoc/download?doi=10.1.1.357.3121&rep=rep1&type=pdf. Accessed 12 Nov 2019
77. Yin, J., Lampert, A., Cameron, M., Robinson, B., Power, R.: Using social media to enhance emergency situation awareness. IEEE Intell. Syst. **27**(6), 52–59 (2012)
78. Zafarani, R., Abbasi, M.A., Liu, H.: Social Media Mining: An Introduction. Cambridge University Press, Cambridge (2014)

Big Data-Driven Citywide Human Mobility Modeling for Emergency Management

Zipei Fan, Xuan Song, and Ryosuke Shibasaki

1 Introduction

With the explosive growth of cities, various urban development issues have emerged. How to guarantee the safety of the people, especially in an emergency situation, is becoming increasingly important to all city regulators. With the popularization of the mobile phones with localization function and the advancement of big data technology, we can collect and analyze human mobility big data at a large scale in real-time, which sheds light on a new era of big data driven citywide human mobility modeling for emergency management.

In general, there are two broad categories of citywide human mobility, routine, composed of daily or periodic travel, and rare, which is essential to many emergency situations, such as big crowd-drawing events or natural disasters. Considering the volume of data and the complexity of the intrinsic patterns, routine human mobility are simpler to model stochastically, while rare human mobility modeling, essential to emergency management, is a much more challenging but unexplored research topic.

In Fig. 1, we show how rare event human mobility different from routine human mobility. Figure 1b shows the population density (represented as number of mobile phone users in the dataset) of Shinjuku area shown in Fig. 1a at 01:30 of each day in 2012 Jan. It is obvious that population density during a big event (the New Year Celebration) drifts far from the routine human mobility. A variety of statistical methods (for example, using a Gaussian or Gamma distribution to model the population density) are suitable for modeling routine human mobility while in the emergency case, the rare human mobility is always treated as noise or outliers.

Z. Fan · X. Song (✉) · R. Shibasaki
SUSTech-UTokyo Joint Research Center on Super Smart City, Southern University of Science
and Technology, University of Tokyo, Tokyo, Japan
e-mail: fanzipei@iis.u-tokyo.ac.jp; songx@sustech.edu.cn

© Springer Nature Switzerland AG 2020   109
R. Akerkar (ed.), *Big Data in Emergency Management: Exploitation Techniques for
Social and Mobile Data*, https://doi.org/10.1007/978-3-030-48099-8_6

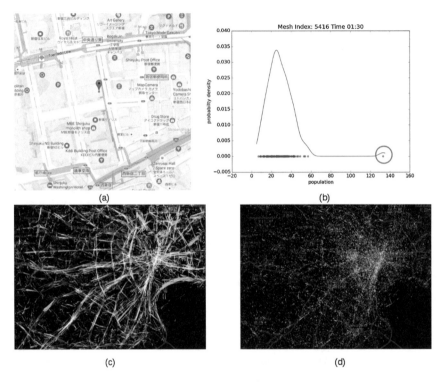

Fig. 1 Comparison of routine human mobility and rare human mobility

On the bottom row, we visualize the human mobility of the Tokyo area on a regular weekday (Fig. 1c) and when the earthquake occurred (Fig. 1d). We can also see a big difference between the mobility patterns of these two, and apparently the model we learned from a regular day is hardly applicable to this emergency situation.

Moreover, the particularity of each emergency situation also adds up to the difficulties in modeling the rare human mobility. For routine human mobility, there are only a few types we could come up with. Two types of routine human mobility, Weekday and weekend, take the largest proportion of the entire citywide human mobility. However, rare human mobility, which take the rest proportion, has a wide range of categories (e.g. New Year Celebration, Olympic Games, big earthquake and mass gathering events like Comiket). What makes this problem more complicated is that even the rare events belong to same category can be quite different from each other. Considering two examples of the greatest earthquakes in Japan, the Great Hanshin Earthquake in 1995, which occurred in the early morning near Osaka and led to the collapse of a large number of buildings, and the Great Tohoku Earthquake in 2011, which occurred in the afternoon in the east part of Japan and was followed by a severe tsunami), we may find that human mobility during these two earthquakes differ considerably because of the disparity in characteristics of the two earthquakes.

Thus we must pay special attention to determining whether it is reasonable to transfer the knowledge from one emergency situation to another, even of the same type.

Bearing these difficulties in mind, in this chapter, we divide the emergency citywide human mobility modeling into three fundamental tasks, which are *analyzing* the emergency human behavior, *predicting* the human mobility in the emergency situation, and *simulating* human mobility in response to an imaginary emergency situation. We review the relevant studies on each task, with real world emergency management case studies.

2 Approaches for Analyzing Human Emergency Behavior

For big crowd-drawing event or natural disaster that happened in the past, what we are interested in is how to learn the human mobility patterns in response to the emergency from the past experience. A simple visualization or do a simple statistics of the human mobility can provide many useful information, but for higher level information (how the life of the people is recovered after the earthquake) turns out to be difficult to extract directly because human mobility is always at a mixing state. Imagine a commercial area at 7 p.m. on a weekend. The people in this region would probably be drinking with friends, shopping, coming or leaving using public transportation. Comparatively, when the disaster occurs, people in this region may gather in the station to wait for the recovery of public transportation. Thus, we assume that a people flow is a mixture of various underlying latent components such as commuting and working patterns. Under this assumption, the objective of analyzing is to infer the underlying components from population density variation.

There are two families of algorithms in finding the latent components. One is topic modeling [5], which assigns a topic to each record of the human mobility data with respect to the coherence of the spatiotemporal topic distributions. Figure 2 shows a case study on applying topic modeling to the call record details data in modeling people behavior changes in Bangladesh during Eid al-Fitr festivals, which is the most important religious festival to the people there.

Another family of algorithms to discover latent components is matrix/tensor factorization [3, 12], which we will introduce in more details. An intuitive example is given in Fig. 3, the upper part of which is a people flow in a mixed state. Some regions are more likely to be a workplace (high density during working hours), other regions are more likely to be a transit station (high density in the morning and evening rush hours), and still some regions may be a combination of the two. Our research objective is to decompose a mixed people flow into a few basic people flows, each of which characterizes one human life pattern in the city, for example, a working pattern or commuting pattern, as shown in the lower part of Fig. 3.

To find the proper "spectrograph" that decomposes the citywide human mobility into basic patterns, Fan et al. [3] proposes a CitySpectrum method to approximate the people flow tensor through a linear combination of a few basic tensors (of rank 1)

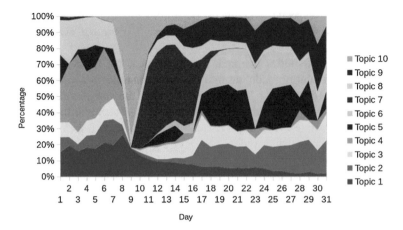

Fig. 2 The topic variation during Eid al-Fitr festival. Figure from [5]

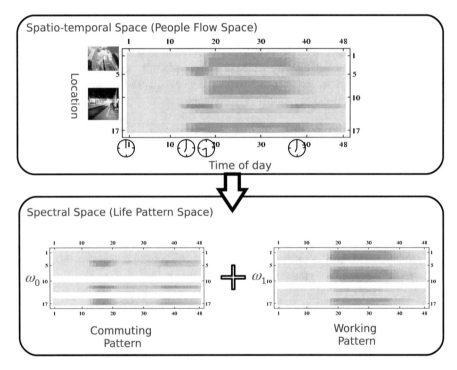

Fig. 3 An intuitive example of analyzing the components of citywide human mobility. Figure from [3]

with constraints (as shown in Fig. 4). There are two commonly used constraints to factorization. The first is the orthogonality (e.g. singular value decomposition), which applies a constraint in that the bases that are factorized out should be

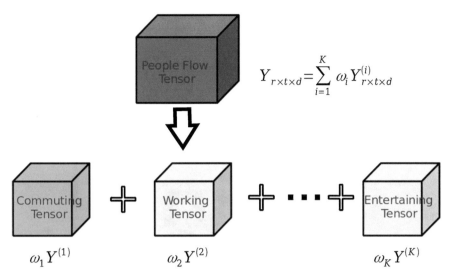

$$Y_{r \times t \times d} = \sum_{i=1}^{K} \omega_i Y^{(i)}_{r \times t \times d}$$

$\omega_1 Y^{(1)}$ $\omega_2 Y^{(2)}$ $\omega_K Y^{(K)}$

Fig. 4 The basic idea of people flow tensor factorization. Figure from [3]

orthogonal to each other. The second is non-negativity (e.g. NTF [1]), which assumes that every entry in the bases have to be non-negative.

Fan et al. [3] claims two reasons why non-negativity is preferred:

- the density of a people flow cannot be negative, and
- the difference between each pattern is not so significant as to be orthogonal.

Each rank-one tensor we discovered can be represented using three vectors, namely, the time-basis, the location-basis and the day-basis. These triple bases describe the spatio-temporal characteristics of the components of a people flow implied by a rank-one tensor. For simplicity and clarity of further analysis, we manually named the labels summarizing what kind of pattern the bases describe. For example, in Fig. 5, we show the bases of the rank-one tensor we factorized out. In the top-right of the figure, the regions with the highest values are the major stations in Tokyo, and we can see that the regions with a high value are approximately aligned along the mainlines (railway) in Tokyo. As for the time-basis, we can see two peaks at about 8:30 and 19:00 which could be interpreted as the morning and evening rush hours. Weekly periodical behavior can be easily observed from the day-basis diagram with the exception of the "golden week" in Japan. In the "golden week", Tuesday to Friday are national holidays. As a result, the people flow behaves similarly as that found on the weekend. Therefore, we labeled the rank-one tensor in Fig. 5 as a "commuting pattern".

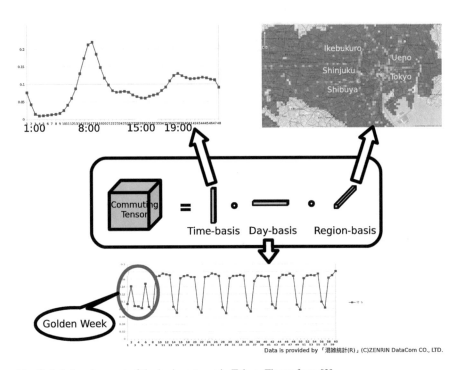

Fig. 5 Label assignment of the basic patterns in Tokyo. Figure from [3]

2.1 Case Studies on Disaster Behavior Analysis

It is difficult for the government to quantitatively evaluate the impact of the disaster on the daily life on the residents. With the help of the human mobility big data, the CitySpectral approach provides a novel perspective in modeling a people flow during a disaster in that disaster impact of the disaster on each basic life pattern can be measured.

The people flow tensors are computed to represent the people flow in Fukushima for four continuous months (ranged from Feb. 1 to May 31, 2011) before and after The Great East Japan Earthquake. In the experiments, nine basic life patterns, annotated as "home (1,2,3,4)", "commercial (1,2)", "working", "entertaining" and "commuting".

Figure 6 shows the days-basis before and after the Great East Japan Earthquake, reflecting the changes of each pattern with days. We can see that the home pattern is affected by the earthquake so significantly that it cannot simply be described as a single basic life patterns. The factorization algorithm separates a home pattern into four sub-patterns, depicting different aspect of home pattern.

The most obvious peak in Fig. 6 is the dramatic increase of "home 1" pattern in the three days following the earthquake. In the first row of Fig. 7, the time-basis (the first column) describes the "home 1" life pattern as "staying at home (or somewhere

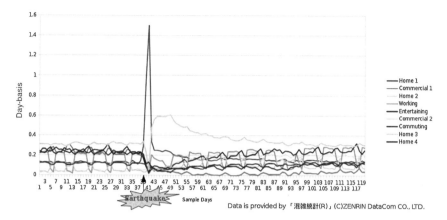

Fig. 6 Diagram of day-basis in Fukushima before and after the Great East Japan Earthquake from Feb. 1 to May 31, 2011 (the earthquake took place on March 11). Figure from [3]

nearby within the region) for the whole day", since there is little variation of the pattern intensity during one day. "Home 3" (on the third row) represents the pattern of "spending most time at home while sometimes going outside during the daytime". As shown in region-basis, "home 1" represents a more concentrated pattern of spatial distribution than "home 3", because "home 1" describes the pattern that people at a very low level of mobility while "home 3" describes the pattern that people mobility is partially recovered. In addition, "home 1" and "home 3" have in common that both have very low intensity in the coastal regions, where are severely damaged by Tsunami.

We can see from Fig. 6 that the peak of "home 1" follows right after the earthquake, this is because after the earthquake the transportation system broke down and the people's movement ability is restricted. In addition, people felt insecure, preferring to stay at home or their temporary shelter. About three days later, "home 1" decreases sharply while "home 3" rises. This is an intermediate state that transiting from heavily affected ("home 1") to regular patterns ("home 3 and 4").

A larger scale (nationwide) spatial disparity of the influence of the earthquake can be analyzed in a quantitative way shown in Fig. 8. We select four areas (inland area of Fukushima prefecture, coastal area of Fukushima prefecture, Tokyo and Osaka) and obtain the CitySpectrum of each area to see the influence of 311 earthquake to the people's daily life. As we can see from Fig. 8, inland and coastal area of Fukushima prefecture are most heavily affected by the earthquake, we could find a dramatic change of the patterns right after the earthquake takes place and it takes about one and a half month for the patterns recover to the normal level. Note that the regeneration process of inland and coastal areas are different. The disastrous Tsunami after the earthquake cause an invertible damage to the coastal area, especially the regions near to Nuclear Power station, we could see from the day-basis that people's life patterns are quite different from that before the

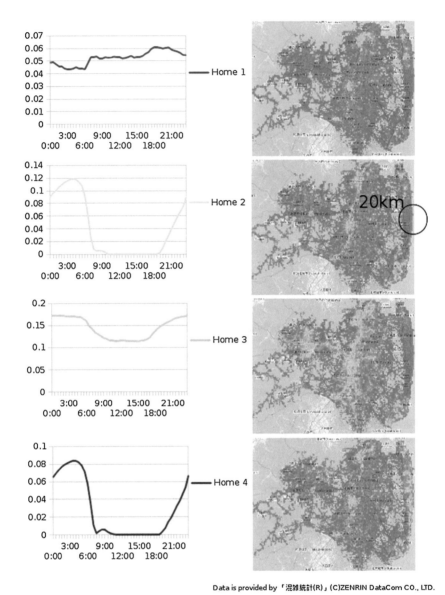

Fig. 7 The time-basis and region-basis of "home" patterns in the Fukushima people flow Tensor before and after the Great East Japan Earthquake. Figure from [3]

earthquake, while in the inland area of Fukushima, though the influence of the earthquake is very strong, it is recoverable and we could observe that after one and half months, people's life patterns have regenerated and indistinguishable from that before the earthquake. We could observe an obvious but much more mild change of

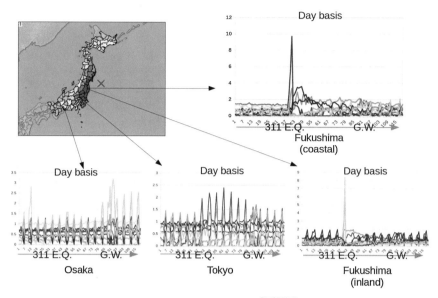

Data is provided by 「混雑統計(R)」(C)ZENRIN DataCom CO., LTD.

Fig. 8 A comparison of the spatial disparity of day-basis at a nationwide scale

people's life patterns compared with those in Fukushima prefecture, while in Osaka, little change due to the earthquake could be observed (the most obvious change is caused by the golden week in May).

3   Approaches for Predicting Human Emergency Mobility

Human mobility is very difficult to predict, especially, when we focus on the human mobility in emergency situation. We can model users' daily routines and predict periodical behaviors by an accumulative observation of their mobility patterns, whereas emergency behaviors, such as the gathering behavior for a crowd-drawing event or responses to the natural disaster, can hardly be predicted and thus they have usually been treated as outliers of the daily routines in most existing studies. However, to guarantee the safety of the people, such rare behaviors intrigue us more than daily routines.

In the scope of citywide, the emergency behavior of each individual is no longer rare and thus it may be predictable. In this section, we explore the probability of making short-term predictions based on the recent movement observations [13, 16], shown in Fig. 9, applies a hidden Markov model on user's past trajectories to learn their behavior pattern, and given the user's current observed movements and disaster states, the future movements are predicted in a particle filtering framework.

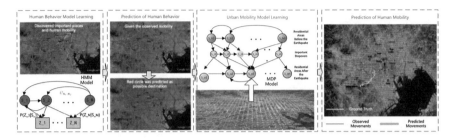

Fig. 9 Overview of the approach for human mobility prediction during an earthquake. Figure from [16]

[14] formulates the human mobility prediction during natural disaster in a Markov decision process to model a better sequential pattern of human trajectories. Konishi et al. [9] uses the characteristics of transit log data, and proposes an algorithm that automatically early detects the rare event and switches the prediction model between regular predictor and emergency predictor. To prevent the tragedy of Shanghai stampede accident [2] from happening again, Zhou et al. [17] detects the irregularity and gives early warning using Baidu map query data.

In the rest of this section, we will detail the following two studies: Fan et al. [4] proposes a novel model called CityMomentum as a predicting-by-clustering framework for sampling future movement using a mixture of multiple random Markov chains, each of which is a Naive Movement Predictive model trained with the movements of the subjects that belong to each cluster. To leverage the historical data and enhance the prediction performance on regular and precedented human mobility, in [7] we take CityMomentum model as one key component, and propose an ensemble prediction framework that copes with both rare (precedented and unprecedented) and regular human mobility.

3.1 CityMomentum

To predict the human mobility during a rare event, Fan et al. [4] makes simplifications based on the following assumptions:

- Social crowds gather gradually so we can collect enough information from those who arrived early to attend gathering to predict late arrivals.
- Subjects sharing similar recent trajectories will have a similar bifurcating pattern in the short-term future.
- The bifurcating behavior can be assumed to be invariant during a short period.

Given these assumptions, this study integrates the GPS logs of mobile phone users based on the current time to predict their future movements at a citywide level. An illustration of the intuition of the proposed model is shown in Fig. 10. Based on observations of the recent trajectory of one user, there is no idea of where he/she

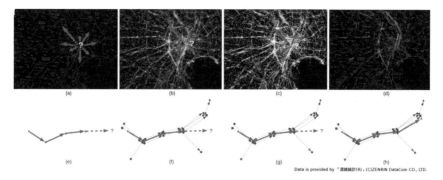

Fig. 10 Overview of the key processes in our CityMomentum model. Figure from [4]

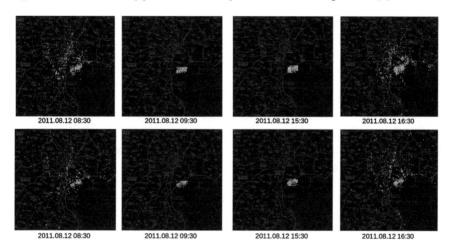

Fig. 11 Predicted sources of visitors to C80 at 1 h later and predicted 1-h-later locations of the visitors at C80 (in the top row) and the actual sources of and 1-h-later locations of visitors in reality (in the bottom row). Figure from [4]

will move next (Fig. 10a). However, in the scope of citywide human mobility, we can make a prediction based on the last location of the subject and the destinations of others from the same location (Fig. 10b and f). Based on the second assumption, we cluster users' recent trajectories so that users within each cluster share similar trajectories (Fig. 10c), and improve our prediction by the movements of the cluster instead of all the users. Then, the predicted movement is generated in a random walk procedure (Fig. 10d).

Here we present the prediction results at a rare event Comiket in Fig. 11. Comiket is the biggest comic fair in the world and is a big challenge to the local transportation system. The left panel of Fig. 11 shows the predicted human movements between 8:30 and 9:30 (top row) based on the momentary movements at 8:30 and a comparison with the ground truth (bottom row). To visualize our prediction of the potential visitors to C80, we select the region around Big Sight at 9:30 and trace back the subjects in this region to find out their locations at 8:30. Our algorithm successfully predict the geographical distribution of the visitors to C80. The bottom row shows that the main sources of the visitors are the two railways to the north-west of Big Sight. These two railways are the most convenient way for reaching Big Sight and they pass through the most important transport hubs in Tokyo (Shinjuku, Tokyo, and Shibuya stations). The results shown in the top row illustrate that most of our predictions agreed with ground truth movements.

At 4 p.m., C80 closed and a large crowd of people were leaving from the Big Sight. In fact, most of the visitors tended to leave earlier because the majority of the best-sellers sold out within the first few hours. As a result, we can obtain some insights into the dispersion behavior of the visitors based on those early leavers. The right panel of Fig. 11 provides an intuitive verification of the predicted of dispersion behavior based on a comparison between the predicted destinations of C80 visitors and their actual destinations.

3.2   Ensemble Human Mobility Predictor

CityMomentum discards all the historical data and make short-term prediction only based on the most recent trajectories. This leads to a great information loss, especially considering the regular and precedented rare human mobility. To enhance the prediction performance on regular and precedented emergency situations, Fan et al. [7] proposes an ensemble models which trains one human mobility predictor for each day of the historical data and most recent data (shown in the lower part of Fig. 12). Thus, each of these can be regarded as an "expert" in predicting the human mobility on its particular day or the most recent trend. All these pre-trained predictors are integrated in a mixture-of-experts way and the weights of the "experts" are adjusted in an online model selection way, as shown in the upper part of Fig. 12.

3.2.1   Case Study on Comiket

Figure 13b shows a typical trajectory that travels along the Joban line from northeast of Tokyo to the Tokyo station. The prediction in shown in Fig. 13c was made using our proposed online predictor for 8:00 a.m. on Aug. 11, 2012, which was the second day of Comiket, while in Fig. 13d, the prediction was made using the predictor for 8:00 a.m. on Aug. 4, 2012, which was one week before Comiket when no big event was being held at Tokyo Big Sight.

As can be seen from Fig. 13c and d, for Aug. 11, 2012, our predictor predicts a significantly higher probability for the Tokyo Big Sight area than the one on Aug. 4. The model selection ability is shown in Fig. 13e and f, on Aug. 11, 2012, the gating function in the ensemble predictor automatically assigned the highest weight to the

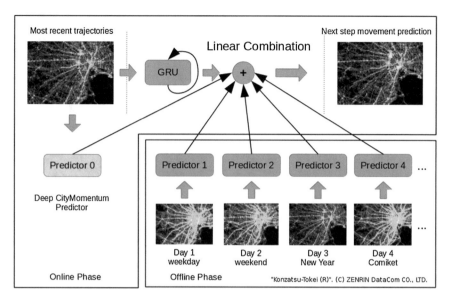

Fig. 12 Overview of the ensemble prediction approach. Figure from [7]

pre-trained predictor for Aug. 14, 2010, which was the second day of the Comiket in Aug 2010, whereas on Aug. 4, 2012, our ensemble predictor only assigned very little weights on the Comiket days in Aug 2010 (indicated by the red box).

3.2.2 Case Study on New Year Countdown

Another case study is on predicting the citywide human mobility at midnight on Jan. 1, 2012 on the New Year eve. Many crowd-drawing events take place on that night, and famous examples include Universal Studios Japan (USJ) Countdown Party, the Kitamido Countdown and Sumiyoshi Taisha Hatsumode. As shown in the left panel of Fig. 14, for each trajectory, we estimated the weight of each pre-trained predictor and colored them based on the predictor with the highest weight. Those trajectories that considered Jan. 1, 2011, as the best predictor are in red, while the others are blue. We can see that the famous New Year's countdown locations are mainly colored red, whereas residential areas, where there are fewer celebration events and the human mobility pattern is not distinguishable from a regular day, are mainly colored blue. In the right panel, we calculated the average weight of each predictor for predicting the human mobility on Jan. 1, 2012. We can see that the best predictor found by the gating function was the one trained using Jan. 1, 2011. It is worth noting that in contrast to classical approaches that label rare events in both the training data and testing data, we did not provide any prior knowledge indicating such a correspondence. In others words, our gating neural network could effectively manipulate the information flow based on the current human mobility to

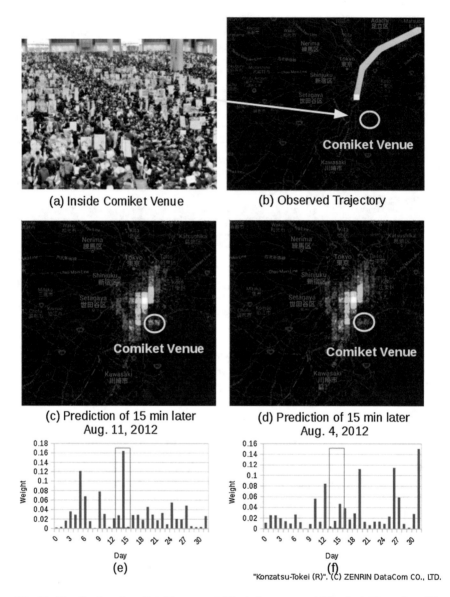

Fig. 13 Visualization of predicted human mobility during rare event (Comiket). Figure from [7]

automatically select the best information from the past, and thus enhance the human mobility prediction at the current stage.

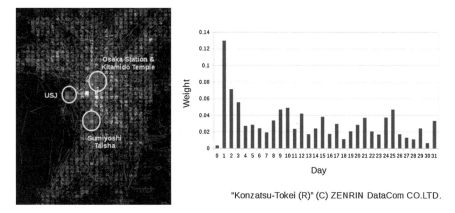

Fig. 14 Visualization of online model selection on New Year Eve. Figure from [7]

3.2.3 Case Study on the 2011 Great East Japan Earthquake

Rare events such as the New Year countdown and Comiket are precedented. Fan et al. [7] tests the performance of our system on unprecedented emergency using the 2011 Great East Japan Earthquake as an unprecedented emergency that could not be found from the historical data. In Fig. 15, we can see that after the earthquake occurred, the citywide human mobility changes significantly (Fig. 15a and b). In response to this, the ensemble model raises the weight of the deep CityMomentum predictor, which is more suitable for predicting unprecedented rare event. It is worth noting that to predict the precedented rare human mobility in Figs. 13 and 14, the ensemble model choose the pre-trained component predictor, while the deep CityMomentum predictor is not activated (the weight of predictor 0 is low).

4   Approaches for Simulating Human Emergency Mobility

When we see the reports of major events on TV, both joyful (e.g. the Olympics Games or the New Year's celebrations), and disastrous (e.g. earthquakes or tsunamis), we may wonder: "What if this happened in my city?" As shown in Fig. 16, when a tremendous earthquake occurs in Tokyo, where hundreds kilometers away from Tokyo, Osaka was only slightly effected by the earthquake. Thus, to learn the lessons from Tokyo and improve the emergency management to minimize the of the government, we may wonder what the human mobility would be in Osaka if the same disaster occurs in Osaka.

We need to address two major problems of transferring the emergency human mobility knowledge from one city to another. The first one is the particularity of each emergency, as we discussed in the examples of two greatest earthquakes in Japan in the introduction section. The second obstacle is the particularity of city

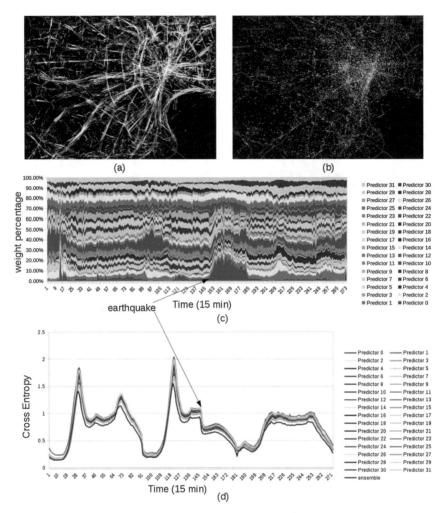

Fig. 15 Visualization of citywide human mobility in Tokyo on regular day (**a**) and when the Great East Japan Earthquake occurred (**b**) (the hue represents the moving direction) (**c**) shows how the weight of each component predictor changes before and after the earthquake took place, and (**d**) shows the cross entropy loss for our ensemble predictor and each component predictor. Figure from [7]

layouts. For example, when we learn lessons from one city in which a transportation hub has been struck by a tremendous earthquake, we must know the details of the corresponding transportation hub in the other city. In previous research, this is done mainly by empirical knowledge with some supportive evidence (e.g. the largest railway station in one city corresponds to the largest railway station in another city); however it is unrealistic to determine city layout alignment manually, because of

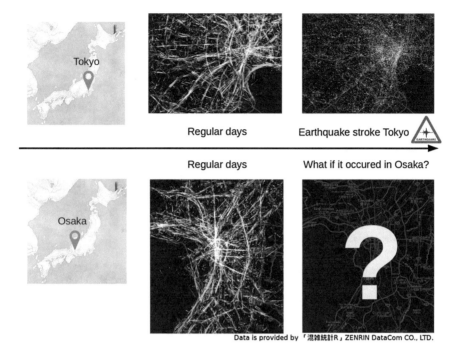

Fig. 16 What if Osaka was struck by the 311 earthquake? Figure from [6]

complex city topologies and multi-modality in intercity layout alignments (that is, one place in a city may correspond to many candidate places in another).

To cope with these difficulties, Fan et al. [6] propose a transfer learning algorithm, CityCoupling, to establish probabilistic intercity spatial mapping, which can be assumed to be invariant with respect to both routine and rare human mobility, that aligns the layouts of two cities in a domain adaptation way. We apply a spatial transformation to rare human mobility, while leaving all the intrinsic factors of human mobility unchanged. Thus, the information of the human mobility at rare events are maximally preserved.

As shown in Fig. 17, the CityCoupling algorithm can be divided into two phases: 1) an expectation maximization (EM) framework for intercity spatial mapping estimation and 2) a hidden Markov model (HMM) that incorporates knowledge transferred from the source city, geographical continuity, and population density prior to generating simulated trajectories. Figure 18 shows an example of how a typical trajectory in Tokyo that travels through Toukaido line corresponds to the locations in Osaka. The four important stations on Toukaido line that connects with Yokohama (the largest city around Tokyo) with Tokyo is mapped to a route that connects Kyoto (one of the largest city near Osaka) with Osaka.

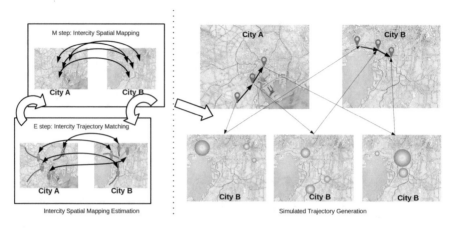

Fig. 17 Overview of our CityCoupling algorithm. Figure from [6]

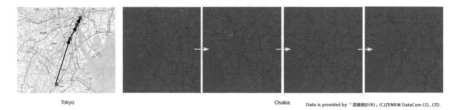

Fig. 18 Visualization of a typical trajectory in Tokyo that travels through Toukaido line (on the left) and the mapping results (on the right) for four important stations on this railway: Kawasaki, Shinbashi, Shimbashi, and Tokyo stations. Figure from [6]

4.1 Case Study on Transferring the Great Eastern Japan Earthquake

As shown in the top row in Fig. 19, Tokyo was heavily affected by the 2011 Great East Japan Earthquake and citywide human mobility was reduced due to severe disruptions of the transportation network. The earthquake occurred at 14:46 on a Friday; therefore, most people were trapped at their workplace, because the transportation network failed to recover until the next morning. However, Osaka was only slightly affect by the earthquake. From the second row in Fig. 19, we can see that in Osaka human mobility on that day did not differ significantly from a regular day.

With the help of the intercity spatial mapping from Tokyo to Osaka, the trajectories in Osaka could be generated to simulate the human mobility in response to the same disaster as in Tokyo. As shown in the third row, our simulated trajectories preserve different phases of the human response to the earthquake "regular → heavily affected by the disaster → gradual recovery". Compared with human mobility in Osaka on that day, we find that our simulation results in the

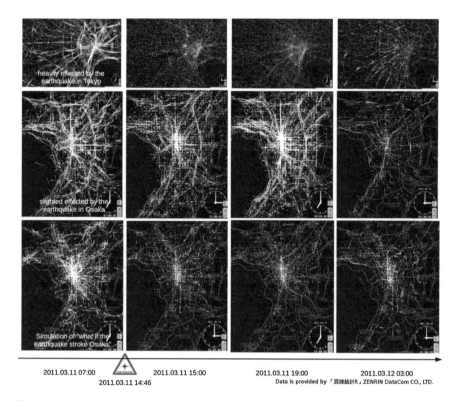

Fig. 19 A visualization transferring human mobility during the Great Eastern Japan Earthquake in Tokyo, where was heavily affected, to Osaka, where was only slightly affected. Figure from [6]

first and fourth columns, which are from before and 12 h after the earthquake (when the transportation network had mostly recovered), are considerably similar to the true human mobility at those times, while those in the second and the third column, which depict transportation network disruption, are substantially different from the second row. Putting the first and third rows together, we find a similar human mobility pattern regardless of city layout.

4.2   Other Studies on Emergency Human Mobility Simulation

There are some other relevant studies on simulating human mobility for emergency management. Traditional approaches are usually multi-agent based human mobility simulation [8, 10], which require a large number of parameter configuration and a rich expertise to make it work properly. Song et al. [13, 15] proposes a data-driven approach for simulating human mobility in response to imaginary disasters described by the disaster parameters. Such learning-to-simulate methods require much fewer parameter configurations (most of the parameters are learned from data), but we need to collect sufficient training samples and the methods are more limited to certain types of emergency that could be parameterized.

5 Conclusion

In this chapter, using the real-world human mobility big data, we give several examples of modeling citywide human mobility for emergency management. The challenges and state-of-the-art solutions to the three basic tasks are introduced.

Considering the limitations of existing studies, some promising future directions in citywide human mobility modeling for emergency management are given as below:

- **Map information**: In general, map information does not draw sufficient attention in the existing studies. The reasons are twofold: the first reason is that map-matching requires a lot of work, and can be quite unstable if the sampling rate of human trajectory is low. However, to make the algorithms more practical, map information should be taken into consideration in the future research (the population density on XXX road is more informative than in grid XXXXX). The second reason is using the map element to represent human mobility implies much more complex constraints, and therefore make the model more difficult to build and work properly.
- **Fusing more sources of data**: Comparing with social network data (e.g. Twitter, Facebook, Weibo), transit app log data (e.g. Google map, Yahoo) or life log data (e.g. Google calendar, survey), GPS points suffer from the problem of lack of semantic information. For emergency management, although we are able to observe irregularities from GPS points data, we are blind about what is happening there. Surveillance camera or twitter data could be very important data providing the semantic information of the emergency to help us know better about what the emergency situation and how people react to it. Besides, for big crowd-drawing event such as Olympic Games, we do not have many cues on whether he/she will attend. Other sources of data, such as search query data, social network data and ticket selling data, can be quite promising in complementing such weakness.
- **Better model that robust to emergency**: From the viewpoint of machine learning, modeling emergency human mobility suffers from the problem that insufficient samples. Emergency situation is always the rare case in the dataset, and we should be very careful about whether we are reasonably generalizing the emergency from our data. Transfer learning [11], which is a hot research topic, sheds light on enabling the rapid learning ability that could even transfer the knowledge between different tasks and learn from insufficient samples.

6   Exercises

Geo-tagged social network data (e.g. Twitter, Foursquare, Instagram) are widely available on the Internet.

1. Write a crawler to collect a geo-tagged social network dataset at least one week in two cities, including at least one crowd-drawing event (e.g. Football match musical festival or New Year Countdown)
2. Implement a CitySpectrum algorithm to find out the latent mobility patterns in the dataset. Try to describe the spatio-temporal characteristics of the big event human mobility
3. Train a predictor on the next move of each user in the dataset, and see how well the human mobility at the big event could be predicted. Popular probability machine learning packages such as PyMC3 or Stan, and deep learning frameworks such as TensorFlow or PyTorch are highly recommended.
4. Find out the intercity spatial mapping between the two cities, and find out the most probable venue of the big event in the other city. Try to simulate the human mobility of the big event in the other city.

References

1. Cichocki, A., Zdunek, R., Phan, A.H., Amari, S.: Nonnegative Matrix and Tensor Factorizations: Applications to Exploratory Multi-Way Data Analysis and Blind Source. Wiley, Chichester (2009)
2. CNN: 'I failed to protect you' – Details emerge of victims in deadly Shanghai stampede. http://edition.cnn.com/2015/01/02/world/asia/china-shanghai-new-years-stampede/
3. Fan, Z., Song, X., Shibasaki, R.: Cityspectrum: a non-negative tensor factorization approach. In: Proceedings of the 2014 ACM International Joint Conference on Pervasive and Ubiquitous Computing, pp. 213–223. ACM, New York (2014)
4. Fan, Z., Song, X., Shibasaki, R., Adachi, R.: Citymomentum: an online approach for crowd behavior prediction at a citywide level. In: Proceedings of the 2015 ACM International Joint Conference on Pervasive and Ubiquitous Computing, pp. 559–569. ACM, New York (2015)
5. Fan, Z., Arai, A., Song, X., Witayangkurn, A., Kanasugi, H., Shibasaki, R.: A collaborative filtering approach to citywide human mobility completion from sparse call records. In: Proceedings of IJCAI, pp. 2500–2506 (2016)
6. Fan, Z., Song, X., Shibasaki, R., Li, T., Kaneda, H.: Citycoupling: bridging intercity human mobility. In: Proceedings of the 2016 ACM International Joint Conference on Pervasive and Ubiquitous Computing, pp. 718–728. ACM, New York (2016)
7. Fan, Z., Song, X., Xia, T., Jiang, R., Shibasaki, R., Ritsu, S.: Online deep ensemble learning for predicting citywide human mobility. In: Proceedings of the 2018 ACM International Joint Conference on Pervasive and Ubiquitous Computing. ACM, New York (2018)
8. Horni, A., Nagel, K., Axhausen, K.W.: The Multi-Agent Transport Simulation MATSim. Ubiquity Press, London (2016)
9. Konishi, T., Maruyama, M., Tsubouchi, K., Shimosaka, M.: Cityprophet: City-scale irregularity prediction using transit app logs. In: Proceedings of the 2016 ACM International Joint Conference on Pervasive and Ubiquitous Computing, UbiComp '16, pp. 752–757. ACM, New York (2016). http://doi.acm.org/10.1145/2971648.2971718

10. Mustapha, K., Mcheick, H., Mellouli, S.: Modeling and simulation agent-based of natural disaster complex systems. Procedia Comput. Sci. **21**, 148–155 (2013). https://doi.org/10.1016/j.procs.2013.09.021. http://www.sciencedirect.com/science/article/pii/S1877050913008144. The 4th International Conference on Emerging Ubiquitous Systems and Pervasive Networks (EUSPN-2013) and the 3rd International Conference on Current and Future Trends of Information and Communication Technologies in Healthcare (ICTH)
11. Pan, S.J., Yang, Q.: A survey on transfer learning. IEEE Trans. Knowl. Data Eng. **22**(10), 1345–1359 (2010)
12. Shimosaka, M., Maeda, K., Tsukiji, T., Tsubouchi, K.: Forecasting urban dynamics with mobility logs by bilinear Poisson regression. In: Proceedings of the 2015 ACM International Joint Conference on Pervasive and Ubiquitous Computing, UbiComp '15, pp. 535–546. ACM, New York (2015)
13. Song, X., Zhang, Q., Sekimoto, Y., Horanont, T., Ueyama, S., Shibasaki, R.: Modeling and probabilistic reasoning of population evacuation during large-scale disaster. In: Proceedings of the 19th ACM SIGKDD International Conference on Knowledge Discovery and Data Mining, pp. 1231–1239. ACM, New York (2013)
14. Song, X., Zhang, Q., Sekimoto, Y., Shibasaki, R.: Prediction of human emergency behavior and their mobility following large-scale disaster. In: Proceedings of the 20th ACM SIGKDD International Conference on Knowledge Discovery and Data Mining, pp. 5–14. ACM, New York (2014)
15. Song, X., Kanasugi, H., Shibasaki, R.: Deeptransport: prediction and simulation of human mobility and transportation mode at a citywide level. In: Proceedings of IJCAI (2016)
16. Song, X., Zhang, Q., Sekimoto, Y., Shibasaki, R., Yuan, N.J., Xie, X.: Prediction and simulation of human mobility following natural disasters. ACM Trans. Intell. Syst. Technol. **8**(2), 29 (2016)
17. Zhou, J., Pei, H., Wu, H.: Early warning of human crowds based on query data from Baidu map: analysis based on Shanghai stampede. CoRR abs/1603.06780 (2016). http://arxiv.org/abs/1603.06780

Smartphone Based Emergency Communication

Huawei Huang and Song Guo

1 Definition of Basic Terms

We first review the definitions of basic terms appeared in this chapter.

- *Emergency Communications* are communication paradigms that are exploited to support one-way and two-way communication of emergency information between two peers, or within a group of peers.
- *Emergency Communication Networks (ECNs)* are networks organized to convey information over multiple types of communication devices, intended to serve disaster-relief missions during emergency situations such as natural disasters.
- *Disruption/Delay Tolerance Network (DTN)* is a type of computer network architecture that aims to solve the technical issues in heterogeneous networks where the continuous network connectivity is not always available [1]. The examples of DTN networks are those operating in mobile terrestrial or space environments.
- *Edge/Fog Computing* is a computing paradigm that brings intelligence and processing capabilities closer to where the data originates from sensors, actuators, relays, etc. Therefore, it does not need to send the data to a remote cloud or other centralized systems for processing. Taking advantage of Edge Computing, the distance and time consumed in sending data to centralized sources can be eliminated, such that the data transportation and service performance are able to much improved.

H. Huang
School of Data and Computer Science, Sun Yat-Sen University, Guangzhou, China
e-mail: huanghw28@mail.sysu.edu.cn

S. Guo (✉)
Department of Computing, The Hong Kong Polytechnic University, Hung Hom, Hong Kong
e-mail: song.guo@polyu.edu.hk

© Springer Nature Switzerland AG 2020
R. Akerkar (ed.), *Big Data in Emergency Management: Exploitation Techniques for Social and Mobile Data*, https://doi.org/10.1007/978-3-030-48099-8_7

2 Introduction to Smartphone Based ECNs

Large-scale disasters such as devastating earthquake, flood, wild fire and tsunami bring severe damages to telecommunication infrastructures, and incur massive blackouts to the affected areas. It usually takes months to recover the damaged infrastructures. Thus, aiming to satisfy the sharply growing communication demands and reduce loss of lives and properties, the ECNs [2] need to be immediately established to response to post-disaster missions. ECNs are designed to provide reliable communications under emergency [3]. For example, the ECN Center can collect messages from disaster areas and notify the rescue team members the required actions for disaster-relief.

2.1 Background of Smartphone Based Networks

Nowadays, smartphones are pervasive in our daily life. In each of them, various sensors such as GPS, cameras, compass, gyroscopes, microphones and light sensors are embedded inside. Thus, when a group of smartphones connect to the Internet through cellular or WiFi networks, or when they connect together under a certain topology using the built-in bluetooth technology, a sensor network is actually constructed and can be exploited to organize ECNs for disaster-relief tasks.

Smartphone based ECNs have attracted enormous attention in recent years. In this chapter, we first review the state-of-the-art smartphone related disaster-relief efforts. We then reveal the open issues and future research directions.

2.2 Overview of ECN Architecture

Through Fig. 1a, we have an overview of the typical smartphone based ECNs. When disasters attack, the affected areas will be usually divided into multiple communities. Due to the damage of the telecommunication infrastructures, these distributed communities potentially disconnect from the Internet and form isolated "islands". As illustrated in Fig. 1a, to build network connection, the approaches exploiting vehicular mobile stations [4–8] and DTN techniques [9–13] have been widely studied. In the communities where vehicular mobile station can go through, people could use the social media apps such as Twitter, Instagram, etc., to communicate with their family members and friends with the Internet connection provided by the mobile stations. In the communities where the mobile stations cannot reach, community residents could share content with their smartphones based on Unmanned Aerial Vehicle (UAV) and Device-to-Device (D2D) technologies. Meanwhile, smartphones can also help to collect data from the Internet of Things

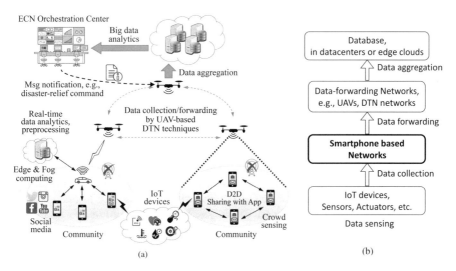

Fig. 1 The overview of smartphone based ECN architecture and the corresponding data-transmission stages. (**a**) Smartphone based ECN architecture. (**b**) Data-transmission stages

(IoT) devices deployed in disaster areas. Then, all the collected data originated from disaster scenes can be gathered by the mobile stations and finally aggregated to the database that locates in remote cloud for big data analytics. By invoking the big data technologies, critical useful information can be mined. For example, the occurring probability of disasters can be predicted using historical records. These useful information is delivered to the ECN Center, which will help make the disaster-relief decisions, e.g., evacuation guidance and rescue commands. In particular, in the edge networks where edge servers are deployed, the real-time data analytics and data preprocessing can be accomplished by exploiting the edge computing technologies [14].

To precisely draw the relationship between ECN components, we use Fig. 1b to illustrate the stages of data-transmission from *sensing* stage to *aggregation* stage. We can observe that the *smartphone based networks* play an important role that bridges the bottom device-layer and the data-forwarding networks. Especially under the ECN scenarios where the UAVs and other DTN network components are constrained by energy limitation, weather conditions and various disaster aftermath, smartphone based networks are much easier to establish comparing with other DTN networks, thanks to the pervasive mobility of smartphone holders, i.e., human. Therefore, smartphone based networks provide the powerful *data collection* functionality for ECN.

2.3 Key Concepts for Emergency Management

2.3.1 Situation Awareness (SA)

Situation Awareness (SA) is a procedure to perceive the environmental events and elements in either time or space dimension, aiming to know the comprehensive understanding of their meaning, and the projection of their future status [15].

The SA information plays a significant role during disaster-relief, because the ECN Center makes rescue planes for rescue teams relying on the onsite situations such as road damages, resident distribution, resource requirement, medical demands, and so on. Thus, it is critical to timely sense the situation awareness information for ECN management. Based on the pervasive sensor-equipped smartphones, the *opportunistic sensing* technology [16] has been considered as the promising paradigm for scalable context monitoring, such as the large-scale crowd-behavioral sensing and environmental monitoring. Especially, the *crowd-mobility* study, such as prediction of crowd mobility in public areas [13], is obviously very useful for guiding evacuation when disaster occurs, to avoid the casualties caused by chaos and panics in the crowd.

2.3.2 DTNs

As we have mentioned, communities in the disaster area may be separated to multiple isolated ECNs, incurring that the end-to-end connection cannot be established. The approaches to construct an ECN by exploiting mobile stations and aerial vehicles [4–8] are options under DTN theories.

2.3.3 Big Data Analytics

A large volume of data can be collected from various sources such as the IoT devices deployed in disaster scenes, smartphone based networks, and social media networks. Then, with the collected data, *big data analytics* is essential to understand the situations in each disaster site, because useful information can be extracted from the collected raw data for situation awareness. For example, a number of recent studies [13, 17–20] have retrieved meaningful information by specifically focusing on analyzing the social media data such as Twitter or Facebook datasets, to response to disasters and manage the emergency networks.

2.3.4 Edge/Fog Computing

As reported in a white paper of Cisco [21], there will be 50 billion things to connect to the Internet by 2020. Such a large number of IoT devices will produce tremendous volume of data that needs to be processed and analyzed. Similarly, as shown in Fig. 1a, in the post-disaster scenes, the IoT devices deployed in the disaster areas and the smartphones themselves can yield a large volume of raw data. To retrieve the real-time useful information for rescue teams, the collected data requires distributed onsite processing. However, the conventional cloud based data processing paradigm needs to direct the data streams to the servers located in the remote cloud for processing or computing. This traditional paradigm results in unacceptable performance under disaster scenarios. *Edge computing* [14] and *fog computing* [22] are proposed to mitigate the workload in conventional datacenter servers by processing local data on the computing nodes located at the edge of networks. Thus, it is necessary to adopt the techniques of edge computing and fog computing to reduce the situation-awareness delay and improve the quality of service in the smartphone based ECNs.

3 Data Source

Generally, any text messages, GPS traces, images and videos reflecting the situations of disasters are greatly helpful for disaster-relief. In this section, we introduce several representative datasets used in ECNs, such as the data for capturing crowd mobility, for estimating the distribution of victims, and for better situation awareness. The brief features of the typical datasets are shown in Table 1.

3.1 Mobility Related Datasets

The mobility pattern analysis towards human or vehicles benefits the evacuation when disaster occurs. For example, to know the road conditions such as blocked, damaged or normal, and the mobility of the crowd determines the rescue plans directly. The typical datasets related to crowd mobility can be found as follows.

The floating car data is sensed and collected from the cars under driving by the mobile devices such as smartphones holding inside cars. For example, to predict the traffics in highway of Rome, Fabritiis et al. [23] successfully estimated the mobility patterns by analyzing the floating car data that was collected from a large number of cars. Then, Ganti et al. [24] studied the movement patterns of the taxi passengers by analyzing the floating car data from taxis.

Table 1 Typical datasets for smartphone based ECNs

Datasets	References	Significance for disaster-relief
Floating car data	[23, 24]	To estimate traffic mobility patterns in disasters
GPS trace data	[25, 26]	To estimate human mobility patterns in disasters
Social media data	[13, 17–20, 27]	To retrieve situation-awareness at disaster scenes

GPS traces of mobile-phone users have been exploited to estimate people who are traveling in urban areas. For instance, in [25], the GPS traces obtained from mobile phones during some social events such as sport games and sudden entry/departure in transport stations, were used to study the correlations between crowd mobility and special events. Horanont et al. [26] analyzed the discerning behavior change during the evacuation after the 2011 Great East Japan Earthquake using the large-scale GPS trace samples.

3.2   Social Media Related Datasets

People who are close to the disaster scenes may post the real-time texts, images, and even videos to the social media such as Twitter, Facebook, Instagram or YouTube. Therefore, social media data captures the first-hand dynamic information at disaster scenes, and it has significant value to disaster-relief. Some examples of using social media data are presented as follows.

The analytics on Twitter dataset has been used in the response to Great East Japan Earthquake [17]. Also, the Twitter dataset has been used to estimate the density of victims via analyzing the distribution of Twitter messages in the post-disaster areas [18]. However, the accuracy of this approach is not convincing, because not everyone has a Twitter account, and not everyone will pose a Twitter when disaster occurs.

Musaev et al. [19] first proposed a rapid ensemble classification system to monitor natural disasters by exploiting the social media texts, such as Twitter data. In this study, the proposed approach specifically addressed an unique challenge caused by multiple meanings of the search word. Furthermore, Musaev et al. [20] developed an online disaster detector that collects keyword related events and particularly supports multiple-language, based on the Twitter social media data.

Higashino et al. [13] presented a smartphone based crowd and event detection architecture, in which the data source from Twitter social media has been used. At first step, the correlation between popular words in the Twitter dataset is analyzed to extract the event keywords. Then, the crowd information is shared among smartphone apps and uploaded to could servers for matching keywords with the event database. In this manner, the presence of crowd in real world could be detected, and the reason behind the crowd event can be also estimated. This is very useful to public safety, because some dangerous events, such as fires and terrorist attacks, could be timely identified to raise an alarm.

In addition, Giridhar et al. [27] developed an adaptive localization algorithm that localizes urban events using the set of pictures retrieved from the Instagram images containing the specified tag keyword.

4   Methodologies and Key Techniques

In this section, we review the state-of-the-art existing methodologies and key techniques in the smartphone based ECNs (Table 2).

4.1   Construct ECNs by Ad-hoc Networks and DTNs

To quickly response to disasters, recent studies [9–13] explored the techniques of ad-hoc networks, opportunistic networks and DTNs to construct ECNs in the affected disaster areas for the survivability and evacuation of victims. For example, Based on the DTN communication techniques, Trono et al. [12] developed a smartphone application called DTN MapEx, which generate and share maps of disaster areas by exploiting multiple nodes in the system. This application can minimize the individual computational workload, since the map generation tasks are shared within all mobile sensing nodes in DTNs. Higashino et al. [13] have launched a research project for disaster mitigation, leveraging the DTN-enabled distributed micro-modules. In their approach, a smartphone-based crowd-event detection architecture has been designed.

4.2   Data Collection and Aggregation in ECNs

4.2.1   Mobile Base Stations

To better understand the situational awareness of disasters, data collection and aggregation are the main tasks in ECNs. A handful number of studies [4–8] realize such missions by applying the vehicle-based or aerial-based mobile base stations. For example, Gomez et al. [4] presented the outcomes of the ABSOLUTE project

Table 2 Key techniques and methodologies of smartphone based ECNs

Contribution	References	Key techniques and methodologies
Construct ECNs	[9–13]	Proposed approaches to communicate in ECNs by ad-hoc networks, Opportunistic networks and DTNs
Data collection and aggregation	[4–8]	Proposed mobile base-station, like UAV, based mechanisms
	[28–31]	Proposed Device-to-Device (D2D) communication based mechanisms
	[32–36]	Proposed crowd-sensing based mechanisms
	[37, 38]	Proposed satellite based technologies for network discovery and connection

[28], in which a low-latency IP mobile network with large coverage has been prototyped by combining aerial, terrestrial and satellites communication networks. In particular, the aerial base stations have been implemented as the main components to provide resilient communications for the mobile devices in disaster scenarios. A low cost balloon based Network [6] has been proposed for the post-earthquake rescue. Li et al. [5, 7] proposed to build a disaster management network based on mobile stations implemented by drones and vehicles, in which sensors and network connection interfaces are equipped. Via this framework, a lot of disaster management tasks can be achieved, such as sensing damage conditions, information collection and message delivery in disaster areas. Then, Narang et al. [8] proposed to build a cyber-physical buses-and-drone based mobile edge infrastructure for the emergency communications in case of large scale disaster, in which the cellular infrastructures have been destroyed.

4.2.2 D2D Communications

Many recent works in the literature have explored D2D communications to extend the network coverage, especially in the context of disasters. For example, Wu et al. [29] exploited smartphones as the medium to collect and disseminate messages in a natural disaster network while the traditional cellular base station is inaccessible. A modified epidemic routing protocol is also proposed to enable smartphones working collaboratively in D2D manner in disaster environments. In the ABSOLUTE project [28], the short-distance D2D communications are applied for rescue teams and emergency agencies when the conventional network infrastructure have been damaged in disasters. Orsino et al. [30] studied the social-aware data collection and information diffusion using D2D communication techniques. The proposed approach can be applied to the emergency networks for public safety. Based on D2D communications in ad-hoc network, Meurisch et al. [31] recently proposed an emergency communication system called NICER911, aiming to provide reliable communication and emergency services in infrastructure-less disaster areas.

4.2.3 Crowd Sensing

To enhance situation-awareness in disaster scenes, the existing studies [32–36] have developed impressive smartphone based crowd sensing techniques. For example, Higuchi et al. [32] proposed a low power cooperative localization algorithm that captures the stop-and-go behavior of indoor pedestrians. Based on the cooperative operations among multiple smartphones, Noh et al. [33] developed an infrastructure-free localization identification technology with high-speed positioning effect. Kojima et al. [34] proposed a new application that estimates the reason behind the scheduled human crowd events using the mobile crowd sensing techniques. To improve the rescue efficiency in terms of bandwidth utilization and energy consumption, Zuo et al. [35] explored the image sharing mechanism that acquires significant onsite situation-awareness information of disasters, e.g., earthquake and Typhoon. In this mechanism, the shared images are collected via the smartphone based crowd-sensing techniques. Based on the fact that a camera can help rescue team well identify the situation-awareness information, e.g., victims trapped in a disaster, Dao et al. [36] implemented a network of cameras with smartphones, which energy-efficiently coordinates among the built-in cameras to transmit the objects detected with high accuracy.

4.2.4 Satellite Based Technologies

Pal et al. [37] proposed a novel WiFi tethering strategy based on smartphones to construct a disaster-relief network architecture, named E-Darwin2. The satellite and its modem in the proposed architecture play the roles of a network gateway and an intermediary cell tower for discovery and connection device. Huang et al. [38] studied an energy-efficient online data upload scheme for geo-distributed IoT networks. Because the low-earth-orbital satellites have global coverage, it is easy to aggregate the data collected by smartphones when satellite modems are configured as gateways in the isolated disaster communities.

5 Real-World Applications and Case Study

In this section, we first review the real-word applications related to the smartphone based ECNs. Then, a case study is presented in the context of disaster management.

5.1 Dedicated Smartphone Apps For Disaster-Relief

Peng et al. [39] developed a bluetooth based smartphone app named "E-Explorer", which can deliver rescue information for the survivors trapped in post-earthquake sites. Then, Han et al. [40] extended the aforementioned iOS based application E-Explorer to other platforms, to better support the emergency communication and fast investigation of damages on the post-earthquake circumstance. Recently, to efficiently response disasters such as large-scale earthquake and tsunami, Miyazaki et al. [41] developed a resilient information management system, which can be executed on Android and iOS platforms and bring convenient information management and data exchange functionalities between rescue teams and victims in disasters. Chiou et al. [42] proposed a mobile emergency system (MES) that can be used in houses, hospitals, and other nursing facilities offering continuous care services for elders and disabilities. The proposed emergency rescue alert system is implemented on Android smartphones, and is able to provide the security and privacy-preserving functionalities, including authentication, location confidentiality, data integrity and anonymity. Kau et al. [43] implemented a smartphone app that can detect the user fall-accidents, perform location positioning, and communicate with the rescue center for assistance.

To detect faces efficiently in a wireless on-demand emergency network, Lampe et al. [44] proposed a smartphone based app, which performs face detection in local mobile devices by exploiting a two-stage combination of existing algorithms.

5.2 Case Study: Resilient Information Management (RIM) System

We now present our previous project named RIM system [41] as a case study for serving ECN. In the proposed RIM system, the smartphone- and UAV-based integrated network aims to provide more delay-efficient and reliable solutions in many harsh disaster environments where conventional cellular communication infrastructures have been almost unavailable or severely damaged. At these crucial scenarios, although the ad-hoc mobile social networks built through mobile devices such as smartphones are the most promising communication approach, the delivery delay could be very large, leading to unacceptable performance for disaster-relief tasks.

As shown in Fig. 2, to reduce the delivery delay, we propose to use the UAVs that are equipped with wireless communication capability. They are controlled to travel along the designed routes, collect the information such as damage conditions, injuries and medical demands, from certain specified sites, and deliver the gathered data to information center. Through this way, the delivery latency of the emergency information can be reduced greatly compared with the systems that rely on the ad-hoc communication paradigm.

Under this smartphone and UAV based architecture, we have designed an integrated information management and sharing mechanism benefiting both rescue teams and victims [41]. Also, an online algorithm that addresses the disaster management tasks with different weights have been proposed by dynamically scheduling mobile stations [5]. Besides, some problems under the RIM system will be studied in the future work, e.g., the energy-efficient schedule of drone-route during the data collection and aggregation missions.

6 Challenges and Open Issues

6.1 Key Challenges of Smartphone Based ECNs

Some notable challenges in smartphone based ECNs can be summarized as follows.

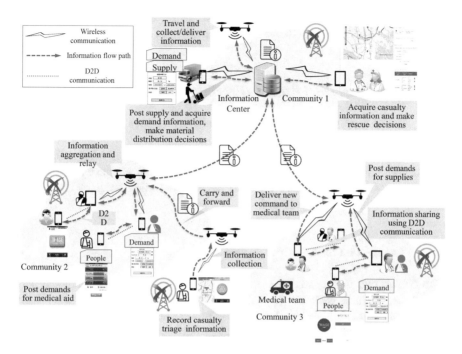

Fig. 2 Case study: the smartphone and drone based resilient information management (RIM) system

- The constrained battery budget of the sensing devices in disasters, e.g., sensors, cameras, smartphones and drones.
- Long delay to grasp the situation of the entire regions in real time. Massive power/network outages make the grasping delay even longer.
- Safe evacuation for the crowd when disaster occurs in the indoor environments.

Disaster possibly destroy the power supply infrastructures and cause massive outage. Thus, maintaining the alive status of the big number of sensing devices with limited power budget becomes an intractable challenge.

Service delay is always the key metric concerned by the literature on DTNs. Although the state-of-the-art techniques and technologies such as UAV based mobile base stations and D2D communications, have been exploited in ECNs, the inter-community delivery delay still cannot be reduced to online service level for disaster communications.

During disaster scenarios in urban districts, for example, big fire occurs in a tall building, or explosive incidents hit the public crowd areas, people are every easy to get into panics and cause casualties. Thus, to provide the efficient evacuation guidance to the crowd is of great significance. This can be realized by studying the mobility of the crowd during disasters. The existing related studies on estimating crowd mobility [32–34] still cannot fulfill the rigorous requirement of safe evacuation for everyone. It can be seen that safe evacuation for the crowd still remains as an intractable challenge in the field of disaster-relief.

6.2 Open Issues and Future Directions

6.2.1 Reliable and Efficient Disaster-Relief Architecture

First, it is an open problem to build a high reliability disaster-relief architecture that can handle the disaster data-sensing and aggregation efficiently in terms of energy and delivery delay. The trade-off between detection accuracy and energy consumption should be emphasized.

6.2.2 Recognition for Indoor Environments

The GPS signal is only available in the outdoor environments, resulting in that GPS based technology is not applicable to the indoor localization and tracking. Therefore, the smartphone based approaches that can actually track human mobility and recognize human behaviors in the indoor environments are in urgent need to satisfy the requirement of disaster-relief applications. For example, Berbakov et al. [45] proposed an indoor positioning system that exploits the built-in inertial sensors of a smartphone to realize the situation awareness in emergency contexts. This work motivates us that various other smartphone sensors are able to be applied to implement the indoor recognition applications.

6.2.3 Fast Data Aggregation

To understand the disaster situations from the collected data, machine learning based classification is a popular approach to recognizing different contexts. On the other hand, to build a machine learning model for classifications, sufficient volume of training data is needed. This implies that to quickly aggregate the required amount of training data samples is a critical problem. Furthermore, since large-volume of sensing data needs to transmit to aggregation gateways, it is crucial to schedule the efficient data delivery such that the data-loss ratio is minimized in DTN based ECNs.

6.2.4 Deployment of Computing Resources

With the collected data that needs to be processed to quickly retrieve the meaningful information for evacuation and rescue, several groups of edge servers might work in a decentralized manner at real-time. Consequently, the deployment of the data processing/computing resources while coordinating with data-collecting devices becomes another open problem.

6.2.5 Privacy

Privacy is an important issue that should not be ignored in the smartphone based ECNs. To achieve situational awareness, data needs to be collected from both public and private sensor networks, and smartphone based applications. This results in privacy issues. Because the existing social medias are used with the annotation functionality, through which some private information of users such as personal home address, daily office routines and social activities could be easily inferred from the multimedia data including images, audio records and videos posted on their social media networks. In order to preserve the privacy of users, social medias usually allow them to tune the privacy level when they are sharing something online. This leads to a trade-off between the privacy-preserving level and situational awareness performance in ECNs: strict privacy control limits the useful information that is aware from disaster scenes.

6.2.6 Emotion Sensing

We notice that the *emotion sensing* [46] is an emerging topic in the smartphone based data analytics. Especially, under disaster scenarios, to know the emotions of victims is great helpful to their emotional care, so as to help them overcome difficulties and recover from disasters. Although some recent studies [47, 48] have conducted the sentiment analysis based on Twitter datasets, it is still a challenge to estimate the psychological status of people with high accuracy in the context of disasters. This poses an interesting open problem for the smartphone based ECN management.

6.2.7 Smart Cities with Integrated Disaster-Relief Infrastructures

Finally, establishing the smart cities with resilient disaster recovery capability is a promising direction for the future sustainable development of human. To achieve this goal, the integrated disaster-relief infrastructure equipped with multiple heterogeneous technologies including satellite communication networks, aerial-vehicle based networks and ground smart-device networks, should be exploited and developed. On the other hand, the efficient distributed algorithms that can work in the decentralized and autonomous environments are also needed to coordinate with the integrated infrastructure.

6.2.8 Bridging IoT Networks and UAV Systems

As illustrated in Figs. 1a and 2, in the isolated disaster communities, smartphone based networks can be treated as the bridge between IoT Networks and the UAV based data collection systems. Although UAVs have flexible flying trajectories, which make them easily aggregate the distributed disaster data to the central database. However, because of the on-board energy limitation, UAVs are impossible to travel every corner to collect data generated from the widely distributed IoT devices. Thus, smartphones can be exploited to bridge the data-transmission between IoT devices and UAVs. With the three primary components of ECN, i.e., smartphone networks, IoT networks, and UAV systems, the time- and energy-efficient collaborative data collection, forwarding and aggregation strategies are expected to design as open issues.

7 Conclusion

In this article, we have reviewed the basics and the state-of-the-art research efforts on smartphone based ECNs. Some key techniques and technologies are summarized. A real-world project, RIM system, is also exhibited as a case study of the smartphone based ECN. Some open problems and future research directions are discussed finally.

Exercises and Mini Projects

At the end of this chapter, we supplement several exercises, programming problems, or mini projects for student readers.

(1) Design an ECN architecture/system that enforces smartphones to collaborate with IoT devices, sensors or actuators for *data collection* stage.
(2) Design an ECN architecture/system that integrates smartphones and UAV based system for *data forwarding* stage.
(3) Develop smartphone applications using open APIs of social media such as Twitter, Facebook, Instagram, etc., to accelerate *data collection* or *data forwarding*.

References

1. Available: https://en.wikipedia.org/wiki/Delay-tolerant_networking
2. Wang, J., Wu, Y., Yen, N., Guo, S., Cheng, Z.: Big data analytics for emergency communication networks: a survey. IEEE Commun. Surv. Tutorials **18**(3), 1758–1778 (2016)
3. Available: https://en.wikipedia.org/wiki/Emergency_communications_network
4. Gomez, K., Kandeepan, S., Vidal, M.M., Boussemart, V., Ramos, R., Hermenier, R., Rasheed, T., Goratti, L., Reynaud, L., Grace, D., et al.: Aerial base stations with opportunistic links for next generation emergency communications. IEEE Commun. Mag. **54**(4), 31–39 (2016)

5. Li, P., Miyazaki, T., Guo, S., Zhuang, W.: Online scheduling of mobile stations for disaster management. In: IEEE Global Communications Conference (GLOBECOM), pp. 1–6 (2016)
6. Thapa, M., Alsadoon, A., Prasad, P., Pham, L., Elchouemi, A.: Impact of using mobile devices in earthquake. In: 13th International Joint Conference on Computer Science and Software Engineering (JCSSE), pp. 1–6. IEEE, Piscataway (2016)
7. Li, P., Miyazaki, T., Wang, K., Guo, S., Zhuang, W.: Vehicle-assist resilient information and network system for disaster management. In: IEEE Transactions on Emerging Topics in Computing, pp. 1–12 (2017)
8. Narang, M., Liu, W., Gutierrez, J., Chiaraviglio, L.: A cyber physical buses-and-drones mobile edge infrastructure for large scale disaster emergency communications. In: 2017 IEEE 37th International Conference on Distributed Computing Systems Workshops (ICDCSW), pp. 53–60. IEEE, Piscataway (2017)
9. George, S.M., Zhou, W., Chenji, H., Won, M., Lee, Y.O., Pazarloglou, A., Stoleru, R., Barooah, P.: Distressnet: a wireless ad hoc and sensor network architecture for situation management in disaster response. IEEE Commun. Mag. **48**(3), 128–136 (2010)
10. Chenji, H., Zhang, W., Stoleru, R., Arnett, C.: Distressnet: a disaster response system providing constant availability cloud-like services. Ad Hoc Netw. **11**(8), 2440–2460 (2013)
11. Fujihara, A., Miwa, H.: Disaster evacuation guidance using opportunistic communication: The potential for opportunity-based service. In: Big Data and Internet of Things: A Roadmap for Smart Environments, pp. 425–446. Springer, Berlin (2014)
12. Trono, E.M., Arakawa, Y., Tamai, M., Yasumoto, K.: Dtn mapex: Disaster area mapping through distributed computing over a delay tolerant network. In: Eighth International Conference on Mobile Computing and Ubiquitous Networking (ICMU), pp. 179–184. IEEE, Piscataway (2015)
13. Higashino, T., Yamaguchi, H., Hiromori, A., Uchiyama, A., Yasumoto, K.: Edge computing and iot based research for building safe smart cities resistant to disasters. In: 2017 IEEE 37th International Conference on Distributed Computing Systems (ICDCS), pp. 1729–1737 (2017)
14. Davis, A., Parikh, J., Weihl, W.E.: Edgecomputing: Extending enterprise applications to the edge of the internet. In: Proceedings of the 13th International World Wide Web Conference on Alternate Track papers & Posters, pp. 180–187. ACM, New York (2004)
15. Available: https://en.wikipedia.org/wiki/Situation_awareness
16. Higuchi, T., Yamaguchi, H., Higashino, T.: Mobile devices as an infrastructure: a survey of opportunistic sensing technology. J. Inf. Proc. **23**(2), 94–104 (2015)
17. Slater, D.H., Nishimura, K., Kindstrand, L.: Social media, information, and political activism in Japan's 3.11 crisis. Asia Pac. J. **10**(24), 1–31 (2012)
18. Wu, Y., Kant, K., Zhang, S., Pal, A., Wang, J.: Disaster network evolution using dynamic clustering of twitter data. In: 2017 IEEE 37th International Conference on Distributed Computing Systems Workshops (ICDCSW), pp. 348–353. IEEE, Piscataway (2017)
19. Musaev, A., Wang, D., Xie, J., Pu, C.: Rex: Rapid ensemble classification system for landslide detection using social media. In: IEEE 37th International Conference on Distributed Computing Systems (ICDCS), pp. 1240–1249 (2017)
20. Musaev, A., Hou, Q., Yang, Y., Pu, C.: Litmus: Towards multilingual reporting of landslides. In: 2017 IEEE 37th International Conference on Distributed Computing Systems (ICDCS), pp. 2494–2496. IEEE, Piscataway (2017)
21. Bradley, J., Barbier, J., Handler, D.: Embracing the internet of everything to capture your share of $14.4 trillion. White Paper, Cisco (2013)
22. Bonomi, F., Milito, R., Zhu, J., Addepalli, S.: Fog computing and its role in the internet of things. In: Proceedings of the First Edition of the MCC Workshop on Mobile Cloud Computing, pp. 13–16. ACM, New York (2012)
23. De Fabritiis, C., Ragona, R., Valenti, G.: Traffic estimation and prediction based on real time floating car data. In: 11th International IEEE Conference on Intelligent Transportation Systems, pp. 197–203 (2008)

24. Ganti, R., Srivatsa, M., Ranganathan, A., Han, J.: Inferring human mobility patterns from taxicab location traces. In: Proceedings of the ACM International Joint Conference on Pervasive and Ubiquitous Computing, pp. 459–468 (2013)
25. Calabrese, F., Pereira, F.C., Di Lorenzo, G., Liang, L., Ratti, C.: The geography of taste: Analyzing cell-phone mobility and social events. In: International Conference on Pervasive Computing, vol. 10, pp. 22–37. Springer, Berlin (2010)
26. Horanont, T., Witayangkurn, A., Sekimoto, Y., Shibasaki, R.: Large-scale auto-GPS analysis for discerning behavior change during crisis. IEEE Intell. Syst. **28**(4), 26–34 (2013)
27. Giridhar, P., Wang, S., Abdelzaher, T., Kaplan, L., George, J., Ganti, R.: On localizing urban events with instagram. In: IEEE Infocom-IEEE Conference on Computer Communications, Atlanta (2017)
28. Valcarce, A., Rasheed, T., Gomez, K., Kandeepan, S., Reynaud, L., Hermenier, R., Munari, A., Mohorcic, M., Smolnikar, M., Bucaille, I.: Airborne base stations for emergency and temporary events. In: International Conference on Personal Satellite Services, pp. 13–25. Springer, Berlin (2013)
29. Wu, X., Mazurowski, M., Chen, Z., Meratnia, N.: Emergency message dissemination system for smartphones during natural disasters. In: 2011 11th International Conference on ITS Telecommunications (ITST), pp. 258–263. IEEE, Piscataway (2011)
30. Orsino, A., Militano, L., Araniti, G., Iera, A.: Social-aware content delivery with D2D communications support for emergency scenarios in 5G systems. In: Proceedings of 22th European Wireless Conference, pp. 1–6. VDE, Frankfurt (2016)
31. Meurisch, C., Nguyen, T.A.B., Wullkotte, S., Niemczyk, S., Kohnhäuser, F., Mühlhäuser, M.: Nicer911: Ad-hoc communication and emergency services using networking smartphones and wireless home routers. In: Proceedings of the 18th ACM International Symposium on Mobile Ad Hoc Networking and Computing (Mobihoc), pp. 33:1–33:2 (2017)
32. Higuchi, T., Fujii, S., Yamaguchi, H., Higashino, T.: Mobile node localization focusing on stop-and-go behavior of indoor pedestrians. IEEE Trans. Mobile Comput. **13**(7), 1564–1578 (2014)
33. Noh, Y., Yamaguchi, H., Lee, U.: Infrastructure-free collaborative indoor positioning scheme for time-critical team operations. IEEE Trans. Syst. Man Cybern. Syst. **48**, 418–432 (2016)
34. Kojima, S., Uchiyama, A., Shirakawa, M., Hiromori, A., Yamaguchi, H., Higashino, T.: Crowd and event detection by fusion of camera images and micro blogs. In: IEEE International Conference on Pervasive Computing and Communications Workshops (PerCom Workshops), pp. 213–218 (2017)
35. Zuo, P., Hua, Y., Liu, X., Feng, D., Xia, W., Cao, S., Wu, J., Sun, Y., Guo Y.: Bees: Bandwidth- and energy-efficient image sharing for real-time situation awareness. In: 2017 IEEE 37th International Conference on Distributed Computing Systems (ICDCS), pp. 1510–1520. IEEE, Piscataway (2017)
36. Dao, T., Khalil, K., Roy-Chowdhury, A.K., Krishnamurthy, S.V., Kaplan L.: Energy efficient object detection in camera sensor networks. In: 2017 IEEE 37th International Conference on Distributed Computing Systems (ICDCS), pp. 1208–1218. IEEE, Piscataway (2017)
37. Pal, A., Kant K.: E-darwin2: A smartphone based disaster recovery network using wifi tethering. In: Proceedings of the 15th IEEE Annual Consumer Communications & Networking Conference (CCNC), pp. 1–5. IEEE, Piscataway (2018)
38. Huang, H., Guo, S., Liang, W., Wang, K.: Online green data gathering from Geo-distributed IoT networks via leo satellites. In: Proceeding of the IEEE International Conference on Communications (ICC), pp. 1–6. IEEE, Piscataway (2018)
39. Peng, D., Zhao, X., Zhao, Q., Yu, Y.: Smartphone based public participant emergency rescue information platform for earthquake zone "e-explorer". Vibroeng. Procedia **5**, 436–439 (2015)

40. Han, R., Zhao, X., Yu, Y., Guan, Q., Peng, D., Li, M., Ou, J.: Emergency communication and quick seismic damage investigation based on smartphone. Adv. Mater. Sci. Eng. **2016**, 1–5 (2016)
41. Miyazaki, T., Anazawa, K., Igarashi, Y., Li, P., Guo, S.: Resilient information management system for disaster situations. In: IEEE International Conference on Information Networking (ICOIN), pp. 1–6 (2017)
42. Chiou, S.-Y., Liao, Z.-Y.: A real-time, automated and privacy-preserving mobile emergency-medical-service network for informing the closest rescuer to rapidly support mobile-emergency-call victims. IEEE Access **6**, 35787–35800 (2018)
43. Kau, L.-J., Chen, C.-S.: A smart phone-based pocket fall accident detection, positioning, and rescue system. IEEE J. Biomed. Health Inf. **19**(1), 44–56 (2015)
44. Lampe, P., Baumgärtner, L., Steinmetz, R., Freisleben, B.: Smartface: Efficient face detection on smartphones for wireless on-demand emergency networks. In: Proceedings of the 24th International Conference on Telecommunications (ICT), pp. 1–7. IEEE, Piscataway (2017)
45. Berbakov, L., Pavkovic, B., Vrane, S.: Smart indoor positioning system for situation awareness in emergency situations. In: Proceedings of the 26th International Workshop on Database and Expert Systems Applications (DEXA), pp. 139–143. IEEE, Piscataway (2015)
46. Chen, M., Zhang, Y., Li, Y., Mao, S., Leung, V.C.: EMC: Emotion-aware mobile cloud computing in 5G. IEEE Netw. **29**(2), 32–38 (2015)
47. Montejo-Ráez, A., Martínez-Cámara, E., Martín-Valdivia, M.T., Ureña-López, L.A.: Ranked wordnet graph for sentiment polarity classification in twitter. Computer Speech Lang. **28**(1), 93–107 (2014)
48. Su, L.Y.-F., Cacciatore, M.A., Liang, X., Brossard, D., Scheufele, D.A., Xenos, M.A.: Analyzing public sentiments online: combining human-and computer-based content analysis. Inf. Commun. Soc. **20**(3), 406–427 (2017)

Emergency Information Visualisation

Hoang Long Nguyen and Rajendra Akerkar

1 From Big Emergency Data to Visualisation

We can leverage big emergency data as the standards and guidelines for emergency management, some of which are smart response systems, early event anticipation, and coordination between end-users (e.g., the connection between authorities, first responders, and local citizens). Emergency data is available in various sources (e.g., social media, mass media, sensor, and linked open data) or local knowledge. In terms of the 6 Vs of big emergency data (i.e., value, volume, velocity, variety, veracity, and variability), they are challenging actually and consume our research efforts in analysing and capturing essential knowledge, especially in urgent circumstances. With manual methods, it may take years for a person to read, process, and understand massive amounts of big emergency data [23]. We, therefore, need to come up with a digital solution, which can deal with the complexity of emergency data, to get meaningful results in a fast response time.

Data visualisation is an excellent approach to solve the problems mentioned above by representing either tangible or intangible emergency data in systematic forms without losing any crucial information [8]. With an enormous amount of complex emergency data, our human brain can understand and process visual information (e.g., diagrams, graphs, or charts) 60,000 times faster than raw documents, spreadsheets, notes, numerical tables, or reports [27]. To identify and deal with an image, we need to spend only 13 ms.[1] Data visualisation is a powerful tool to discover latent correlations and unexpected relationships, which is impossible by

---

[1] http://news.mit.edu/2014/in-the-blink-of-an-eye-0116.

H. L. Nguyen (✉) · R. Akerkar
Big Data Research Group, Western Norway Research Institute, Sogndal, Norway
e-mail: hln@vestforsk.no; rak@vestforsk.no

© Springer Nature Switzerland AG 2020
R. Akerkar (ed.), *Big Data in Emergency Management: Exploitation Techniques for Social and Mobile Data*, https://doi.org/10.1007/978-3-030-48099-8_8

manually exploring or traditional descriptive statistics [14]. It can bring us surprising patterns that we may never imaginable.

One of the key discoveries in science that disease was passed through germs, rather than through pollution resulted from perception derived from a visualisation of the location of London cholera outbreaks near the Broad Street pump. The visualisation of cholera outbreaks changed how we saw a disease. Present-day Information visualisation can be used to create similar ideas: understanding the spread of a COVID-19 pandemic, spotting terrorist movement, or evaluating the emergency impact on a town. But, there are some notable challenges: several things may be utilised and visualised, often derived or aggregated from vast data sets, or created by algorithms for analytics.

Moreover, we can leverage data visualisation for performing prediction [1] and feature selection [29] in machine learning and artificial intelligence. We can do the data visualisation even before, during, or after data analysis. Visualising data before and during data analysis provides better insights into our data. It supports discovering underlying knowledge quickly and comprehensively; for example, conducting time-series visualisation may help recognise abnormal patterns and spot trends on which we should focus. On the other hand, performing visualisation after analysing data may make it easier, quicker, and more precise to communicate any results and insights to audiences. Even though data visualisation is enormously useful, but inappropriate methods can drive our decisions in negative ways. Hence, we must deeply understand our data, target audiences, and particular scenarios to select visualisation techniques correctly and carefully for achieving the most powerful insights.

Our motivation in this chapter is to provide crucial knowledge to let readers understand how big emergency data should be visualised to overcome challenges, what visualisation techniques are available to support data analytics, and in which situations we can apply. Based on these critical questions, we address in detailed multiple design strategies for an excellent viewing, different methods to display emergency information in various conditions, and several exercises at the final for understanding how to bring proposed theories into practical problems. The knowledge in this chapter can support a wide range of emergency applications that is vital for our community to derive optimal decision-making criteria and strategies, as our world is becoming more and more complex. Besides, we complete this chapter to be used different end-users, from academic researchers to practitioners, from natural to social science areas, and from inhabitants to authorities. The visualisation of emergency information is a must for any community today to increase their resilience [3].

We introduced the problem and emphasised our motivation for researching about emergency information visualisation in this section. In Sect. 2, we present visualisation design objectives for the sake of efficiency in further sections. Next, Sect. 3 summarises different visualising methods for content-based, geospatial, and temporal information along with details of dashboards. Then, we introduce some pertinent research issues in Sect. 4. Last but not least, we provide practical exercises in Sect. 6.

2 Visualisation Design Objectives

The main objective of the visualisation is to explore, develop and provide insight into a data set. However, there are several essential challenges [28] that data visualisation techniques have to face with, especially towards big data. Some of which are mentioned as follows.

- **Understanding our data:** to create an effective visualisation, it is vital to understand our data comprehensively, for example, manifest and latent context, underlying meaning, and hidden patterns. However, following our data has never been easy. In the era of big data, we have to deal with the sheer volume of both structured and unstructured emergency data. A data type is very diverse, as well. It can be content-based, geospatial, and temporal data. Misunderstanding our data can lead to inefficient visualisation or, also, missing or giving wrong information.
- **Dealing with outliers:** outliers are exceptional values that are inconsistent with other observations in a data set on account of measurement variability, sampling problems, wrong number crunching, natural variation or experimental errors. We should remove outliers from our data set because they may create a degree of complexity and ambiguity, which could be the main problems affecting our visualisation, leading us to make the wrong decision. On the opposite, outlier can contain useful information about abnormal properties of entities. We need practical approaches to tackle with and evaluate on that abnormal values to determine whether we should keep or exclude them. However, detecting, analysing, and assessing anomalous instances might be not always easy. Neural networks, support vector machine, logistic regression, and clustering-based algorithms are basic methods to handle outliers.
- **Fast response time:** high accuracy is essential; however, fast response time is a crucial attribute of a good visualisation as well. There are always challenges of querying the overabundant amount of data in a short time to capture and display useful information. In real-time systems, we have to decide a trade-off between discovering the data accurately and visualising it quickly.
- **Displaying meaningful results:** even we can capture all useful information quickly, displaying significant results is the problem of selecting what to display when dealing with enormous amounts of information. We have to define what type of information is displayed, how to show, and in which order. Stuffing everything at the same place can cause audiences confusingly.

Visualisation design objectives can be considered as good starts for brightening the way of people in avoiding these problems as above mentioned and creating useful visualisations. For transforming complicated scientific information into an expression that is meaningful and helpful towards every user group, visualisation techniques should satisfy the following objectives.

- **Setting your target:** to do a visualisation successfully, the first objective is to acknowledge our end goal. We need to identify which our audience prefers by always asking ourselves what our audience is expecting to derive. There may have some information that is so obvious and seems to be redundant to us; however, the viewer may need to understand the visualisation comprehensively. Determining an explicit target can guarantee that we do everything purposively, reasonably, and understandably.

- **Choosing the right visualisation:** selecting an inappropriate visualisation may demolish all of your hard efforts. There may have several ways to visualise our data. In this circumstance, it is crucial to follow our determined end goal and choose a visualisation methodology that is best suited to the targets of our work and the requirements of our intended audience.
- **Simple is the best:** this is a critical objective to create an effective visualisation. Remembering not to put so much information in your visualisation. This will make audiences challenging to capture their necessary information. If we make the visualisation too complicated and tedious, the audience is going to spend much time understanding the diagram instead of getting hidden knowledge. This is not what we want to have. Instead of cramming all of the information in the same place, you should categorise them into groups and visualise them in different graphs or diagrams. Do not waste our time on futile decorations. We use labels only if they do not cover any essential information on the chart.
- **Be consistent:** a piece of advice, especially for beginners, is to ensure that every design feature (e.g., the use of shapes and symbols, the choice of colour scheme, the order of items, and the selection of position and font of labels) is consistent within your visualisation. A visualisation guaranteeing the consistency can help readers get an overview at a glance.
- **Easy comparison:** one good motivation when using visualisation is the ability to conduct the comparison. Our visualisation will be more helpful if we can compare valuables in the same diagram or even between different diagrams easily and comprehensively. We then can capture the strengths and weaknesses of variables over space or time-periods.
- **Ensuring the clarity:** last but not least, we must verify that every information is visible. The contrast between colours, especially adjacent ones, must be high enough. The placement of all labels on data points and lines must be easy to determine. If there is any text in our visualisation, we should make sure to create high descriptive text and not over-explain. Every duplicated and redundant information should be removed as well.

In the emergency area, visualisation can enable end-users (e.g., authorities, first responders, and inhabitants) to utilise captured information by presenting it in significant ways. This can enhance the value of information and increase decision-making potential. To deal with complications of emergency information visualisation, we provide adequate techniques for a successful data visualisation in the next section.

3   Visualisation Techniques

In this section, we aim at providing different visualisation techniques corresponding to the types of information that we wish to process which are content-based, geospatial, and temporal information.

3.1   Content-Based Information Visualisation

What may we do if we were given a massive raw data set? Content-based analysis can be the first step for providing a deep analysing with a variety of methodologies to capture valuable knowledge, to discover hidden patterns, and to identify complex relationships. It is also known as content-based mining and knowledge discovery. In the field of emergency, we can apply content-based analysis for anticipating risks, determining impacts, and comprehending triggered actions. The integration of content-based analysis and visualisation can convert from structured and unstructured data (e.g., corpora, spreadsheets, and social media data) to comprehensible diagrams and charts. These diagrams and charts can enhance the ability of people to explore, capture essential information promptly and come up with more application solutions, as well. In this section, we provide useful visualisation techniques supporting content-based information, which are correlated and hierarchical visualisation.

3.1.1   Visualising Correlation

Correlation visualisations are very helpful to determine whether there is any relationship between variables.

Matrix Chart This is a compelling visualisation method for analysing, expressing, and understanding the relationship from two to four groups in a matrix format. Numbers or symbols in each cell of the matrix indicate the strength of the relationship between variables of groups. The matrix diagram allows us to compare, match, and search for variables between groups to derive better decisions. For example, the local community and first responders can choose the most effective strategies among possible solutions to behave in and after disasters. There are various types of matrix chart which are L-shaped, T-shaped, Y-shaped, C-shaped, and X-shaped matrices [21], each of them is used depending on how many groups you want to compare. Among these five types of matrix chart, people frequently use the L-shaped matrix chart.

- **L-shaped matrix chart:** among the types of matrix chart, this is the basic, simplest, and most popular matrix diagram to capture a critical relationship between two groups of variables by using a two-dimensional table. The variables of the first group and second group are placed on the left column and the top row of the table, respectively. The value in the intersection between rows and columns indicates how related between pairs of variables of two groups.

- **T-shaped matrix chart:** it is the combination of two L-shaped matrices to compare one core group with two other groups (e.g., we use the T-shaped matrix to compare two cities that are related to a list of resilient indicators). In this type of matrix chart, we usually represent variables of the core group as columns and variables of the other two groups as rows.
- **Y-shaped matrix chart:** the Y-shaped matrix chart is used for identifying interactions among three groups in a circular manner. Assuming that three groups are a,b,c respectively, we can discover the relationships among these following pairs of groups: (a,b), (b,c), and (a,c).
- **C-shaped matrix chart:** the C in the name of this matrix chart is the abbreviation for *Cube*. This is the extension of the Y-shaped matrix chart. We may use the C-shaped matrix chart for representing and comparing three groups concurrently in a three-dimensional space.
- **X-shaped matrix chart:** this is the extension of the T-shaped matrix, allowing you to conduct the comparison among four different groups. Each group is related to two other groups that are immediately adjacent to it (i.e., two groups, which are opposite, are not related to each other).

Node-Link Diagram Node-link diagram is also known as a network graph or a relationship map. The node-link diagram illuminates interconnections and relationships between a set of entities through the use of nodes and links (or vertices and edges in a graph). Nodes are often displayed as points, dots or circles, but we can use squares, icons, and symbols instead. We connect nodes by links, which are usually straight lines, or curved lines in complicated diagrams. Labels can be used to provide additional information to nodes and links. If there are multiple relationships between two nodes, we may use more than one line. The line colour is useful to show different types of relations as well. Besides, not all of the nodes and links are same in all node-link diagrams. They can have different sizes, shapes, and orientations, depending on the type of node-link diagram that we are using. There are four features of node-link diagram categorised into two groups, which are *weighted and unweighted*, and *directed and undirected*. We can express the weight of node and line by node size and line thickness, respectively. One-way or two-way arrows can represent the direction of relations. Based on four features, there are four significant types of node-link diagram which are: (1) unweighted and undirected, (2) unweighted and directed, (3) weighted and undirected, and (4) weighted and directed node-link diagrams. The node-link diagram is a powerful method to show how entities connect and which entities are more important. To derive useful insights from a node-link diagram, we should focus on nodes with many connections to discover clusters, central nodes, trivial correlations, and connectivity patterns. However, the use of so many nodes and links will reduce the legibility, and we are in trouble to explore new information. In this case, we should focus on particular sub-diagrams or eliminate some nodes and links with pre-defined rules. Also, we can leverage two traditional approaches which are force-directed layouts and edge bundling [12] to construct a better node-link diagram with many nodes and connections. There also have other similar diagrams which are the chord diagram, the Sankey diagram, and the arc diagram. We may use these types of diagram instead if your data set does not work with the node-link diagram well.

Word Cloud Word cloud given a textual corpus, we may have to tackle with a hundred thousand different words that seem to have no clue for exploring their correlation. Word cloud, otherwise called text cloud or tag cloud, may be useful in this situation. This is a visualisation method to show a collection of words appearing in different sizes. The larger size of a word (or sometimes the bold of text), the higher frequency this word appears in the document; with the assumption that words with higher frequency are more important. The colours in the word cloud are often used for aesthetic or classifying types of words. We can use word cloud visualisation to identify wording, recognise semantic similarity, analyse and understand users' sentiment, discover underlying patterns, and optimise search engines. Remembering to pre-process your textual data before visualising with word cloud; otherwise, we may be unable to derive useful information. There are different pre-processing tasks which we can do at the first step to remove noise, some of which are lowercasing, lemmatisation, stop-words deletion, and word normalisation [18]. Word cloud visualisation, in general, are effortless, fast, attractive, and easy to understand. Nevertheless, there are several situations that we should not use the word cloud. That is when the frequency of words is not adequate different, when words in a document are not variable enough, and when our textual data is too noisy. Besides, long words may get over-attention than short ones. The designs of the word cloud are also vital points to consider. The use of so many fonts (or tangled fonts) and colours, the cramped distance between words, the large number and messy direction of words, and the complicated shape of a word cloud can affect audiences in recognising importance information as well. We must guarantee that we understand our data and design objectives comprehensively before deciding to use word cloud visualisation.

3.1.2 Visualising Hierarchy

Hierarchical data visualisations are used for displaying multiple groups of data in organisational order. In this section, we present two popular hierarchical data visualisation techniques that are tree diagram and sunburst diagram.

Tree Diagram The tree diagram is a method of visualising the organisational hierarchy of data in a tree-like structure without containing any cycle. Typically a tree diagram consists of nodes (including root nodes, nodes, and leaf nodes) and links; every node has at least one relationship. The root node is the highest one with no parent nodes. From a root node, there are many branches leads to nodes that are connected by links. Each node has either parent or child nodes. We call nodes at the same level and share the same parent node as sibling nodes. The leaf nodes, which are the ending points of a tree diagram, do not have any further child nodes. We usually use rectangles or circles as nodes, straight or elbowed lines as links, and descriptive text inside or around nodes. With the recursively defined property, any subtree is also a completed tree diagram. The root node usually has an overall meaning. From top nodes to leaf nodes, the content becomes more specific and detailed. Tree diagram visualisation appears in various applications, from computer science, biology, and mathematics to business, information management, and emergency management. For example, we can build a tree diagram for quick disaster responses with leaf nodes are specific actions. An alternation of tree diagram is the treemap that shows hierarchical variables by rectangle areas. In the treemap, all the categories are represented as rectangle areas. The rectangle area of a parent category will contain all its child categories inside. Comparing to the tree diagram, we can easier recognise the differences between groups in the treemap.

Sunburst Diagram This is a multi-level pie chart through the use of a series of rings. The sunburst diagram will become the doughnut chart if there are no hierarchical relationships. The root node is at the centre, child nodes moving outward from there and placing on top of each other, and leaf nodes stay at the outermost of the circle. Each ring in the sunburst diagram represents for a level of the hierarchy. The slices of every ring are divided based on hierarchical relationships with their parents. The angle of slices having the same parent can be either equal or proportion to their parent/the whole diagram slices. Different colours can categorise different types of variables or hierarchical levels. Utilising sunburst diagram helps us understand the hierarchical relationship between outer and inner rings. Along with hierarchical information, sunburst diagram can be sufficient to show the part-to-whole relationships, i.e., between a variable with either its parent variable or the whole chart. We should not use sunburst diagram if there are so many slices in each ring because this can skew our perception. Besides, labels will be ineffective and useless if the space of slices is too cramped. Instead of using a label for every slice, we may use for inner ones only (e.g., at the first or second level) because they will have a larger area.

3.2   Visualising Geospatial Information

Visualising geospatial information is one of the earliest approaches in the history of information visualisation. This is the process of representing objects, elements, and events using their location. The location is a diverse range of areas; from a small place such as an office, a building, or a street; to a large region like a city, a nation, or a continent. On the opposite with static information, as we mentioned, the location can also be dynamic. It means the movement from a location to the others, referred to as spatial interactions [9, 24]. For example, the movement of a storm, the expansion of a fire forest, or the spread of disease. Geospatial data can be captured either by humans (e.g., geologists, land surveyors, photographers, or polices) or by machines (e.g., sensors or GPS-enabled smartphones). Leveraging geospatial information can bring us a lot of benefits in various applications [15].

3.2.1 Geospatial Data Types

After collecting, we can represent and store geospatial information in various forms including vector, raster, compressed raster, geographic database, relational database, light detection and ranging (LiDAR), computer-assisted drafting (CAD), elevation, web, multi-temporal, cartographic, 3D, and interchange file formats.[2] For the sake of simplicity, we only provide the most commonly used forms as follows.

Vector Vector data is beneficial for modelling discrete objects such as streets, rivers or buildings. This is the basic type of data that people always start thinking of when they face with spatial data. It is the combination of vertices and paths for representing location and shape of geographic features, by three geometric shapes which are points, lines, and polygons (or areas). Ubiquitous online mapping application, some of which are Google Maps and Open Street Maps, represent their geospatial data using this format.

- **Vector point:** each point has its location using (X, Y) coordinate or longitude and latitude values. Each vector point can describe information itself. In the topic of emergency, we can describe a traffic accident, a destructed building, or a victim location as a point.
- **Vector line:** is the connection by at least two points with or without direction. A vector line starts and ends with nodes and changes its directions through vertices. Information can be attached to a specific point, node, or ever an entire line. Examples of emergency events which are represented well by vector lines are the shifting of a storm and the movement of rescuers.
- **Vector polygon:** polygons join a set of points which share the same starting and ending coordinates. We usually place information of a polygon in its centre, be independent of the shape of this polygon. A flooding risk, a forest fire, or a dam breach are well modelled by vector polygon.

Raster In contrast with vector data, we use raster data to store and represent connected objects such as population distribution and temperature of an area. Raster data consists of a set regular grid array, pixels, or cells. Each cell in the raster has a coordinate value that means the position of the centre of this cell. The coordinate value depends on its dimension, in 2-D is width and height, in 3-D is width, height, and depth. The shape of a cell can be square or rectangular; however, it is usually represented as a square. The continuous rasters have associated values gradually changing in a defined manner. We find it essential to take into account the resolution of a raster (i.e., the size of a cell). The resolution can express how large area a raster

---

[2]https://gisgeography.com/gis-formats.

can cover. If the resolution is too high, a cell will include a small area; therefore, the information is a cell is less. If we zoom in to the map utmostly, we can observe separated cells, each of them brings a particular colour. This concept is especially crucial towards geospatial visualisation. By selecting the optimal size of a cell, we can effectively and efficiently express necessary information while minimising file size.

Web Files As we are living in the area of internet and big data, publishing geographic features over the internet is an essential requirement. The GeoJSON and the GeoRSS file formats were built to store and display geographic features over the internet effectively. GeoJSON is designed based on the JSON (JavaScript Object Notation) standard format that contains both geospatial and attribute data. The GeoJSON filename usually ends with *.geojson*. This web file data has been widened used by popular services and systems (e.g., the QGIS, the ArcGIS, the Tableau, and the Spotzi). Meanwhile, GeoRSS is developed based on Geography Markup Language (GML) for describing and pinpointing geographic information on Internet content. These two formats can well describe complex natural features such as canyons, lakes and rivers to human-made creations such as buildings, universities, and cities. Besides that, there exist cloud-based platforms (e.g., Esri ArcGIS Online Web Services) that allow individuals and organisations to publish their contents in shareable and recoverable environments.

3D 3D data is the extension of 2D data by adding Z-aspect to the dimension for creating a triple coordinate (X, Y, Z); therefore, it is similar with vector data and raster data in term of concept. Z-value can be either a tangible value (e.g., geological depth) or an intangible value (e.g., the suitability of a place, the level of pollution, or concentration values). A 3D geospatial surface can be represented by a connected triangle. There are two basic types of 3D data which are feature data and surface data.

- **3D feature:** represents 3D geospatial information for discrete objects.
- **3D surface:** expresses continuous phenomena by having height values over a specific area.

Overall, types of geospatial data in which we select are depend on our input data, expected output, and targeted audiences. Each type is not higher-level than the others, but each can maximise efficiency when it is used in the right demand and context. If the output is close to traditional cartographic representations, then vector data would be appropriate. Meanwhile, raster data is more suitable in term of representing a surface, physical phenomena, or mathematical context.

3.2.2 Techniques

Geospatial data convey a physical context, mostly in 2D space, like geographical maps or floor plans. The primary form of visualising geospatial data is mapping. In *choropleth* maps, colour encoding is used to add represent one data attribute.

Cartograms aim to encode the attribute value with the size of regions by distorting the underlying physical space. Tile grid maps reduce each geospatial area to a uniform size and shape (e.g., a square) so that the colour coded data are easier to observe and compare, and they arrange the tiles to approximate the neighbour relations between physical locations. Grid maps also make a selection of smaller areas (such as small cities or states) easier. Contour (isopleth) maps connect areas with similar measurements and colour each one separately. Network maps aim to show network connectivity between locations, such as flights to/from many regions of the world. Spatial data can also be presented with a non-geospatial emphasis (e.g., as a hierarchy of continents, countries, and cities). Maps are commonly combined with other visualisations. Based on types of geospatial data, i.e., data which contains geo-referencing, there are popular visualisation techniques to show and leverage full advantage of geospatial information as follows.

Cartogram   A cartogram describes information by using the forms of geographical regions. Nevertheless, we can distort or modify the actual shapes of geographic areas (i.e., expanding or reducing the actual size of the geographical regions) to best fit with our data. Although a cartogram is not correct in term of geographic size, it still preserves the spatial relationships of objects. There are several popular types of cartogram which are non-contiguous cartogram, contiguous cartogram, and Dorling cartogram.[3]

– **Non-contiguous cartogram:** this is the simplest one among different types of the cartogram. Non-contiguous cartogram does not conserve the connectivity of adjacent objects. This detachment allows geographical objects to expand or shrink their size without distorting their natural shape. There are two types of non-contiguous cartogram which are non-overlapping (for avoiding overlapping but affecting the distance of objects) and overlapping (for maintaining centroid coordinates of objects). Among the two types, people usually prefer to use non-overlapping because we can observe objects comprehensively.
– **Contiguous cartogram:** comparing to non-contiguous, the contiguous cartogram is more complicated to construct because we must preserve the topology between geographical objects. This type of cartogram immensely distorts the shape of geographic regions to represent attribute value associated with this region. The higher value, the more distorted the size of geographical areas will be affected.
– **Dorling cartogram:** in Dorling cartogram, we represent the geographical objects as uniform non-overlapping shape circles, with appropriate positions and suitable size that can maintain their original topology effectively. The Dorling cartogram can preserve not only the topology but also the shape, and centroid of geographical objects. Similar to Dorling cartogram is the Demers cartogram in which circles are replaced by squares to decrease the distance between terrestrial objects.

---

[3]http://www.ncgia.ucsb.edu/projects/Cartogram$_$Central/types.html.

There are other types of a cartogram, including the hexmaps cartogram, the tilegrams cartogram, and the distance cartogram as well; however, we only describe a more detailed for popular types as above mentioned. Every kind of cartogram can represent geographical objects from a different perspective. Although we can gain many advantages by visualisation geospatial information as a cartogram, it also has limitations in shape recognition and area magnitude estimation. In [6], authors suggested overcoming these problems by (1) representing the shapes of the enumeration units as irregular polygons and (2) "at least one square legend symbol should be used at the lower end of the data range. It is best to provide three squares in the legend, one at the low end, one at the middle, and one at the high end of the data range".

Flow Map A flow map is a combination between a flow chart and a map to represent the movement of objects between different areas and geographically express the distribution. In a flow map, the arrow depicts the direction, and the thickness of lines represents for the magnitude or amount of phenomena of objects. The use of flow lines is similar to other graduated symbols on other thematic maps [2].

One of the benefits of a flow map is that it enables users to easily recognise the differences in magnitude or amount of a wide diversity of items across areas without many map-clutters [20]. This allows cartographers and Geographic Information Systems (GIS) analysts to see the majority of the movement of objects, and then they can discover implicit patterns. Almost flow maps are created with vector, instead of raster data, because the changes of objects usually shown as lines. In vector-based flow maps, the vectors are points or lines that represent information about the direction and magnitude of items which are transferring. There are three different types of flow maps[4] as follows.

- **Radial flow map:** this type of flow map represents the relationships between one source towards many destinations. It uses different lines radiating out from a starting point to express the movements.
- **Network flow map:** network flow map depicts the quantity of flow in an existing network; hence, this type of flow map can effectively show transportation systems or communication networks.
- **Distributive flow map:** similar with radial flow map, the distributive flow map show relationships between a single source and many destinations; however, this map often has a large, single line from one source and this line is divided into different parts when reaching its destination.

We can use a flow map for showing dynamic geospatial information of people, weather phenomena, and other living things (e.g., the migration of people, the movement of storms across space, or river flow).

---

[4]https://www.gislounge.com/overview-flow-mapping/.

Density Map Density map is sufficient for visualising the density differences between areas. To represent how different between objects, people usually use colour scale either with a linear mapping [13] or with a non-linear mapping [10]. This type of visualisation brings many advantages towards big dynamic data because we can have valuable insight at the application level. We can create a density map by using either point or line data. The way we choose radius value can affect the representation of the density map. With larger values of the radius value, the density map is more generalised. On the opposite, the smaller values of the radius can show information more detail. There are different methods for calculating magnitude, which is point density and line density. These two interpolation methods can provide quantitative values to represent the concentration of points and poly-lines.

– **Point density**: this method calculates the magnitude-per-unit area of point features that fall within a neighbourhood around each cell. We consider only points that fall within the neighbourhood, if there is not exist any point, we understand as no data.
– **Line density**: this method is similar to point density; nevertheless, it calculates based on poly-line features instead of point features. To obtain an appropriate value of density, we need to select a suitable area unit scale factor (e.g., square kilometres and square meters). The larger the value of area unit scale factor, the more significant value of density we have.

The magnitude of point or line at every sample location is spread through the study area. Density map can determine which locations are greater or fewer numbers of data points or lines. We can utilise density map for visualising different information, some of which are population, urban [25], bomb, crisis [7], and even unhealthy behavior of men [22]. One practical example is the use of a density map for tornado monitoring and analysis in the United States from 1950 to 2017.[5] This visualisation is extremely useful for meteorologists to anticipate weather and to estimate where a tornado may move to have a good preparedness, response, and mitigation of damages [5]. Density map is more effective in case there are many data points (or data lines) in a small geographic area.

With the development of social networking services and smart devices, there emerge many applications of density mapping using geo-located Twitter data to discover hidden patterns of social events. In [19], authors collect geo-located tweets in 1×1 km grid cells over 2 months in Indonesia. By applying random forests-based census dis-aggregation method to the geospatial data and density mapping, we can comprehend population distributions at a particular time. Governments can take advance of this work for having adjustments promptly to increase the citizen's quality of life. In another work, authors create a density map of Manhattan urban using the data of billion taxi trips for over 7 years [30]. This research is useful for detecting and understanding civic events given specific locations.

---

[5]http://maxfelsenstein.com/gis-maps/tornado-density-map-1950-2017/.

3.3   Visualising Temporal Information

Time is a distinctive dimension in real world. It gradually moves forward without our control. But, we often record it as a moment or interval. We can represent it in different ways, for instance year, month, day, hour, and minute. As we calculate time based on cyclic (day/night) incidents in environment, our representations are cyclic too. For example, May follows April and so on. The cyclic way of representation can be described by circular visual encodings, such as the typical clock. Time series data is data that is collected at different points in time, such as stock market or weather data. Data points in time series are gathered at adjacent time periods and has potential for correlation between observations. The emphasis of the analysis is on exploring temporal trends and anomalies, probing for precise patterns, or prediction. The statistical attributes of time series data often violate the notions of standard statistical methods. Thus, analysing time series data requires a unique set of tools and techniques, mutually known as time series analysis. Temporal analysis is comprehending the sequences of events. In our day-to-day life we analyse event sequences. In the analysis of event sequences, uncovering the most common patterns, perceiving unique patterns, searching for certain sequences, or knowing what directs to certain kind of incidents is important (e.g., what situations lead to a unrest during the football match). In this section, we mention different methods for visualising temporal information effectively, which are a line graph, area chart, polar area diagram, and the Gantt chart.

Line Graph We use a line graph to show how quantitative values of something changed over a continuous interval or period. A line graph is constructed by connecting individual data points in the Cartesian coordinate system, consisting of a horizontal x-axis to show a timescale or a sequence of intervals (e.g., hours, days, weeks, or months) and a vertical y-axis to show quantitative values of data. The values on the x-axis are independent because it remains unaffected by other values. On the other hand, the values on the y-axis are dependent because a y-value must correspond to an x-value. Hence, we can call x-axis as independent axis and y-axis as the dependent axis. At a particular time, each x-value only has one y-value associated with it; nevertheless, different x-values may have the same y-value (e.g., a country only has one value of the population at a specific time). Typically, the y-value is positive, but we can express negative values under the x-axis as well. The label in each axis should be selected and divided into suitable units according to different data sets; for example, the x-axis would represent the time measured in years for the population of a country and in months, days, or hours for average temperature. The line graph may lose its clarity if there are so many points in a tiny area.

Besides, we can draw more than one line in the same chart to discover how different between variables, for example, we can compare the temperature, the number of storms, or the population between countries. In this circumstance, the lines should have different colours, shapes, or patterns. However, we should avoid drawing too many lines in a graph because the line chart becomes denser, challenging to see, and impossible to get insights from. A good number of lines to represent information effectively and efficiently is under five.

Area Chart Area chart is the mixing between the line graph and bar chart. Similar to the line graph, an area chart can show the changes or patterns of quantitative values over time. For example, we can comprehend seasonal peaks in the area chart as a periodic pattern. The x-axis typically represents time, and the y-axis is for another variable that depends on the x-axis. We connect discrete data points by straight lines or smooth curves. An area chart which connects points by a fitted curve is defined as the spline-area chart. The difference with a line graph is that the space between line and x-axis in an area chart is filled up with specific colours, shadings, or patterns. By filling the area under the curve, we can observe the trend from data more apparent. This is also a limitation of the area chart. Comparing to the line graph, we find it harder to add data labels because of less available space.

To use or not to use the area chart will depend on our data set. An area chart can work best if we meet the following requirements: (1) the comparison between values towards the total value is essential, (2) the difference between values are adequate, and (3) the data set is represented over a long period with many values of the time. Though the basic area chart is good at showing how values develop over time, it will not be effective when tackling with multiple attributes. In addition to the primary area chart, there are extended versions as follows.

– **Stacked area chart:** this is the extension of a basic area chart, which can deal with several groups on the same graph by placing each group on top of another one. When only one attribute is presented, the stacked area chart becomes the basic area chart. The stacked area chart is useful for figuring out how the total value is distributed to groups. We may use the stacked area chart for negative numbers, but typically people use positive values instead. By normalising values at each timestamp to the range between 0 and 100%, we can draw a percent stacked area chart. It is precisely the same thing, but the y-values are always on the 0–100% scale. The percent stacked area chart can represent the performance of each segment concerning the total, but we will be unable to find information about the trend of the total.
– **Stream graph:** a stream graph is a modification of the stacked area chart to display high-volume datasets along a different central horizontal axis. As the name, this type of visualisation represents the changes of values of several groups over time by resembling a themed river with the use of flowing and organic shapes; therefore, there is no fixed, straight corner, axis, or angle as in the stacked area chart. This makes the stream graph more interesting and entices users to see the graph. We should use the stream graph when groups are possible to start and finish at different time points. In a stream graph, the height of stream shapes is corresponding to the values of groups. The vertical dimension does not imply positive or negative values. There may not exist even a y-axis to use as a reference

in many stream graphs. Hence, we should focus on the general view of the stream graph rather than spending much time to concentrate on a slice at a particular time point.

Polar Area Diagram Polar area diagram can display data occurring in cycles (e.g., months, years, and seasons) cleanly and effectively. It is also known as a rose chart or a coxcomb chart. A polar area diagram is the combination of a radar chart and a stacked column chart. It is similar to a traditional pie chart; however, sectors have the same size of angles. The distance that extends out from the centre of the circle representing the value of each variable. We can express multiple groups by continuously stacking each on the others in a sector of the pie. To create an excellent and correct polar area diagram, we should keep in mind these experience carefully: (1) each the data set has to follow the part-to-whole relationship (i.e., the sum of values in a group is 100%), (2) selecting appropriate colours (e.g., the colours between groups should be disparate, using darker colours for groups having higher value), (3) we should avoid using too many numbers of sectors to ensure the visibility and legibility, (4) a functional polar area diagram should have the area of sector corresponding to the value of the variable that is representing, and (5) adding data labels may not useful towards polar area chart because of the limited space. Comparing to the traditional pie chart, the polar area diagram is a little harder-to-understand; however, it can display multiple data sets in the same graph, instead of using a series of traditional pie charts.

Gantt Chart The Gantt chart is an organisational visualisation tool allowing you to keep track of and update statuses of various activities/tasks/events to guarantee that we can complete them entirely and punctually [17]. This is extremely useful for emergency management in any size. Nowadays, the Gantt charts are widely used for every management activities due to its efficiency and simplicity. There are two primary components of a Gantt chart that are activity and time duration. Very simple, we put on the left of the Gantt chart a list of all activities and on the top a timescale. Based on the original bar chart, the Gantt chart uses the horizontal axis to display the progress of all events that need to be accomplished, with each one is a bar. The position and length of horizontal bars represent for the starting time, ending time, and duration of activities. We can use different colours for categorising different types of events. In Gantt charts, we may display additional information such as the contributors, milestones, or dependency relationships (i.e., how an action relates to the others by connecting arrows). The current status in the Gantt chart can represent by using different colours or shadings, filling in partially, or plotting a vertical line of the present day. Because activities can run in parallel; it is crucial to control and ensure that there are not so many activities overlapping at a particular time point. With the Gantt chart, we can recognise overlapping events efficiently and promptly. There are two popular types of Gantt chart which are the progress Gantt charts and the linked Gantt charts.

– **Progress Gantt charts:** in progress Gantt chart, we shade horizontal bars until the positions where the tasks have completed (i.e., a job that has completed 50%

should be 50% shaded). We can use a vertical line as the current time to monitor the progress of all task. If parts of horizontal bars of all tasks at the left side of the vertical line shaded, everything is processing punctually. This type of Gantt chart provides an excellent visual representation of the progress of tasks to determine which ones should be taken into account soon. Being unable to manipulate workflow is one disadvantage of the progress Gantt chart because it does not display the dependencies between tasks explicitly.

– **Linked Gantt charts:** the linked Gantt charts represents the connection between tasks by lines. Nevertheless, linked Gantt charts can be very cluttered and lose its clarity if a project has many tasks that are strongly dependent on the others. This is also a limitation of the linked Gantt chart in expressing complex interdependencies between tasks, which may usually happen in large emergency projects.

Temporal information visualisations are the simplest and quickest techniques to represent important information about features and attributes regarding the duration of time [4]. The visualisation can enable and enhance the ability to discover different social events and phenomena in term of temporal data (e.g., crime trends, disaster patterns, and temperature changes). Temporal data is simply data that contains temporal information, usually having a staring and a finishing time. There may have overlap between events. We create temporal data in almost activities, for records, management, and presentations. To obtain temporal data, we can collect from different sources manually and automatically; some sources are mass media source, social networking services [11], observational sensors and simulation models. Comparing to geospatial information, we can obtain temporal information more efficiently and seamlessly. With the personally-identifiable nature of the data, we can not access geospatial information in several situations.

3.4 Dashboards

Dashboards can increase situational awareness so that problems can be noticed and solved early and better decisions can be made with up-to-date information [26]. A dashboard exhibits a smart overview of your most crucial information. Dashboards allow you to display your data, gain a new bird's-eye view on emergency response or management and share information with your team. We define dashboard as:

> A dashboard is a glimpse of geographic information that helps you observe incidents or activities. Dashboards are designed to exhibit multiple visualisations that work together on a single screen. They offer a comprehensive and engaging view of collected data, to provide key insights for immediate decision making.

Dashboards are a visual design pattern that integrates components (dashlets) that can be interconnected or independent. The dashboard is powered by data from different sources via a pivot (service), with which the components (dashlets) exchange synchronously or asynchronously, delayed or in real-time. Interactivity can be expound at both levels-individual dashlet and dashboard. The latter is based on the dependencies defined between the components. The data that you visualise can be processed both in the pivot and/or during visualisation. There are also dashboard implementations as stand-alone systems in the organisation's information infrastructure. For the effective application of a dashboard in infrastructure, whether as a standalone element or as part of a specific software solution, the following aspects should be taken into account:

– **Data adaptation:** very rarely a dashboard exhibits data from a single source. Adaptation to the different formats is needed for data to be processed for visualisation.
– **Adaptation of the visualisation:** the variety of visuals often makes it hard to choose the right presentation. Adaptation implies evaluating variants that are at hand for visualisation, which further reflects on the data format.
– **Navigation adaptation:** interplay in a dashboard can be divided into two groups- the first in terms of the data defining the set of actions available with the dashboard at a time, and the second in view of the way in which it can be executed. Dashboard navigation is an rigorous process in terms of computing and communication through dashboard pivot down to the data sources.
– **Supporting context:** the context of the dashboard is determined by the selected sources, the current users, the selected indicators, and the navigation actions carried out so far. Upholding a complex context affects cognitive integration. Through it in the different components (dashlets) on a dashboard, the diverse aspects of the related data are interpreted and visualised.
– **Managing complexity:** to efficiently design and develop a dashboard in management processes, it is essential to manage the complexity that has many dimensions such as semantic transparency, perceptual discrimination, cognitive capability etc.

The utilisation of dashboard holds significant benefit for those with emergency management responsibilities. Emergency managers rely on a wide variety of location-based data to assist their mitigation, preparedness, response, and recovery tasks. However, it can be a ominous task to figure out how to credibly turn the overwhelming flood of raw data into reliable information that can be analysed and shared.

One tool that is helping emergency managers is the use of GIS operational dashboards. GIS technologies are not new; they have facilitated the emergency management community for many years and have become vital elements in modern emergency management practice. GIS takes data that is referenced to an Earth coordinate system and stores, analyses and produces spatial data and information. This information can be collated into a dashboard, which is an interactive visualisation of the information exhibited in a variety of formats, including graphical, maps, or numerical. The strength of a dashboard is that it can convey a vast amount of actionable information on one screen, whether it's a computer or mobile device.

In a very lucid account of how to create a GIS-enabled operational dashboard, creating a dashboard is begun by identifying the desired near-live data feeds, which could come from a location-enabled mobile application, such as a Twitter feed. Connections are then formulated between the GIS and those data feeds. The data from the different sources are then processed and analysed, and the dashboard exhibited on a computer with the ability to access the dashboard on mobile field devices.

The operational dashboards allow emergency managers to comprehend better data from complex, near-real-time data feeds. Also, visualised presentation of information allows emergency managers to gain insights from data that helps them make more informed decisions, take precise actions, and create detailed strategies during a disaster.

4   Research Issues and Readings

The fields of visualisation rely on methods from scientific, geospatial, and information analytics. It benefits from the knowledge out of the field of interaction as well as of cognitive and perceptual science. We continuously see more increasing amounts of data: new sensors, faster-recording methods and decreasing prices for storage capacities in the previous years allow storing huge amounts of data that used to be unthinkable a decade ago. In this section, we will discuss some significant research issues or challenges in the field of data or information visualisation.

Scalability   The scalability problem is a enduring challenge for information visualisation. Visual scalability is defined as the capability of visualisation tools to smartly exhibit large data sets in terms of either the number or the dimension of single data elements. Most visualisations handle relatively small data sets but scaling visualisations from millions to billions of records does require cautious coordination of analytic algorithms to filter data or perform fast aggregation, effective visual summary designs, and rapid refreshing of displays. To accommodate a billion records, aggregate markers (which may represent thousands of records) and density plots are valuable. In some cases, the large volume of data can be collected meaningfully into a small number of pixels. For example Google Maps and its visualisation of traffic conditions. A quick glance at the map allows drivers to use a highly aggregated synopsis of the speed of a large number of vehicles and only a few red pixels are enough to decide when to get on the road. Maintaining interactive rates in querying big data sources is a challenge, with a distinct of methods proposed, such as approximations and compact caching of aggregated query results.

Scalability is a major challenge of data visualisation as it establishes the power to process large datasets by means of computational overhead as well as pertinent rendering techniques. Information visualisation has recently developed numerous techniques to visualise datasets, but only some of them are scalable to the huge data sets used in visualisation. It is the task of visualisation (analytics) to build a higher-level view of the dataset to acquire insight while maximising the number of additional information simultaneously.

Contrary to the field of scientific visualisation, supercomputers have not been the primary source of data providers for information visualisation. Parallel computing and other high-performance computing techniques have not been used in the field of information visualisation as much as in scientific visualisation. In addition to the standard approach of developing increasingly better ways to scale up sequential computing algorithms, the scalability issue should be studied at different levels- such as the hardware and the high-performance computing levels-as well as that of individual users. Additionally, the challenge of visualising data streams is due to the pattern of the data stream and the necessity to comprehend its contents.

Data Deluge Increasing access to disruptive technologies and the increasing application of sensors are generating massive volumes of data. Such Big Data has huge relevance for emergency management. However, the growing amount of data poses challenges for data management, analysis and verification.

Causality Visual representation, reasoning, and analytics stress the role of information visualisation as the key medium for detecting causality, forming hypotheses, and assessing accessible evidence. The challenge is to derive highly sensitive and selective algorithms that can resolve conflicting evidence and suppress background noises. Complex network analysis and link analysis are crucial in this matter. Due to the exploratory and decision-making nature of such tasks, users need to voluntarily interact with raw data as well as its visualisations to find causality. Methods such as multiple coordinated views will boost the discovery process. Features that facilitate users in detecting what-ifs and test their hypotheses should be given.

Visual Impairment Colour impairment is a common condition that needs to be taken into consideration. For example, red and green are appealing or their intuitive mapping to positive or negative outcomes (also depending on cultural associations); however, users with red-green colour blindness one of the most common forms, would not be able to differentiate such scales distinctly.

Interpretability The ability to recognise and understand the data is one of the key challenges in the visualisation. Creating a visually correct output from raw data and drawing the right conclusions largely depends on the quality of the used data and methods. Several potential quality problems (e.g., data capture errors, noise, outliers, low precision, missing values, coverage errors, double counts) can be hold in the raw data. Also, the preprocessing of data in order to use it for visual analysis shows several possible quality problems. Data can be inherently incomplete or out dated. The challenges are to determine and to minimise these errors on the pre-processing side, and to provide a flexible yet stable design of the visual analytics application to manage with data quality problems. For example, Homeland Security applications, in particular, have to deal with missing values and uncertainty. Suppose a screening program in the context of Homeland Security in a sensitive area. The system should identify potential attackers, but also try to minimise false positives in order to avoid incorrectly targeting innocent commuters. A falsely inserted data record should not influence the primary manner in which the system observes and analyses different people. Moreover, updated data of a potential attacker might not be available in the database, but the visual monitoring and analysis of patterns should still work even though the records in the database are largely incomplete.

Aesthetics The aim of information visualisation is the insights into data that it provides. It is important to comprehend the representation of insights in order to comprehend how insights and aesthetics interact, and how these two goals could sustain insightful and visually appealing information visualisation. Much of the aesthetics wisdom consists more of heuristics than empirical evidence at the elementary level of perceptual-cognitive activity. Research in this area mostly focuses on graph-theoretical properties and hardly ever involves the semantics associated with the data. Insights should be detected in the data modelling phase of the process. Incorporating aesthetics into information visualisation still remains a challenge.

Semantics Another challenge in the context of information visualisation is to furnish semantics for analysis tasks and decision making visualisation. Semantic meta data extracted from heterogeneous sources may capture associations and complex relationships. Hence, providing approaches to analyse and detect this information is important to visualisation applications. Ontology-driven approaches and systems have allowed new semantic applications in financial services, web services, business intelligence, and national security. Nevertheless, more research is necessary in order to increase capabilities for creating and maintaining large domain ontologies and automatic extraction of semantic meta data, since the integration process between different ontologies to link various datasets is not fully automated yet. To perform more effective analysis of heterogeneous data sources, more advanced methods for the extraction of semantics from heterogeneous data are a key requirement. Thus, research challenges arise from the size of ontologies, content diversity, heterogeneity as well as from computation of complex queries and link analysis over ontology instances and meta data. New ways to resolve semantic heterogeneities to discover complex relationships are crucial.

Evaluation Human-centric evaluation of visualisation techniques can give rise to qualitative and quantitative assessments of their potential quality, with previous researches focus on the effectiveness of basic visual variables. Evaluations can aim to measure and study the size and value of the insights divulged by the employing of exploratory visualisation tools. Diagnostic usability evaluation is a core of user-centred design. Usability studies can be carried out at different phases of the development process to verify that users are able to complete benchmark tasks with adequate speed and accuracy. Resemblances with the technology earlier used by target users may also be possible to verify improvements. Metrics need to address the learnability and utility of the system, in addition to performance and user satisfaction. Usage data logging, user interviews, and surveys can also assist in spotting potential enhancements in visualisation design and developments.

5   Social Media Data Visualisation and Filtering

In the following section an overview of the methods used for social media data visualisation related to emergency events will be given.

5.1   Sorted List

A simple way of displaying posts and other news is to arrange them in a simple list. An advantage of this presentation is the easy (re-)arrangement, for example in a chronological, geographical or relevance (based on more complex metrics) order. The posts can also be shown with accompanying pictures (e.g., of authors) or timestamps.

5.2   Table

A more structured approach to visualise data in comparison to a list is a table with several columns like frequency, post content, author, etc. In general, a table can be ordered by clicking a column header. The items in the table are then ordered ascending or descending according to the attributes in the selected column.

5.3   Timeline

A timeline is a form of visualisation where one axis represents the time. The other axis can represent various types of information like events or posts. The advantage in comparison to a list is a better visualisation of the chronological order as the temporal relationships between events can be easily visualised and understood.

The displayed data can be as simple as points just representing an event ("something took place at this point in time") but can also be more complex such as a visual representation of what happened at this point in time (i.e., a photo).

5.4   Structural

A structural visualisation collects various node-link network layouts to illustrate the structure of a network. It supports the exploration of connectivity in large graph structures. In the case of social media data for example the spreading (reposting) of posts by actors can be shown. Colours can be used to emphasise links or present additional information. In addition to node-link diagrams there is also a matrix orientated approach that compresses information to get a better use of limited space. This gives them an advantage over node-link diagrams which rapidly clutter when the network grows.

The map is the most often used visualisation method. This is understandable as a map is a medium that can be intuitively understood and is appropriate for visualising geographical information. However most maps contain only basic features such as displaying a marker for every post, maps displaying enhanced data are used less often.

Statistical information is also frequently used as it provides a visual way of understanding data. Humans can use this visual display e.g., to detect anomalies or track the time progression of an event.

Lists and tables are often used since they provide the most basic way of displaying simple information. This makes them suitable for displaying data that cannot or does not need to be visualised like simple content of posts.

Other visualisation methods such as structural or temporal visualisation are not frequently used although they provide great potential for displaying important information. This might be due to the fact that the data required for them is harder to gather and mine.

5.5 Filtering

When trying to visualise too much data at once the visualisation might get cluttered. Therefore filtering options are needed that reduce the information or adjust it dynamically to the user's focus. In dependence to the form of visualisation, filter mechanics might regard time, location, keywords, quality metrics and other attributes of posts.

In time-based filtering, the user can select a start- and end date, a start time and the length of the time window to be displayed. In addition, the user can specify how the data should be replayed (Movie/Loop) and control the replay (Start/Stop). In addition to simple selection elements for the time another visualisation component can be used for defining a time interval where a timeline is used as a filter element and a data visualisation element at the same time.

Moreover, a map can be used for filtering a dataset based on location as the map's viewport defines a (normally rectangular) geographical area. It is also possible to create more precise location filters on the map by defining an area with markers. The selected area can be used to restrict the dataset to events that occurred within the area, allowing queries such as "What is the sentiment of users in this region?" or "Was there a sharp influx of posts in this city?".

Keywords (and especially tags) are an easy to use method to restrict a large dataset to data that is only relevant for a specific topic. Further, information quality metrics can be automatically computed to determine the quality of an information.

Therefore they can be used to restrict the dataset to data that matches certain quality criteria.

Time, location and keywords were frequently used for filtering, presumable because they provide a simple way to filter out messages concerning a specific event out of a larger dataset.

6 Exercises

In this section, we provide some general guidances of how to apply visualisation techniques mentioned above into possible emergencies using a real dataset collected from social data sources.

6.1 Data Set

To provide practical exercises, we use a real dataset collected from Twitter in 2012 about the Hurricane Sandy 2012. Twitter is an useful source to support managing and analysing emergency situations [16]. The Hurricane Sandy (also known as Superstorm Sandy) was the deadliest, strongest, and the most destructive hurricane of the Atlantic hurricane season in 2012. According to the record, is was inflicted almost $70 billion USD in damage. It was also the second-costliest hurricane towards the United States until now (the first ranking belongs to the hurricanes Harvey and Maria in 2017). Along the path of this storm through eight different countries, at least 233 people were passed away. This dataset collected for the REVEAL project includes around 2,000 tweets with enough textual, geospatial, and temporal information. Besides, each tweet in the dataset was labelled with location entries at the building, street and region levels manually to provide a gold standard for evaluation work. We can obtain this dataset directly on the website of the REVEAL project.[6] Each tweet has various information encoded as JSON as follows.

Listing 1 A tweet with various information encoded as JSON

```
1  {
2    "favorited":false,
3    "in_reply_to_user_id":null,
4    "contributors":null,
5    "truncated":false,
6    "text":"Seeing the midtown tunnel flooded and with water
          just flowing down was scary",
7    "created_at":"Tue Oct 30 04:04:41 +0000 2012",
```

[6]https://revealproject.eu/geoparse-benchmark-open-dataset/.

```
 8    "retweeted":false,
 9    "in_reply_to_status_id_str":null,
10    "coordinates":{
11      "type":"Point",
12      "coordinates":[-73.95240391, 40.74147806]
13    },
14    "in_reply_to_user_id_str":null,
15    "entities":{
16      "user_mentions":[],
17      "mentions":[
18      {
19        "indices":[11, 24],
20        "class":"Location",
21        "subclass":"building",
22        "name":"Midtown Tunnel"
23      }
24      ],
25      "hashtags":[],
26      "urls":[]
27    },
28    "in_reply_to_status_id":null,
29    "id_str":"263129269520195585",
30    "place":{
31      "full_name":"Queens, NY",
32      "url":"http://api.twitter.com/1/geo/id/b6ea2e341ba4356f.
              json",
33      "country":"United States",
34      "place_type":"city",
35      "bounding_box":{
36        "type":"Polygon",
37        "coordinates":[
38          [
39            [-74.042112, 40.489794],
40            [-73.700272, 40.489794],
41            [-73.700272, 40.812242],
42            [-74.042112, 40.812242]
43          ]
44        ]
45      },
46      "country_code":"US",
47      "attributes":{},
48      "id":"b6ea2e341ba4356f",
49      "name":"Queens"
50    },
51    "user":{
52      "follow_request_sent":null,
53      "profile_use_background_image":true,
54      "geo_enabled":true,
55      "verified":false,
56      "profile_image_url_https":"https://si0.twimg.com/
              profile_images/2659914767/511
              c11c3bd2a216ed19378592d5b35dc_normal.jpeg",
57      "profile_sidebar_fill_color":"f6ffd1",
58      "is_translator":false,
```

```json
59      "id":480979191,
60      "profile_text_color":"333333",
61      "followers_count":80,
62      "profile_sidebar_border_color":"fff8ad",
63      "id_str":"480979191",
64      "default_profile_image":false,
65      "location":"",
66      "utc_offset":-14400,
67      "statuses_count":3764,
68      "description":"24.Virgo.NewYorker.Queens",
69      "friends_count":112,
70      "profile_link_color":"0099CC",
71      "profile_image_url":"http://a0.twimg.com/profile_images
          /2659914767/511c11c3bd2a216ed19378592d5b35dc_normal.
          jpeg",
72      "notifications":null,
73      "profile_background_image_url_https":"https://si0.twimg.
          com/images/themes/theme19/bg.gif",
74      "profile_background_color":"FFF04D",
75      "profile_background_image_url":"http://a0.twimg.com/
          images/themes/theme19/bg.gif",
76      "screen_name":"xnancyi",
77      "lang":"en",
78      "profile_background_tile":false,
79      "favourites_count":96,
80      "name":"Nancy",
81      "url":null,
82      "created_at":"Thu Feb 02 04:39:37 +0000 2012",
83      "contributors_enabled":false,
84      "time_zone":"Atlantic Time (Canada)",
85      "protected":false,
86      "default_profile":false,
87      "following":null,
88      "listed_count":0
89    },
90    "in_reply_to_screen_name":null,
91    "retweet_count":0,
92    "geo":{
93      "type":"Point",
94      "coordinates":[40.74147806, -73.95240391]
95    },
96    "id":263129269520195585,
97    "source":"<a href=\"http://twitter.com/download/iphone\"
          rel=\"nofollow\">Twitter for iPhone</a>"
98  }
```

6.2   Visualisation Tool

Visualisation tools can organise data in a meaningful way that lowers the cognitive and analytical effort required to make sense of the data and make data-driven decisions. Users can scan, recognise, understand, and recall visually structured representations more rapidly than they can process non-structured representations. The science of visualisation draws on multiple fields such as perceptual psychology, statistics, and graphic design to present information, and on advances in rapid processing and dynamic displays to design user interfaces that permit robust interactive visual analysis.

In this section, we use the D3 library as the visualisation tool. The D3 is a very popular JavaScript (JS) library to give different visualisation techniques for various types of information. The reason for choosing D3.js because JS is a light-weight, interpreted, and just-in-time compiled programming language and compatible with every systems and device. Besides, the D3 library gives us the freedom to modify their source code to adapt to our particular requirements.

To start using the D3 library, we need to download the regular version[7] or the minified version[8] (i.e., all the white-space were wiped to reduce file size and time loading) from their website. This exercise is writing for the *5.12.0* version; however, it will be mostly similar to the other versions. After downloading and getting the file d3.v5.min.js, we should create a folder for containing this JS file. For the sake of simplicity, I will name this folder as *exercises*. The next step is to create an HTML file, name it as *demo.html*, and place into the same folder with the JS file. The folder *exercises* now contains two files as shown in Fig. 1.

Now copying this source code and put into the file *demo.html*. You then only need to open the file *demo.html* with any browser to run the program.

Fig. 1 The folder structure for this exercise

d3.v5.js   demo.html

---

[7]https://d3js.org/d3.v5.js.
[8]https://d3js.org/d3.v5.min.js.

Listing 2 Template for making visualisation with the D3 library

```
 1  <html lang="en">
 2    <head>
 3      <meta charset="utf-8">
 4      <title>Emergency Visualisation Demo</title>
 5      <script type="text/javascript" src="d3.v5.js"></script>
 6    </head>
 7    <body>
 8      // The D3 code will come here
 9      // ..........................
10    </body>
11
12  </html>
```

For any D3 script providing in the next section, we should put into the place that we noted as *"The D3 code will come here"*. This D3 JavaScript code will then generate other necessary HTML elements for the visualisation automatically.

Towards beginning users that do not have much experience in the D3 library, it is beneficial to visit their website[9] and follow their instructions. In the gallery, different authors modified and extended the original D3 library to adapt to their specific visualisation requirements. After we self-determined our visualisation targets, we may search in the collection of examples to pick up the most similar ones.

6.3   A Case Study with the Hurricane Sandy 2012

In this section, we focus on providing different visualisations that can support end-users understanding useful information about Hurricane Sandy 2012 quickly and efficiently. To derive a helpful visualisation, pre-processing and analysing data are beneficial. For the sake of simplicity, we only mention about pre-processing and analysing data briefly here and leave other space for describing visualisation methods. In the previous section, we introduced different visualisation techniques that can deal with content-based, geospatial, and temporal information.

Given no prior knowledge of an event, the word cloud is beneficial that should be conducted at the first step to derive an overview of what has happened. The input of the word cloud visualisation is a set of non-duplicated words extracting from the attribute "text" in the dataset. This set of words should not contain stop words, which are commonly used words (e.g., the, a, an, and in) but empty of meaning. Besides stop word removal, we can do the stemming or lemmatisation to convert words to their base forms. Stemming considers removing the last few characters, but this may lead to incorrect meanings and spelling errors. Otherwise, lemmatisation focuses more on the context and tries to revise words to their meaningful original form. To split a text into words, we may use a unigram, bigram or trigram model or combining

---

[9]https://github.com/d3/d3/wiki/Gallery.

these models. In addition to the processes as mentioned earlier, we also delete hyperlinks, remove all punctuation marks, and change all the letters to lowercase for reducing noise and redundancy. Finally, we obtain 30 highest frequency words in ascending order as follows: *school, news, coastal, high, wind, crazy, good, warning, live, rain, subway, safe, street, hope, bad, manhattan, storm, basement, east, people, house, tsunami, hurricane, city, water, power, sandy, movie, flood, and newyork.* The source code for visualising these words along with their frequency is given as below.

Listing 3 Source codes for the word cloud visualisation

```
1   <div id="visualisation">
2     // The HTML will be generated here
3   </div>
4   <script src="https://cdn.jsdelivr.net/gh/holtzy/D3-graph-
        gallery@master/LIB/d3.layout.cloud.js"></script>
5   <script type="text/javascript">
6   // List of words
7   var words = [{word: "school", size: "10"}, {word: "news",
        size: "10"}, {word: "coastal", size: "10"}, {word: "high"
        , size: "10"}, {word: "wind", size: "10"}, {word: "crazy"
        , size: "15"}, {word: "good", size: "15"}, {word: "
        warning", size: "15"}, {word: "live", size: "15"}, {word:
        "rain", size: "15"}, {word: "subway", size: "15"}, {word
        : "safe", size: "15"}, {word: "street", size: "20"}, {
        word: "hope", size: "20"}, {word: "bad", size: "20"}, {
        word: "manhattan", size: "20"}, {word: "storm", size: "20
        "}, {word: "basement", size: "25"}, {word: "east", size:
        "25"}, {word: "people", size: "30"}, {word: "house", size
        : "35"}, {word: "tsunami", size: "35"}, {word: "hurricane
        ", size: "40"}, {word: "city", size: "40"}, {word: "water
        ", size: "45"}, {word: "power", size: "55"}, {word: "
        sandy", size: "60"}, {word: "movie", size: "70"}, {word:
        "flood", size: "80"}, {word: "newyork", size: "90"}]
8
9   // set the dimensions and margins of the graph
10  var m = {top: 10, right: 10, bottom: 10, left: 10},
11      w = 850 - m.left - m.right,
12      h = 850 - m.top - m.bottom;
13
14  // append the svg object to the body of the page
15  var svg = d3.select("#visualisation")
16              .append("svg")
17                .attr("width", w + m.left + m.right)
18                .attr("height", h + m.top + m.bottom)
19              .append("g")
20                .attr("transform",
21                    "translate(" + m.left + "," + m.top + ")");
22
23  // Constructs a new cloud layout instance.
24  // An algorithm to find position of words that suits the
        needs.
25  // The different from one word to the other must be here.
26  var layout = d3.layout.cloud()
```

```
27        .size([w, h])
28        .words(words.map(function(d) {return{text: d.word, size:
               d.size};}))
29        .padding(6) //space between words
30        .rotate(function() {return ~~(Math.random() * 2) * 90;})
31        .fontSize(function(d) {return d.size;}) // font size
32        .on("end", draw);
33   layout.start();
34
35   // Takes the output of 'layout' above and draw the words.
36   // THE SAME from one word to the other can be here.
37   function draw(words) {
38     svg
39       .append("g")
40         .attr("transform", "translate(" + layout.size()[0] / 2
               + "," + layout.size()[1] / 2 + ")")
41         .selectAll("text")
42           .data(words)
43         .enter().append("text")
44           .style("font-size", function(d) { return d.size; })
45           .style("fill", "#69b3a2")
46           .attr("text-anchor", "middle")
47           .style("font-family", "Impact")
48           .attr("transform", function(d) {
49             return "translate(" + [d.x, d.y] + ")rotate(" + d.
                   rotate + ")";
50           })
51           .text(function(d) { return d.text; });
52   }
53   </script>
```

Figure 2 depicts the word cloud, which is referred from the D3 examples.[10] To use this source code, we need to define an array containing different words and their frequency (e.g., {word: "school", size: "10"}). Because the frequency of appearance of words extracted from tweets in the Hurricane Sandy 2012 is very high and deviant, the visualisation may lose its clarity (i.e., some words are too big while the others can be too small). To obtain a better appearance of words, we normalise the frequency of words to values lower than 100 following a defined scaling function. We may change the fonts, colours, sizes, and directions of words in the word cloud by modifying the source codes as well. From this visualisation, we can quickly have an insight in where this event might happen (i.e., New York), what is this event (i.e., hurricane and tsunami), and what is effect of the Hurricane Sandy 2012 (i.e., flood, water, city, house, power, and so on).

For the next visualisation, we consider representing geospatial information. With the development of smart devices, there are more tweets posted with geotagged locations; however, the number of geotagged tweets is still in limitation due to users'

---

[10]https://www.d3-graph-gallery.com/graph/wordcloud_size.html.

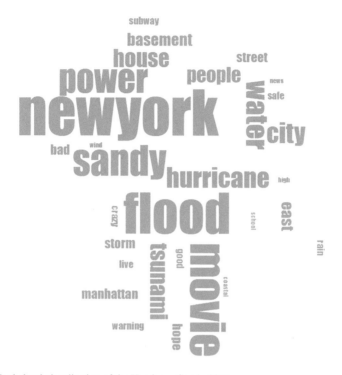

Fig. 2 Word cloud visualisation of the Hurricane Sandy 2012

privacy. In this dataset, we can get the geospatial information by extracting from the attribute "full_name" in "place" (e.g., *Queens, NY*. With the assumption that the number of tweets is corresponding to the effect of the Hurricane Sandy 2012 towards different states in the US (i.e., the longer time and more severe of the hurricane, the more people posted tweets to Twitter), density map is an excellent selection to express this information. The source code for density map visualisation is given as below.

Listing 4 Source codes for the density map visualisation

```
1  // Create US map.
2  <script src="http://bl.ocks.org/NPashaP/raw/
       a74faf20b492ad377312/uStates.js"></script> <!-- . -->
3  <svg width="960" height="600" id="statesvg">
4    // The HTML will be generated here
5  </svg>
6  <style>
7  .state{
8    fill: none;
9    stroke: #a9a9a9;
10   stroke-width: 1;
11 }
12 </style>
```

```
13
14  <script>
15  var sampleData = {"HI": {"color": "#ffffff"},"AK": {"color":
        "#ffffff"},"FL": {"color": "#ffff00"},"SC": {"color": "#
        ffffff"},"GA": {"color": "#ffffff"},"AL": {"color": "#
        ffffff"},"NC": {"color": "#008000"},"TN": {"color": "#
        ffffff"},"RI": {"color": "#ffffff"},"CT": {"color": "
        #008000"},"MA": {"color": "#008000"},"ME": {"color": "#
        ffffff"},"NH": {"color": "#ffffff"},"VT": {"color": "#
        ffffff"},"NY": {"color": "#ff0000"},"NJ": {"color": "#
        ffb266"},"PA": {"color": "#ffff00"},"DE": {"color": "#
        ffffff"},"MD": {"color": "#ffff00"},"WV": {"color": "#
        ffffff"},"KY": {"color": "#ffffff"},"OH": {"color": "#
        ffff00"},"MI": {"color": "#ffffff"},"WY": {"color": "#
        ffffff"},"MT": {"color": "#ffffff"},"ID": {"color": "#
        ffffff"},"WA": {"color": "#ffff00"},"DC": {"color": "#
        ffffff"},"TX": {"color": "#ffff00"},"CA": {"color": "#
        ffff00"},"AZ": {"color": "#ffffff"},"NV": {"color": "#
        ffffff"},"UT": {"color": "#ffffff"},"CO": {"color": "
        #008000"},"NM": {"color": "#008000"},"OR": {"color": "#
        ffffff"},"ND": {"color": "#ffffff"},"SD": {"color": "#
        ffffff"},"NE": {"color": "#ffffff"},"IA": {"color": "#
        ffffff"},"MS": {"color": "#ffffff"},"IN": {"color": "#
        ffffff"},"IL": {"color": "#ffff00"},"MN": {"color": "
        #008000"},"WI": {"color": "#008000"},"MO": {"color": "#
        ffff00"},"AR": {"color": "#ffffff"},"OK": {"color": "#
        ffffff"},"KS": {"color": "#ffffff"},"LS": {"color": "#
        ffffff"},"VA": {"color": "#ffff00"}};
16
17  // Fill colour for above states.
18  uStates.draw("#statesvg", sampleData);
19  d3.select(self.frameElement).style("height", "600px");
20  </script>
```

We use the example of the density map in the D3 gallery for our visualisation.[11] For the sake of simplicity, we removed the tooltip function for reducing the length of this source code. Besides, we modified the source code for users to customise the colours of the density map easily. What we need as the input is an array of US states with their respective colours (e.g., "HI": "color": "#ffffff"). Here, the colours represent levels of emergencies. We used five different colours as the descending of risks including red (i.e., significant risk to lives exist and significant damage and disruption), orange (i.e., more certain that there is to personal and property safety), yellow (i.e., hazard is possible, be aware of the potential impacts of the hazard), and green (i.e., non-urgent or not serious), and white (i.e., no hazards expected). The colour codes of these five colour are #ff0000, #ffb266, #ffff00, #008000, and #ffffff respectively. Based on extracted locations in the dataset and their frequency of appearance, the red group includes *NY*, the orange group comprises *NJ*, the yellow

---

[11] http://bl.ocks.org/NPashaP/a74faf20b492ad377312.

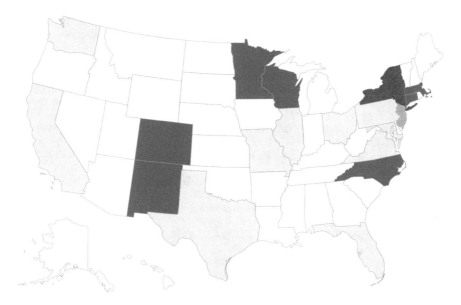

Fig. 3 Density map visualisation of the Hurricane Sandy 2012

group contains *FL, PA, MD, OH, WA, TX, CA, IL, MO, VA*, the green group consists of *NC, CT, MA, CO, NM, MN, WI*, and the rest states belong to the white group.

From the density map in Fig. 3, we may recognise the state under the highest risk was New York, following by New Jersey. However, the dataset may contain noise because the tweets can be posted by not only people in areas of the hurricane but also any person at any state in the US. In case of temporal visualisation, it is not useful towards this dataset because authors collected these tweets in a very short time (i.e., in only 10 minutes from 04:00 to 04:10). In a short duration of time, we find it difficult to express the differences or changes using temporal information. In order to understand the data comprehensively, of course, we need higher-level data analysis with a certain amount of time and effort. Therefore, the former visualisations (i.e., word cloud and density map in this exercise) are very compelling, which can be considered as a roadmap to guide further data analytics.

Acknowledgments The work is funded from the Research Council of Norway (RCN) and the Norwegian Agency for International Cooperation and Quality Enhancement in Higher Education (Diku) grant through INTPART programme.

References

1. Brady, G.P., Stouten, P.F.: Fast prediction and visualization of protein binding pockets with pass. J. Comput. Aided Mol. Des. **14**(4), 383–401 (2000)
2. Chang, K.T.: Introduction to Geographic Information Systems. McGraw-Hill, Boston (2008)

3. Chen, A.S., Khoury, M., Vamvakeridou-Lyroudia, L., Stewart, D., Wood, M., Savic, D.A., Djordjevic, S.: 3d visualisation tool for improving the resilience to urban and coastal flooding in Torbay, UK. Procedia Eng. **212**, 809–815 (2018)
4. Chittaro, L., Combi, C.: Representation of temporal intervals and relations: information visualization aspects and their evaluation. In: Proceedings of the 8th International Symposium on Temporal Representation and Reasoning (TIME 2001), pp. 13–20. IEEE, Piscataway (2001)
5. Deng, Y., Wallace, B., Maassen, D., Werner, J.: A few GIS clarifications on tornado density mapping. J. Appl. Meteorol. Climatol. **55**(2), 283–296 (2016)
6. Dent, B.D., Torguson, J.S., Hodler, T.W.: Cartography: Thematic Map Design, vol. 5. McGraw-Hill, New York (1999)
7. Fitterer, J., Nelson, T.A., Nathoo, F.: Predictive crime mapping. Police Pract. Res. **16**(2), 121–135 (2015)
8. Grinstein, U.M.F.G.G., Wierse, A.: Information Visualization in Data Mining and Knowledge Discovery. Morgan Kaufmann, San Francisco (2002)
9. Guo, D.: Flow mapping and multivariate visualization of large spatial interaction data. IEEE Trans. Vis. Comput. Graph. **15**(6), 1041–1048 (2009)
10. Herman, I., Marshall, M.S., Melançon, G.: Density functions for visual attributes and effective partitioning in graph visualization. In: Proceedings of the 6th IEEE Symposium on Information Visualization (InfoVis 2000), pp. 49–56. IEEE, Piscataway (2000)
11. Hoang Long, N., Jung, J.J.: Privacy-aware framework for matching online social identities in multiple social networking services. Cybern. Syst. **46**(1–2), 69–83 (2015)
12. Holten, D., van Wijk, J.J.: Force-directed edge bundling for graph visualization. Comput. Graph. Forum **28**(3), 983–990 (2009)
13. Jerding, D.F., Stasko, J.T.: The information mural: a technique for displaying and navigating large information spaces. IEEE Trans. Vis. Comput. Graph. **4**(3), 257–271 (1998)
14. Keim, D., Qu, H., Ma, K.L.: Big-data visualization. IEEE Comput. Graph. Appl. **33**(4), 20–21 (2013)
15. Lee, J.G., Kang, M.: Geospatial big data: challenges and opportunities. Big Data Res. **2**(2), 74–81 (2015)
16. Martinez-Rojas, M., del Carmen Pardo-Ferreira, M., Rubio-Romero, J.C.: Twitter as a tool for the management and analysis of emergency situations: a systematic literature review. Int. J. Inf. Manag. **43**, 196–208 (2018)
17. Maylor, H.: Beyond the Gantt chart: project management moving on. Eur. Manag. J. **19**(1), 92–100 (2001)
18. Nguyen, H.L., Jung, J.E.: Statistical approach for figurative sentiment analysis on social networking services: a case study on twitter. Multimedia Tools Appl. **76**(6), 8901–8914 (2017)
19. Patel, N.N., Stevens, F.R., Huang, Z., Gaughan, A.E., Elyazar, I., Tatem, A.J.: Improving large area population mapping using geotweet densities. Trans. GIS **21**(2), 317–331 (2017)
20. Phan, D., Xiao, L., Yeh, R., Hanrahan, P.: Flow map layout. In: Proceedings of the 11th IEEE Symposium on Information Visualization (InfoVis 2005), pp. 219–224. IEEE, Piscataway (2005)
21. Ryan, T.P.: Statistical Methods for Quality Improvement. Wiley, Hoboken (2011)
22. Silva, J.P.: Mapping unhealthy behavior among economically active men using GIS in suburban and rural areas of Sri Lanka. Asia Pac. J. Public Health **28**(1 Suppl), 10S–16S (2016)
23. Sivarajah, U., Kamal, M.M., Irani, Z., Weerakkody, V.: Critical analysis of big data challenges and analytical methods. J. Bus. Res. **70**, 263–286 (2017)
24. Stock, K., Guesgen, H.: Geospatial reasoning with open data. In: Automating Open Source Intelligence, pp. 171–204. Elsevier, Amsterdam (2016)
25. Susaki, J., Kajimoto, M., Kishimoto, M.: Urban density mapping of global megacities from polarimetric SAR images. Remote Sens. Environ. **155**, 334–348 (2014)
26. Verbert, K., Govaerts, S., Duval, E., Santos, J.L., Assche, F., Parra, G., Klerkx, J.: Learning dashboards: an overview and future research opportunities. Pers. Ubiquit. Comput. **18**(6), 1499–1514 (2014)

27. Vogel, D.R., Dickson, G.W., Lehman, J.A., et al.: Persuasion and the role of visual presentation support: the UM/3M study. Management Information Systems Research Center, School of Management, University of Minnesota (1986)
28. Wang, L., Wang, G., Alexander, C.A.: Big data and visualization: methods, challenges and technology progress. Digit. Technol. **1**(1), 33–38 (2015)
29. Yang, H.H., Moody, J.: Data visualization and feature selection: new algorithms for non-gaussian data. In: Proceedings of the 12th International Conference on Advances in Neural Information Processing Systems (NIPS 1999), pp. 687–693 (2000)
30. Zhu, X., Guo, D.: Urban event detection with big data of taxi od trips: a time series decomposition approach. Trans. GIS **21**(3), 560–574 (2017)

Printed in the United States
by Baker & Taylor Publisher Services